Feeling Democracy

The Feminist Bookshelf: Ideas for the 21st Century
A project of the Institute for Research on Women at
Rutgers University

Series titles are edited by Sarah Tobias and Arlene Stein

The Perils of Populism
Feeling Democracy: Emotional Politics in the New Millennium

Feeling Democracy

Emotional Politics in the New Millennium

EDITED BY SARAH TOBIAS
AND ARLENE STEIN

Rutgers University Press

New Brunswick, Camden, and Newark, New Jersey

London and Oxford

Rutgers University Press is a department of Rutgers, The State University of New Jersey, one of the leading public research universities in the nation. By publishing worldwide, it furthers the University's mission of dedication to excellence in teaching, scholarship, research, and clinical care.

Library of Congress Cataloging-in-Publication Data
Names: Tobias, Sarah, 1963– editor. | Stein, Arlene, editor.
Title: Feeling democracy : emotional politics in the new millennium / edited by Sarah Tobias and Arlene Stein.
Description: New Brunswick, New Jersey : Rutgers University Press, [2024]. | Series: The feminist bookshelf : ideas for the 21st century | Includes bibliographical references and index.
Identifiers: LCCN 2023044050 | ISBN 9781978835450 (paperback) | ISBN 9781978835467 (hardback) | ISBN 9781978835474 (epub) | ISBN 9781978835481 (pdf)
Subjects: LCSH: Women—Political activity—Cross-cultural studies. | Women and democracy—Cross-cultural studies. | BISAC: POLITICAL SCIENCE / Political Process / Political Advocacy | SOCIAL SCIENCE / Feminism & Feminist Theory
Classification: LCC HQ1236 .F435 2024 | DDC 320.90082—dc23/ eng/20240122
LC record available at https://lccn.loc.gov/2023044050

A British Cataloging-in-Publication record for this book is available from the British Library.

References to internet websites (URLs) were accurate at the time of writing. Neither the author nor Rutgers University Press is responsible for URLs that may have expired or changed since the manuscript was prepared.

♾ The paper used in this publication meets the requirements of the American National Standard for Information Sciences—Permanence of Paper for Printed Library Materials, ANSI Z39.48-1992.

rutgersuniversitypress.org

Contents

Introduction   1
SARAH TOBIAS AND ARLENE STEIN

1. Social Movements and Emotion Cultures:
   Learning from the Undocumented
   Immigrants' Movement   26
   KATHRYN ABRAMS

2. "The Women of Egypt Are a Red Line":
   Anger and Women's Collective Action   58
   NERMIN ALLAM

3. Our Paranoid Politics   85
   NOËLLE MCAFEE

4. The Political Branding of COVID-19   114
   CIARA TORRES-SPELLISCY

5. Toward a Decolonial Democracy: Rageful
   Hope in the 1961 and 1972 Afro-Asian
   Women's Conferences   167
   KIRIN GUPTA

6. "The Kind of World We Wanted to Be In": "Protocol Feminism" and Participatory Democracy in Intersectional Consciousness-Raising Groups   192
ILEANA NACHESCU

Acknowledgments   225

Notes on Contributors   227

Index   231

Feeling Democracy

Introduction

SARAH TOBIAS AND ARLENE STEIN

When Ukrainian President Vlodymir Zelensky rallied the West to support his country against Russia's invading forces in March 2022, he depicted the war in his homeland as a battle for freedom and democracy. In a powerful video address to the U.S. Congress that was designed to evoke sympathy, he invoked Dr. Martin Luther King Jr.'s "I Have a Dream" speech. Congresspeople, some in tears, rose to give Zelensky a standing ovation. Many *felt* the depth of his passion and the immediacy of his appeal. In subsequent discussions of the Russia–Ukraine conflict, talk of feelings was ever-present.

Some observers pictured the conflict between Russia and Ukraine as a "battle between two competing masculinities: the mighty, bare-chested Putin, whose hyper-masculine strength . . . [was] being challenged, and the kind, gentle, but still strong protector, Zelenskyy [*sic*]" (Friedman 2022). Others tied Putin's putative hypermasculinity, and his primal fear of NATO's expansion, to irrationality. "The mistake we made was to think that Putin is a rational actor, with rationality being defined in terms of tangible, material costs and benefits," declared political scientist Alexander Motyl. When it comes to Ukraine, Putin is "driven by passions, appetites, fears and emotions" (Motyl 2022). Yet rationality and irrationality, cognitions and emotions, are never wholly separate from one another (Jasper 2018). As the late cultural critic Lauren Berlant has noted, "politics is always emotional." It is an arena where conflicting interests "are described in rhetoric that intensifies the fantasy of vulnerable and possible worlds" (2016).

That we have an abundance of "political feelings" should come as no surprise in the second decade of the twenty-first century, an era marked by the global resurgence of right-wing populism and the fear, anger, and resentment that scholars often associate with that phenomenon (Graff and Korolczuk 2021; Demertzis 2020; Rico, Guinjoan, and Anduzia 2017; Salmela and Von Scheve 2017). Also unsurprising is that analysts often juxtapose the emotional and the rational, alluding to a dichotomy in the history of Western political thought that is often seen in gendered terms: men as rational, women as emotional. Gender norms and the emotions they embody frequently come to symbolize the nation and are used to entrench state power (Sperling 2014). As emotions and affect have emerged as a rich field of inquiry in the social sciences and humanities, feminist and queer scholars such as Sara Ahmed (2004), Lauren Berlant (2011), Ann Cvetkovich (2012), Deborah Gould (2009), Arlie Hochschild (1979, 2016), Sianne Ngai (2005), and Eve Sedgwick (2003) have explored the social and political dimensions of feelings. But scholars have paid little attention to the ways emotions are entangled with the idea and practice of democracy.

This lacuna seemed especially stark at the start of the Trump administration, when emotions—those of supporters, opponents, and the president himself—were particularly intense.[1] In January 2017, millions of women in the United States and abroad took the streets chanting: "Show me what democracy looks like! This is what democracy looks like!," channeling mass anger at the incoming president's misogyny and racism. Politicized emotions can galvanize participation and inspire democratic renewal, as witnessed during the civil rights movement in the United States. But these appeals can also undermine democratic stability, as demonstrated by populist leaders who use emotion to motivate their volatile supporters.

This volume had its origins in an April 2020 conference at the Institute for Research on Women (IRW) at Rutgers University that considered how feminism helps us make sense of the complex relationship between emotions, politics, and social movements. The conference explored the ways in which emotions are entangled with the public sphere, a realm that is historically associated with reason rather than emotion and gendered as masculine. We also considered the dimensions of gender, race, and sexuality, and the ways solidarities around them at times act as catalysts for a passionate democratic politics. Their contributions are informed by psychoanalytic, sociological, historical, intersectional, and other approaches. As an interdisciplinary feminist research institute that advances conversations across the humanities and social sciences, this volume bridges work on affects and emotions, the two primary conceptual frames that currently guide research in this area.

Beyond Affects vs. Emotions

Scholars in the humanities speak of the power of affect, which they understand to be a preconscious "intensity" that is "irreducibly bodily and autonomic," according to philosopher Brian Massumi, whose scholarship draws on the writings of Spinoza, Deleuze, and Guattari (1995, 88, 89). Affect is neither subjectively interpreted nor "capturable," he says. It "escapes confinement in the particular body whose vitality, or potential for interaction, it is" (Massumi 1995, 96). As prepersonal (rather than personal), affect corresponds to "the passage from one experiential state of the body to another," which implies "an augmentation or diminution in that body's capacity to act" (Massumi 1987, xvi).

In contrast, interpretive social scientists such as Deborah Gould, Arlie Hochschild, and Eva Iloux are concerned with the terrain of the emotions. They begin with the assumption that humans are meaning-seeking creatures rather than embodiments of affective states. Emotion, writes Hochschild (1979, 552), "is not an unmediated response but an arena of social performance entailing systems of meanings, norms, motivation, and social reaction." Moreover, social norms deeply affect the individual, shaping embodied feelings. Social scientists often examine specific emotions such as shame and pride, love and hate, to ask how they are culturally patterned, experienced, acquired, legitimated, and managed in daily life. They are interested in linkages among feelings and culture, structure, and modes of interaction.

Though their objects of inquiry differ—affect theorists tend to focus on cultural objects and texts, and interpretive social scientists on interactions—they share the belief that the world is shaped by narratives and arguments, but also by nonlinguistic feelings. In the interest of forging an interdisciplinary feminist conversation between these approaches, this volume is ecumenical about the relationship between emotion and affect. We question the need to see affect and emotion as dichotomous categories. As feminist scholar Sara Ahmed has astutely observed, "the activity of separating affect from emotion could be understood as rather like breaking an egg in order to separate the yolk from the white. . . . That we can separate them does not mean they are separate" (2004, 210). Similarly, feminist scholar Sianne Ngai uses the terms affect and emotion "more or less interchangeably" and argues that the difference between these concepts is not one of "quality or kind" but of "degree" (2005, 27). Following cultural analyst Ann Cvetkovich's lead, we use the term affect in a way that is "intentionally imprecise" and intended to incorporate "emotion, and feeling . . . impulses, [and] desires" (2012, 4).

We adopt this more flexible approach recognizing that how we feel is often conditioned by social context and "feeling rules" (Hochschild 1979; Jaggar 1989). Social context also dictates if (and how) we differentiate between thought and feeling. Indeed, the feminist adage that "the personal is political" suggests that we should also be wary of understandings of "prepersonal" (or prepolitical) embodiment. How emotions are constructed and "what emotions do politically" are of central importance for any feminist analysis, especially since they may be contagious (Åhäll 2018, 38; Sedgwick 2003). This collection of essays seeks to explore, from feminist perspectives, how emotions shape power dynamics and political practices, and how power shapes emotions.

The Meaning of Democracy

Before addressing the ways in which emotions shape power and democratic practices, it is worth examining the meaning of democracy itself. The term derives from the combination of two Greek words, *demos*, meaning the people, and *kratos*, meaning power. Democracy is therefore interpreted as people power, or rule by the people. As a type of government, modern democracy typically takes a representative form, with those who govern theoretically being "held accountable for their actions in the public realm by citizens, acting indirectly through the competition and cooperation of their elected representatives" (Schmitter and Karl 1991, 76).

But throughout its history, democracy has had multiple meanings, and until the mid- to late eighteenth century, many of these had negative connotations (Williams 2014; Innes and Philip 2013).

Democracy is simultaneously empirical and normative. It organizes and permits power to be exercised in different ways: from the process of deliberation used to assess different options, to "the actual decision mechanism," and, finally, to the way in which these decisions are effectuated (Geuss 2001, 112–114). Within these categories, there are variations in how people exert power, connected to whether these individuals are directly deciding and acting or using representative mechanisms to empower others to take action (Geuss 2001).

Crucial to the practice of democracy is how "the people" are defined and constituted. In ancient Greece, adult men alone could participate in the process of direct, deliberative decision making that connoted democracy in that era. Women were routinely excluded from the franchise until the suffrage movements of the early twentieth century bore fruit. In the United States, the Fifteenth Amendment (1870) enabled Black men to vote in theory, but the pervasiveness of literacy tests and poll taxes prohibited many from casting ballots in practice until after the passage of the 1965 Voting Rights Act. Even in the twenty-first century, many Americans with felony convictions—predominantly people of color—are denied the right to vote.

Like its empirical counterpart, the normative understanding of democracy derives from ancient Greece. This view of democracy holds that "the highest moral demand . . . is that a person be free and self-legislating, and avoid dependence on the will of others." The creation of "a self-legislating political system" is the preferred way to preclude such dependence (Geuss 2001, 123). Proponents of normative democracy believe that "even if democracy were to turn out to be inherently inefficient, ill-informed, [and] corrupt . . . it would still have an absolute moral advantage over other forms of politics" because "for people to have the power to decide for themselves what they will do is a good in itself" (2001, 123).

This normative approach to democracy is bound to affects. As the cultural critic Raymond Williams notes, "to be democratic, to have democratic manners or feelings, is to be unconscious of class distinctions, or consciously to disregard or overcome them in everyday behaviour: acting as if all people were equal, and deserved equal respect, whether this is really so or not" (Williams 2014, 58). No wonder some scholars describe democracy itself as a fantasy, or "the means by which people hoard idealizing theories and tableaux about how they and the world 'add up to something'" (Berlant 2011, 2). Indeed, sometimes these fantasies can turn into nightmares. "Democracy is the name that has been assigned to a dream as well as to certain already existing realities that are lived, by many people, as a nightmare," writes poet and cultural critic Fred Moten (2014), alluding to how democracy operates in the United States, a country shaped by its deep history of slavery and racial capitalism. This history helps explain why only some Americans experienced an overwhelming sense of shock and loss when Donald Trump, that champion of misogyny and white supremacy, took over the White House and lurched sharply toward authoritarianism. As political theorist Juliet Hooker puts it: "democracy grief is indeed real," but for Black Americans, who encounter "a racist criminal justice system and mass incarceration policies that demonize them as a group and routinely subject them to lethal police violence . . . being dehumanized . . . is nothing new" (McIvor et al. 2021).

For Moten, democracy is multivalent and consequently elicits both "both mourning and optimism" (2014). We must distinguish between "what exists and what is yet to come under the name of democracy," he writes, and do so "while inhabiting a state that constantly announces itself to be democracy's very incarnation" (Moten 2014). He suggests that feelings about democracy are most palpable at the interstices between democracy's paltry present and fantasized future, or between normative democracy and its empirical manifestation. The essays in this volume address the relationship between emotion and democracy at this critical nexus.

Emotions and Democracy

"All societies are full of emotions," writes philosopher Martha Nussbaum. "The story of any day or week in the life of even a relatively stable democracy would include a host of emotions—anger, fear, sympathy, disgust, envy, guilt, grief, many forms of love" (2013, 1–2). Yet for centuries, emotions have been regarded as undesirable in political life and subordinate to the rational. Indeed, as political theorist Barbara Koziak trenchantly notes, "The political realm has often been construed as open only to those who possess reason. In various ways Plato, Aristotle, Hobbes, Locke, and Kant all built their political constructions on a demand for a society governed by reason, apparently maligning emotion" (1999, 4).

Aristotle, for instance, maintains that man, as a "political animal," should be obligated "to bring his passions under the control and the limitation of reason" (Barker 1959, 321). Plato understands the demise of democracy—a form of government that he describes as "charming" and "full of variety and disorder, dispensing a sort of equality to equals and unequals alike"—to be linked to excess passion (2017, 558). In Book Eight of *The Republic*, he writes that those living in democracies are led by their appetites or desires "from day to day indulging the appetite of the hour" and encounter "a distracted existence . . . [called] joy and bliss and freedom" (2017, 561). It is this "insatiable desire" for happiness and freedom, a politics led by affect, that ultimately results in democracy's demise and transition into tyranny (2017, 562).[2]

If emotions have largely been seen as undesirable within the political realm, it is often because they are seen as feminine. This negative association has historically been used to justify women's exclusion from democratic participation. "As the constitutive other of 'reason' (as well as the objective, the mind, the masculine) in Western, binary modes of thinking," feminist theorist Linda Åhäll writes, "'emotion' has been (and still is) a political strategy keeping women and the feminine out of politics and political spheres" (2018, 37). It is not just that "'emotion' has been viewed as 'beneath' the faculties of thought and reason," as Sara Ahmed correctly observes. "To be emotional is . . . to be reactive rather than active, dependent rather than autonomous," and even, when viewed through a Darwinian lens, as "primitive" (2004, 3).

Political scientists often argue that democracy is a regime type that implies "progress," especially when compared to authoritarian "backsliding." Combine this with the historical association of emotion with nature (as the philosopher Kant notes, "For feeling, whatever may arouse it, always belongs to the *order of nature*") and it is easy to see how democracy was designed to exclude women, who have often been relegated to the domain of the "natural," and designated as "primitive" and "dependent" by politicians and political philosophers alike (Kant 1991, 182). Of course, when emotions are experienced collectively, they can be used to feminize and marginalize "others" on the basis of race, sexuality, and a host of other characteristics. Ahmed, for instance, writes about racism as a political manifestation of "the affective economies of hate" (2004, 44). Little wonder, then, that feminists reject binaries, arguing that they are inappropriately naturalized and frequently associated with the consolidation of preexisting power relations.

Feminist scholars regularly offer alternative interpretations of the relationship between emotion and politics. For instance, feminist philosopher Alison Jaggar argues that emotions are "historical products, bearing the marks of the society that constructed them." It is a mistake to think of emotions as "necessarily passive," because we often use emotions to "engage actively" in world building, which includes the construction of social and political norms (1989, 159). Jaggar observes that "within a hierarchical society, the norms and values that predominate tend to serve the interest of the dominant groups." It follows that in "a capitalist, white-supremacist, and male-dominant society," dominant norms will "serve the interests of rich white men" (1989, 165). We imbibe these norms, she writes, "in the very process of learning the language of emotion, and those standards and values are built into the foundation of our emotional constitution" (1989, 165). Our norms, then, have an emotional component that is inextricable from their power to compel.

Yet as Sara Ahmed notes, neither emotions nor their associated politics are reified. Examining what our feelings *do* reveals the working of power, which, like emotion, "shapes the very surfaces of bodies as well as worlds." Studying emotion therefore becomes a mechanism to show "how subjects become *invested* in particular structures" such as racism, colonialism, and slavery (2004, 12, 202). We can upend norms by developing "a different affective relation" to them, which sometimes entails "'feeling' their costs as a collective loss" (2004, 10–12, 196). Emotions therefore have the potential to "open up futures, in the ways they involve different orientations to others" (2004, 202).

Emotions are often most compelling when interwoven with narrative—and for feminists, this entails telling counterstories. Philosopher Hilde Lindemann notes that "the counterstory sets out to uproot some part of the oppressive story and replace it with a more accurate one" (Lindemann 2020, 286). Critical race theorists and critical race feminists have long relied on the use of storytelling to challenge "the bundle of presuppositions, received wisdoms, and shared understandings against a background of which legal and political discourse takes place" (Delgado 1989, 2143). Emotion in storytelling therefore becomes part of the method of social and legal change.

When collectivities use narrative to pursue change, they often do so in social movements, which serve as intermediaries between the "people," broadly defined, and the law. Legal theorists Lani Guinier and Gerald Torres argue that social movements successfully effect change "when they (1) shift the rules that govern social institutions, (2) transform the culture that controls the meaning of legal changes, and (3) affect the interpretation of those legal changes by providing the foundation for naturalizing those changes into the doctrinal structure of law and legal analysis" (2014, 2755). For Guinier and Torres, the term "demosprudence" captures the analysis of such shifts and processes. Demosprudence is a study of "the creation of authoritative meaning within a democratic polity" (Guinier and Torres 2014, 2755). The role of emotion in creating "authoritative meaning" in democracies is a main concern of this volume.

Emotional Movements

As many feminist scholars have observed, emotions are a central component of social movements. Indeed, as sociologist Deborah Gould notes, "emotion work" pervades social movements, where attempts "to alter one's emotion, to evoke or heighten or suppress a feeling," are key to creating collectivities primed to take action (quoted in Kinsman 2009).

Some analysts of social movements have been critical of emotional expressions on the grounds that they threaten the project of democracy and the redistributive politics at its heart. Displays of feelings, they suggest, are at odds with rational self-interest. But if democracy is defined more broadly, as a quest for recognition as well as redistribution (Fraser and Honneth 2003), emotions are often a key element. Social movements bring to public consciousness stories that have been silenced, untold, and denied. Such storytelling is often emotional in focus, mobilizing narrative communities to display anger and rage, bringing personal feelings into the public sphere (Goodwin, Jasper, and Poletta 2001).

While emotions do not translate neatly into strategic action, since a movement's success is defined partially in relation to its ability to elicit mass participation, displaying and eliciting emotions is often crucial. The mobilization of emotions energizes movements, opening up discursive spaces and empowering individuals who had previously been marginalized and voiceless. This is clearly apparent in relation to second-wave feminism, which encouraged the public revelation of one's darkest secrets, bringing emotions that were typically seen as private into public view (Illouz 2008).

Women coming of age in the wake of the feminist and gay/lesbian movements used emotionally rich autobiographical accounts to challenge dominant medicalized definitions of lesbianism (Stein 1997). Emotional storytelling also helped facilitate the rise of movements for comprehensive sex education, and against sexual violence. In the 1960s, the sexual revolution, the human potential movement, and sex education activists waged a battle against repression and sexual shame—informed by the psychology of Wilhelm Reich and other variants of humanistic psychology, along with Eastern mysticism, reshaping our emotional culture (Irvine 2009).

Movements against rape and other forms of intimate violence opened up space for the acknowledgment of shame and suffering, battling a profound lack of knowledge about the problem. They mobilized individuals to tell their stories and "break the silence," and urged law enforcement and treatment agencies to alter their understandings of sexual abuse in the family (Whittier 2009). Some of the most sweeping institutional gains in recognizing and addressing child sexual abuse occurred in the 1980s as the mainstream self-help and recovery movements focused on emotional healing and adopted feminist and therapeutic insights.

Feminists called upon individuals who are confronted with events that are, in the clinical definition, "outside the range of usual human experience" to master that trauma by speaking about it with others (Herman 2015). The discursive space opened up by feminism, with its focus on emotional storytelling, influenced other social formations, such as descendants of Holocaust survivors (Stein 2009), who urged their peers to break the silence about their familial legacy and make storytelling a vehicle for self-transformation, collective identification, and social action.

Some critics on the left suggested that displaying emotions in public is tantamount to embracing a permanent victim identity and furthering a "political sentimentality" in which brooding over one's losses prevents one from seizing possibilities for radical change in the present (Berlant 2011; Brown 1995). Yet a common cultural trope uniting the women's, LGBT, and recovery movements, writes sociologist Ken Plummer, is the modernist logic of the triumphant individual—one who has "suffered, survived, and surpassed" (1995, 76).

Perceiving that victimhood confers moral authority, the right has seized upon the victim trope, using it to argue that white Christian men are the "true" victims (Hochschild 2016; Stern 2019). During the 1990s, right-wing campaigns organized by evangelical Protestant and conservative Catholic organizations cast gays and lesbians, supporters of women's abortion rights, and proponents of sexual education as immoral individuals who challenge the "natural" dichotomy of the sexes and the authority of fathers. They charged that an undeserving elite exerts an outsized influence upon the state and its institutions, manipulating it to carry out their liberal agenda. And they used emotions such as anger, shame, and rage to amplify their message and to gain adherents for their "culture war" against secular liberalism (Hunter 1991; Stein 2022).

In the new millennium, right-wing populist campaigns have become globalized, more secularized, and animated in part by the goal of overturning "gender ideology." Like their counterparts elsewhere, American anti-gender activists argue that feminist and queer notions of gender threaten a presumed natural social order, promote heterosexuality, and induce gender confusion. They use secular and faith-based arguments to assert that efforts to question the essential nature of gender and sexuality are unscientific and dangerous. These campaigns enlist parents, particularly mothers, as warriors for the so-called traditional patriarchal, heteronormative family. Animating their struggles is the figure of the innocent, vulnerable child who is the unwitting victim of liberal indoctrination and symbolizes national purity, and at times racial purity too (Gill-Peterson 2021; Stern 2019).

These symbolic struggles, which often elicit displays of strong emotions in public, seek to consolidate power on the right and undermine democracy. Rather than encourage democratic debate, a better representative system, and economic redistribution, they embolden right-wing activists and distract others from acting on pressing social issues. They elevate authoritarian leaders who have much more in common with the corrupt elite than with ordinary people. And yet they claim to represent "the people"—those segments of the population that they value as patriotic bearers of common sense.

Feeling Democracy

Our volume recognizes that democracy's form—both actual and imaginary—as well as its meaning(s), and how people "feel" about it, are contextually contingent. We begin with two chapters that demonstrate the powerful role of emotions in pro-democracy movements in the United States and Egypt. Collective action—and what inspires new activists to undertake it—is a central theme of legal scholar Kathryn Abrams's chapter, "Social Movements and Emotion Cultures: Learning from the Undocumented Immigrants' Movement." Abrams's research focuses on the state of Arizona, where noncitizens make claims on a hostile state that denies them "any material or subjective attribute of belonging." Drawing on Lynette Chua's concept of "emotion culture," Abrams argues that the "experience, understanding, expression, and management of emotion" are crucial to helping an undocumented person evolve from "aggrieved target to engaged participant in collective action." Storytelling is an essential component of this transformation; it "teaches people to *turn toward, not away from* each other . . . [and] shows them that even the manifestation of painful emotion is an important way to connect with others." Organizers' use of emotion-laden aphorisms—for example, "DREAMers never quit"—plays an important role in this process, validating specific emotions that are useful for activists. Socialization in "emotion cultures" teaches new activists "to be resourceful, to manage their fears, to be resilient in the face of disappointment or frustration, and to be unafraid of vulnerability." Standing in solidarity with their peers, they acquire political agency in a democracy that is formally structured to exclude them.

In "'The Women of Egypt Are a Red Line': Anger and Women's Collective Action," Nermin Allam analyzes the ethical significance of women's anger in politics. She focuses specifically on the emotions expressed by Egyptian women during a transitional period of army rule between the ousting of President Hosni Mubarak in 2011 and the election of President Mohamed Morsi in 2012. After a woman demonstrator was beaten and disrobed by the army and vilified by the media, protesters organized a 10,000-person women's march, the largest in Egyptian history. Furious, women demanded an end to army rule and to violence against them. By shaming the army and releasing the victim from blame, Allam argues that women's expression of anger was productive. Women's anger also led to the creation of movements to end sexual harassment and violence, and enable their political participation. Unlike philosopher Martha Nussbaum, who condemns "garden-variety anger" for being retaliatory and unable to "restore what is lost," Allam finds value in women's anger. Anger, she maintains, facilitates the recognition of wrongs and subsequently leads to a broader focus on social welfare; Nussbaum denies the significance of the former and only sees value in the latter.

Given this volume's temporal and geographical origins, it should come as no surprise that two chapters address the intense emotions circulating in the United States during the Trump era. In "Our Paranoid Politics," philosopher Noëlle McAfee discusses the "persecutory anxieties" that attract people to conspiracy theories. She argues that people drawn to conspiracy thinking—such as those who are convinced that the 2020 election was stolen—are not easily swayed by facts. These people typically suffer from a "fear of breakdown," or concern that a large group they identify with is becoming increasingly (and intolerably) less significant. Conspiracy theories are particularly attractive when group members are undergoing stress, which may cause them to regress. Their fears, according to McAfee, cause some to seek a "phobic object" or "fetish" to become the "external substitute" for their "source of anxiety." They associate unwanted feelings with "malevolent" others outside the group, whom they diminish and sometimes even seek to destroy. In the contemporary United States, white supremacists typically project their "intolerable anxieties" onto people of color and other colonized peoples, says McAfee. But "the real enemy of white civilization," she emphasizes, "is the fragile and anxious identity of the colonizers themselves, their own other within." The implication of McAfee's argument is clear: conspiracy theories are related to unbearable feelings and have the potential to imperil American democracy.

In "The Political Branding of COVID-19," Ciara Torres-Spelliscy discusses the Trump administration's catastrophic response to the COVID-19 pandemic, which she calls "a partisan disaster." She focuses on the administration's efforts to brand, and thereby politicize, the virus. Political branding, she argues, involves the manipulation of emotion, a process that "can pathologize or normalize nearly any topic—even a deadly contagion." Trump's insistent repetition of "what his audience wanted to hear: that COVID-19 was not that serious" and a "Democratic hoax," helped promote "a soothing myth that was emotionally attractive to his followers." Torres-Spelliscy argues that Trump's public displays of emotion accentuated partisan silos, diminishing discussion of the pandemic's dangers and causing millions to suffer and needlessly die.

Democracy and its imaginary are not monolithic. In "Toward a Decolonial Democracy: Rageful Hope in the 1961 and 1972 Afro-Asian Women's Conferences," Kirin Gupta describes a forgotten history of women's pro-democracy organizing tied to the "emerging postcolonial" in Asia and Africa. This history has been obscured in the United States, where only one report of the 1961 women's conference exists and documents related to regional organizing between Asia and Africa have been "redacted from library records" because of possible ties to communism. Gupta remarks that Afro-Asian women believed that "national liberation was the pathway to women's liberation." These women were inspired by the idea of "communist, sovereign democracies—allied and united into a democracy of color—outside of the dominion of the capitalist West." While we now associate democracy with whiteness and capitalism, Gupta laments that we have lost this "alternative imaginary," and with it a vision of political society that is "innovatively socialist, gender-egalitarian, [and] democratic."

Even within the United States, democracy manifests variously, sometimes as a practice only peripherally related to formal legislative structures. Ileana Nachescu draws our attention to the work of the Chicago-based National Alliance of Black Feminists (NABF) in the 1960s and 1970s to offer a corrective to histories of the women's movement that focus predominantly on white women. Nachescu explores the second-wave feminist practices of assertiveness training and consciousness raising as methods that link emotion to politics. According to Nachescu, assertiveness training is a type of "protocol feminism" (Murphy 2012), a top-down approach to self-help fashioned through a psychotherapeutic "procedural script." It utilizes "role-playing," with the goal of creating "behavioral change." Consciousness raising, by contrast, is a more expansive modality; it is "polyvalent," with a variety of potential outcomes. Black feminists used consciousness raising to theorize from their experiences while also working "to erase internalized racism and sexism in a collective way." Nachescu argues that consciousness raising, especially when "led by those multiply oppressed," is best understood as a beneficiary of the civil rights movement and its ethos of participatory democracy. It uses democratic practices "to move away from seeing pain as a personal problem," understand it in a wider social and political context, and develop a more equitable political vision.

Conclusion

The essays in this volume show that emotions shape norms, power, and practices in democracies—both for those at its center, and for those struggling for inclusion at its margins. Some of the chapters in this volume tell a story about democracy's vulnerability. They illustrate that emotions are pivotal to attacks on contemporary democracies, as evidenced by the virulent affects fomented by Trumpian populism in the United States. Other essays tell a different story, suggesting the veracity of Clare Hemmings's claim that "in order to know differently, we have to feel differently" (2012, 150). Feeling differently—and as a feminist—can shift the dynamics of democratic practice, challenge preexisting hierarchies, and create openings for progressive policies, whether through the development of new emotion-based solidarities or the collective expression of emotions such as anger. Finally, emotions can help reshape the "authoritative meaning" of democracy itself. As the DREAMers' struggle suggests, emotion can empower noncitizens to claim democratic agency despite being formally denied the vote, which is often considered to be the hallmark of democratic citizenship. Emotions therefore play a role in enlarging democratic norms and closing the gap between these norms and the empirical realities that so often betray them.

Feeling Democracy demonstrates that we do not only think about democracy; we have feelings about it. We love it, hate it, are indifferent toward it, mourn it, feel betrayed by it, oppressed by it, inspired by it, angered to fight for (or against, or to be incorporated within) it—and more. We are awash in feeling, and any compelling analysis of democracy, feminist or otherwise, will be richer for recognizing its relation to the affective dimensions of our lives. We hope that *Feeling Democracy* encourages other scholars to undertake further explorations into this potentially rich field.

Notes

1. Indeed, as *New York Times* White House correspondent Maggie Haberman wrote in early 2021, "much of the past four years have been marked by discussion of Trump's feelings" (Haberman, Schmidt, et al. 2021).
2. This is not to imply temporal consistency about how the concepts of passion, emotion, feeling, and sentiment have been employed. As Amelie Rorty (1982) notes, between the periods in which Descartes and Rousseau were writing, the concept of "mind" changed significantly, as did the relationship of these affective states to cognition. Moreover, the earliest uses of the term emotion were associated with disorder, both of the mind and in the public realm ("Keyword Emotion").

References

Åhäll, Linda. 2018. "Affect as Methodology: Feminism and the Politics of Emotion." *International Political Sociology* 12: 36–52. https://doi: 10.1093/ips/olx024.

Ahmed, Sara. 2004. *The Cultural Politics of Emotion*. Edinburgh: Edinburgh University Press.

———. 2010. "Happy Objects." In *The Affect Theory Reader*, edited by Melissa Gregg and Gregory J. Seigworth, 29–51. Durham, NC: Duke University Press.

———. 2017. *Living a Feminist Life*. Durham, NC: Duke University Press.

Barker, Ernest. 1959. *The Political Thought of Plato and Aristotle*. London: Methuen.

Berlant, Lauren. 2011. *Cruel Optimism*. Durham, NC: Duke University Press.

———. 2016. "Trump, or Political Emotions." *Supervalent Thought*, August 4. https://supervalentthought.com/2016/08/04/trump-or -political-emotions/.

Brown, Wendy. 1995. *States of Injury: Power and Reason in Late Modernity*. Princeton, NJ: Princeton University Press.

———. 2015. *Undoing the Demos: Neoliberalism's Stealth Revolution*. Cambridge, MA: MIT Press.

Cvetkovich, Ann. 2003. *An Archive of Feelings: Trauma, Sexuality, and Lesbian Public Cultures*. Durham, NC: Duke University Press.

———. 2012. *Depression: A Public Feeling*. Durham, NC: Duke University Press.

Delgado, Richard. 1989. "Storytelling for Oppositionists and Others: A Plea for Narrative." *Michigan Law Review* 87, no. 8: 2411–2441.

Demertzis, Nicolas. 2020. *The Political Sociology of Emotions: Essays on Trauma and Ressentiment*. London: Taylor & Francis.

Fraser, Nancy, and Axel Honneth. 2003. *Redistribution or Recognition?* New York: Verso.

Friedman, Rebecca. 2022. "Macho Macho Man: Russia's Politics of Manhood Drive Putin's Invasion of Ukraine." *Miami Herald*, March 7. https://www.miamiherald.com/opinion/op-ed /article259157823.html.

Geuss, Raymond. 2001. *History and Illusion in Politics*. Cambridge: Cambridge University Press.

Gill-Peterson, Jules. 2021. "The Anti-Trans Lobby's Real Agenda." *Jewish Currents*, April 27. https://jewishcurrents.org/the-anti -trans-lobbys-real-agenda.

Goodwin, Jeff, James M. Jasper, and Francesca Polletta. 2001. *Passionate Politics: Emotions and Social Movements*. Chicago: University of Chicago Press.

Gould, Deborah. 2009. *Moving Politics: Emotion and ACT-UP's Fight against AIDS*. Chicago: University of Chicago Press.

Graff, Agnieszka, and Elzbieta Korolczuk. 2021. "Anxious Parents and Children in Danger: The Family as a Refuge from Neoliberalism." In *Anti-Gender Politics in the Populist Movement*, edited by Agnieszka Graff and Elzbieta Korolczuk, 114–136. New York: Routledge.

Guinier, Lani, and Gerald Torres. 2014. "Changing the Wind: Notes toward a Demosprudence of Law and Social Movements." *Yale Law Journal* 123, no. 8: 2740–2804.

Haberman, Maggie, Mike Schmidt, Carl Hulse, Mark Leibovich, Catie Edmonson, Jim Rutenberg, Charlie Savage, and Alan Rappeport. 2021. "Vote Certification Proceedings Restart after Siege at Capitol: Reporter Analysis." *New York Times*, January 6. https://www.nytimes.com/interactive/2021/01/06/us/politics /electoral-college-certification-live-stream.html.

Hemmings, Clare. 2005. "Invoking Affect: Cultural Theory and the Ontological Turn." *Cultural Studies* 19, no. 5: 548–567.

———. 2012. "Affective Solidarity: Feminist Reflexivity and Political Transformation." *Feminist Theory* 13, no. 2: 147–161.

Herman, Judith. 2015. *Trauma and Recovery*. New York: Basic Books.

Hochschild, Arlie R. 1979. "Work, Feeling Rules, and Social Structure." *American Journal of Sociology* 85, no. 3: 551–575.

———. 2016. *Strangers in Their Own Land*. New York: New Press.

Hunter, James Davison. 1991. *Culture Wars: The Struggle to Define America*. New York: Basic Books.

Illouz, Eva. 2008. *Saving the Modern Soul: Therapy, Emotions, and the Culture of Self-Help*. Berkeley: University of California Press.

Innes, Joanna, and Mark Philip. 2013. *Reimagining Democracy in the Age of Revolutions*. Oxford: Oxford University Press.

Irvine, Janice M. 2009. "Shame Comes Out of the Closet," *Sexuality Research & Social Policy* 6, no. 1: 70–79.

Jaggar, Alison. 1989. "Love and Knowledge: Emotion in Feminist Epistemology." *Inquiry* 32, no. 2: 151–176.

Jasper, James. 2018. *The Emotions of Protest*. Chicago: University of Chicago Press.

Kant, Immanuel. 1991 (1797). *The Metaphysics of Morals*. Translated by Mary Gregor. Cambridge: Cambridge University Press.

"Keyword: Emotion." n.d. University of Pittsburgh and Jesus College, Cambridge Keywords Project. https://keywords.pitt.edu/keywords_defined/emotion.html.

Kinsman, Gary. 2009. "AIDS Activism and the Politics of Emotion: An Interview with Deborah Gould." *Upping the Anti*, October 26. https://uppingtheanti.org/journal/article/08-aids-activism-and-the-politics-of-emotion.

Koziak, Barbara. 1999. *Retrieving Political Emotion: Thumos, Aristotle, and Gender*. University Park: Pennsylvania State University Press.

Lawrence, Charles R., III. "'Acting Our Color': Racial Re-Construction and Identity as Acts of Resistance." *UCLA Asian Pacific American Law Journal* 18, no. 1: 21–34.

Lindemann, Hilde. 2020. "Counter the Counterstory: Narrative Approaches to Narratives." *Journal of Ethics and Social Philosophy* 17, no. 3: 286–298. https://doi.org/10.26556/jesp.v17i3.1172.

Massumi, Brian. 1987. "Notes on the Translation and Acknowl-edgments." In *A Thousand Plateaus: Capitalism and Schizophrenia*, by Gilles Deleuze and Félix Guattari, xvi–xx. Minneapolis: University of Minnesota Press.

————. 1995. "The Autonomy of Affect." *Cultural Critique* 31, part 2 (Autumn): 83–109.

McIvor, David W., Juliet Hooker, Ashley Atkins, Athena Athanasiou, and George Shulman. 2021. "Mourning Work: Death and Democracy during a Pandemic." *Contemporary Political Theory* 20, no. 1: 165–99.

Moten, Fred. 2014. "Democracy." In *Keywords for American Studies*, edited by Bruce Burgett and Glenn Hendler. New York: NYU Press. https://keywords.nyupress.org/american-cultural-studies /essay/democracy/.

Motyl, Alexander, J. 2022. "Being Wrong about Putin." *The Hill*, March 7. https://thehill.com/opinion/national-security/597093 -being-wrong-about-putin/.

Murphy, Michelle. 2012. *Seizing the Means of Reproduction: Entanglements of Feminism, Health, and Technoscience*. Durham, NC: Duke University Press.

Ngai, Sianne. 2005. *Ugly Feelings*. Cambridge, MA: Harvard University Press.

Nussbaum, Martha. 2013. *Political Emotions: Why Love Matters for Justice*. Cambridge, MA: Belknap Press.

Pedwell, Carolyn, and Anne Whitehead. 2012. "Affecting Feminism: Questions of Feeling in Feminist Theory." *Feminist Theory* 13, no. 2: 115–129.

Plato. 2017 (360 BCE). *The Republic of Plato*. Translated by Benjamin Jowett. Urbana, IL: Project Guttenberg. https://www.gutenberg .org/files/55201/55201-h/55201-h.htm.

Plummer, Ken. 1995. *Telling Sexual Stories*. New York: Routledge.

Rico, Guillem, Marc Guinjoan, and Eva Anduzia. 2017. "The Emotional Underpinnings of Populism: How Anger and Fear Affect Populist Attitudes." *Swiss Political Science Review* 23, no. 4: 444–461. https://onlinelibrary.wiley.com/doi/full/10.1111 /spsr.12261.

Rorty, Amelie. 1982. "From Passions to Emotions and Sentiments." *Philosophy* 57, no. 220: 159–172.

Salmela, Mikko, and Christian von Scheve. 2017. "Emotional Roots of Right-Wing Political Populism." *Social Science Information* 56, no. 4: 567–595. https://doi.org/10.1177/0539018417734419.

Schmitter, Philippe C., and Terry Lynn Karl. 1991. "What Democracy Is . . . and Is Not." *Journal of Democracy* 2, no. 3: 75–88.

Sedgwick, Eve Kosofsky. 2003. *Touching Feeling: Affect, Pedagogy, Performativity.* Durham, NC: Duke University Press.

Sperling, Valerie. 2014. *Sex, Politics, and Putin: Political Legitimacy in Russia.* Oxford: Oxford University Press.

Stein, Arlene. 1997. *Sex and Sensibility: Stories of a Lesbian Generation.* Berkeley: University of California Press.

———. 2009. "Feminism, Therapeutic Culture, and the Holocaust in the United States: The Second-Generation Phenomenon." *Jewish Social Studies: History, Culture, Society* 16, no. 1: 27–53.

———. 2022 (2001). *The Stranger Next Door: The Story of a Small Community's Battle over Sex, Faith, and Civil Rights.* Boston: Beacon Press.

Stern, Alexandra Minna. 2019. *Proud Boys and the White Ethnostate: How the Alt-Right Is Warping the American Imagination.* Boston: Beacon Press.

Whittier, Nancy. 2009. *The Politics of Sexual Abuse.* New York: Oxford.

Williams, Raymond. 2014. *Keywords: A Vocabulary of Culture and Society.* Oxford: Oxford University Press.

1

Social Movements and Emotion Cultures

Learning from the Undocumented Immigrants' Movement

KATHRYN ABRAMS

How does a group of people with a shared grievance become a movement of committed, coordinated activists capable of mobilizing communities and influencing decision makers and the public? This is a question that social movement theorists and organizers have long struggled with. To explore this question, some analysts have focused on objective features of the environment surrounding participants: the relative openness of the political system to their central claims, or the resources they can marshal from external sources or their own communities. Others have focused on subjective factors such as the self-understandings of activists, or the resonance of their claims with the values and assumptions of the public.

Several decades ago, Doug McAdam—a social movement theorist whose work has greatly influenced my own—proposed a three-part theory: he analyzed the openness of the political system, along with the resources (both external and indigenous) that could be mobilized by a prospective social movement. But he placed particular emphasis on an element that he called "cognitive liberation": a mental state among prospective activists that combines the recognition of an urgent need for change with a sense of individual and group capacity to bring that change about.[1] This focus on the self-understandings of prospective activists was a precursor to the "cultural turn" in social movement analysis, which emphasizes subjective factors in explaining social movement emergence.

In this chapter, I take up the vital focus on the self-conception of prospective activists, arguing that liberation, particularly the sense of one's capacity and authorization to act as a change maker, is not entirely a cognitive process. A crucial vehicle for the socialization of activists—that is, for their transformation from aggrieved targets to engaged participants in collective action—is the experience, understanding, expression, and management of emotion. The kinds of emotions that participants experience can influence whether their disadvantage mires them in discouragement, self-isolation, and passivity, or catapults them into collectivity and mobilization. Social movement groups or organizations themselves create emotional environments, what legal sociologist Lynette Chua has termed "emotion cultures" (2018), which orient new participants toward collectivity and self-assertion, and prepare them for the outward-facing work of activism. In this chapter I explain how emotion cultures have been a key influence upon the movement of undocumented immigrants in the state of Arizona.[2]

This movement challenges some of the central scholarly assumptions about social movements, including the dominant notion that social movements are primarily the province of citizens. Citizens, who can exercise the right to vote, are the ones to whom lawmakers and other elected officials are structurally obliged to listen. Virtually all of the major social movements of the twentieth century were composed of citizens who could claim that their differential treatment or devaluation by agents of the state denied them the equal status to which they were formally entitled. Moreover, social movement scholars frequently argue that social movements tend to emerge in the face of a "political opening": a growing institutional receptivity to the claims of a particular group (Meyer 2004). Although some scholars have argued that the threat of harm, by increasing the costs of quiescence, has the potential to galvanize social movements too, this claim is less well developed and has typically been used to explain singular protest events rather than sustained movements (Almeida 2019; Zepeda-Millan 2016). In Arizona, a group of people lacking any form of legal status emerged as a social movement at a time when they were facing a systematically hostile state response— which not only rendered them vulnerable but deprived them of any material or subjective attribute of belonging. This unlikely emergence framed the central question of my research: *How does a group of people without legal status who are deprived of virtually all incidents of belonging by state authorities develop the sense of authorization necessary to create and sustain a robust and effective social movement?* A big part of the answer lies in how *undocumented participants are socialized by social movement organizations.* As I will explain here, this process is shaped by the practices and related "feeling rules"—of undocumented organizations, which hold the potential to revise and reenergize our understandings of participation in a democracy (Hochschild 1979; Meyer and Fine 2017).

Emotion Cultures and Undocumented Organizations

That members of organizations perform "feeling work," or emotional labor, or that those organizations have resulting "emotion cultures"—understandings about what feelings are valued, or are appropriate to feel under particular circumstances—is not a new insight. Sociologist Arlie Hochschild (1983) wrote about the emotion work of commercial organizations more than thirty years ago in *The Managed Heart*. The understanding that social movements draw on emotional responses is also not new: scholars such as James Jasper, Jeff Goodwin, and Francesca Polletta have written about the kinds of emotions that are mobilizing and demobilizing; the reciprocal emotions that grow up between members of a movement; and the emotions that are communicated from participants to observers or members of the public through public protest or demonstrative action (Jasper 2008; Goodwin, Jasper, and Polletta 2001). But until recently, little attention had been given to the environment or practices through which members of social movements build "emotion cultures" that facilitate activism. This work is now beginning: Almost a decade ago Deborah Gould (2009) discussed the "emotional habitus" of the LGBT anti-AIDS movement and how changes in that habitus—from an environment that fostered grief and compassion to one that fostered outrage and defiance—permitted the formation of the confrontational direct-action organization ACT-UP. And more recently, Lynette Chua in *The Politics of Love* (2018) has written about how the distinctive emotion culture of the LGBT movement in Burma helped to form a new kind of queer activist. Chua's thesis, in particular, provides a useful template for thinking about the undocumented immigrants' movement.

Chua focuses on two major tasks that LGBT organizations undertake to transform those who have simply become interested in or curious about LGBT activism into robust collectivities. First, organizations undertake a process of "grievance transformation"; this helps change participants' understanding of what it means to be oppressed as an LGBT person, so that they are more inclined to mobilize. Second, organizations facilitate a process of "community building," which connects participants to each other and to a new LGBT identity; this fosters a commitment to each other, and to more sustained participation in the movement. Although these processes are partly cognitive—activists learn about human rights conventions and come to understand the varieties of sexual and gender nonconformity that constitute LGBT identity—they are also importantly emotional. They are structured by "feeling rules" that instruct new activists how to feel about their queer identity and how to respond to their oppression. For example, activists learn not to view discrimination against queer people through a karmic lens—as punishment for bad acts in a previous life to be borne with a combination of shame and resignation. Instead, they come to view discrimination as a violation of their human rights to be addressed with a mixture of hope and confidence. Participants also come to understand themselves not as femmes or butches or trans men or women (or the terms that capture their Burmese equivalents), but as members of an encompassing, mutually supportive "LGBT" community. These two emotional features arising from the goal-oriented work of the movement—the affective response to oppression of LGBT individuals, and the inclusive bonding across LBGT identity—define for Chua the "emotion culture" of the movement.

The undocumented immigrants' movement in the United States differs from the LGBT movement in Burma. Those who come to undocumented organizations understand the state as an important source of their suffering.

But because federal and state governments systematically target undocumented people, many must first be persuaded that they are equipped to take action against governmental actors (Abrego 2011). This requires changes in self-perception and emotions. But, as with the transformations described by Chua, "emotion cultures" must be developed within undocumented organizations themselves. How do social movement organizations led by and for undocumented immigrants achieve this?

The first stage in this process prepares immigrants, who may be powerfully shaped by exclusion and oppression by state actors, to be confident, outward-facing political activists. This change, in turn, requires two kinds of transitions in participants' sense of self. First, new participants must be encouraged to replace their individual feelings of fear, shame, or powerlessness with emotions that are more conducive to mobilization. Second, they must also come to see their identities—which have been stigmatized by the state and isolated and individuated through immigration enforcement—as situated within a collectivity. This collectivization of identity continues to transform their sense of self and fosters positive emotions such as solidarity and even joy, which encourage them to become more visible. To grasp these transformations more fully, it is necessary to understand the political context in Arizona in the early twenty-first century.

Attrition through Enforcement in Arizona

Arizona was one of the first states in the United States to implement a legislative program referred to as "attrition through enforcement." The explicit goal of this program was to make life so miserable for undocumented people who had crossed into, or overstayed visas in, the United States that they would "self-deport," or leave for their countries of origin.[3] Attrition by enforcement had several different features, accomplished through legislative action and implemented by law enforcement activity.

The first step was the statutory withdrawal of state benefits from undocumented residents. This change, which was enacted through a series of statewide ballot issues, encompassed the denial of a variety of benefits including state-run adult education (such as English classes), in-state tuition and public scholarships for undocumented students, and the ability to post bail for undocumented individuals held for certain crimes. The second step included intrusive police surveillance and enforcement. This enforcement power was premised on a statute, known as SB 1070, which criminalized undocumented presence and employment in the state (Arizona State Senate 2010). That same statute authorized any state law enforcement agent to ask someone they suspected of being undocumented to show their papers during any kind of legal interaction (this could be a workplace investigation or something as banal as a traffic stop, including being stopped for squeaky brakes or a broken taillight). This practice not only terrorized immigrant communities, leading many people to leave preemptively; it also resulted in the police apprehending many more undocumented immigrants. In Maricopa County, in metropolitan Phoenix, the virulently anti-immigrant Sheriff Joe Arpaio used this power to conduct workplace raids and neighborhood saturation patrols, both of which brought dozens of cruisers and law enforcement personnel into immigrant-rich environments and resulted in a demand for identification from virtually everyone they encountered. A final, notable feature was the imposition of substantial penalties on anyone who harbored, transported, or assisted a person who was undocumented. This feature of SB 1070 cut undocumented people off, both practically and symbolically, from the solidarity and assistance of their fellow residents.[4]

These policies were so severe that an estimated several hundred thousand undocumented people left the state. Many more suffered what sociologists Cecilia Menjívar and Leisy Abrego (2012) have called "legal violence." They began to isolate themselves from any contact with the state, even if it might have helped them, such as to report being victims of crime to police, or to secure benefits for their citizen children. And they began to respond, internally, to the stigmatizing depictions of undocumented immigrants as criminals bringing violence to communities, or economic opportunists undeservedly burdening the state finances. Some immigrants felt hopeless and anticipated hostility from those around them; others began to perceive themselves as less worthy of opportunity or even respect.[5] But even as "legal violence" occurred, an increasingly visible social movement composed of undocumented people and their (largely, but not exclusively Latino) allies emerged across the state.

The Emotion Cultures of Youth Organizations

In Phoenix, youth first organized against state laws denying in-state tuition to undocumented students; they then joined a national movement supporting the DREAM Act, and the path to citizenship for childhood arrivals that it offered.[6] Youth activists also sought political changes at the state level through "civic engagement," organizing to register new Latino voters with the goal of replacing anti-immigrant officials or enacting pro-immigrant policies. In preparation for both kinds of efforts, youth organizations helped participants to embrace new understandings of self that were contingent on positive emotional associations with their undocumented status and collective or solidaristic notions of identity.

The shift away from self-conceptions that fuel shame, fear, or self-isolation began with the practice of storytelling. Since the first DREAMers told their stories to Congress in the early 2000s, experiential storytelling has been a prominent feature of outward-facing undocumented youth activism.[7] Storytelling also plays a vital role in socializing activists and building emotion cultures within youth organizations. Most youth organizations feature storytelling as a staple of their internal meetings. Some include storytelling by current members as a regular feature of general meetings, to reassure and reorient new participants; others teach volunteers to share stories with each other as preparation for sharing them with prospective voters in civic engagement campaigns, or other intended audiences.

Framed by identifiable narrative structures, these stories feature hardship, which is ubiquitous in undocumented communities, along with persistence, resourcefulness, and accomplishment. A member may relate her struggle to fund her education when in-state tuition was denied, but share the sense of possibility and accomplishment she experienced as a college student; another may highlight the confidence and skills he acquired as he was forced to take care of younger brothers and sisters when a parent was detained. These stories are not simply about individual attainment; they also describe the empowerment that can arise from coalescing with others. A story shared by an Arizona youth leader reflects these signature elements, offering a narrative of hardship and individual effort:

> I remember being in the eighth grade classroom. I didn't
> know a word of English. I felt that everything I had built
> was taken away. As a kid, I was a little social butterfly,
> I was [doing well] in grades. As soon as I came into the
> eighth grade classroom, I didn't speak, I was paralyzed.

And at that moment I felt that I had to prove people wrong, I felt that people were valuing who I was because I didn't speak a language. . . . I learned English pretty fast and I was pretty much able to join the mainstream English classes. But at that moment I remember feeling shame, and being so mad at my parents for bringing me to a place that I didn't like and that I didn't belong.[8]

The narrative also emphasizes the role of collectivity in fostering agency: "It wasn't until I got to college that I got to meet people that were in my same shoes. . . . I got to see in their faces all the fear that they had for being worried that like driving to school . . . they could immediately be put in deportation proceedings. . . . But I also got to witness the beautiful power that it has to be working with community, and being able to find your own voice" (Montoya 2019). Hearing these stories, new activists learn what undocumented people are capable of accomplishing. These narratives of undocumented life combat a sense of powerlessness and the internalization of stigma, making it possible for participants to envision themselves as change makers, or as fighters for themselves and their communities.

One of the most painful and demobilizing effects of undocumented status, particularly under a regime like Arizona's, is the tendency to turn inward—from the state and from other members of one's own community. Many undocumented people do not acknowledge their status outside their family. In the face of "enforcement by attrition," some literally sequester themselves in their homes, emerging only for work, school, and groceries. In contrast, storytelling teaches people to *turn toward, not away from* each other; it shows them that even the manifestation of painful emotion is an important way to connect with others. Storytelling does this by conferring an immediate emotional reward on both teller and listener. Listeners learn that sharing stories leads to connection with numerous others with very similar life experiences. As one Arizona youth described it: "It was the first time that you could speak to somebody that would understand you. Your family members are undocumented as well, but . . . my mom didn't go to college, and . . . my brother didn't, and he was the one who was living with us. Not that you can't relate, but sometimes they don't understand you when you're talking about college. . . . [But here] it was like automatically. Like when we had these group meetings, it felt like we knew each other for years, even though we had just met."[9] Storytellers learn that revealing themselves to others—and expressing emotions of pain or vulnerability—is not a sign of weakness. Rather, by doing so they acknowledge formative, shared experience that can trigger supportive, solidaristic responses from their peers. One young woman who had shared her story in an organization recounted: "It was amazing to me to just be sitting there and having all these people stare at me, and there I am exposing myself and being very vulnerable. And then surviving from that. They held my hand, and they told me and my sister that it would be okay. And that's when I knew that I wanted to create that kind of safe space for other people as well. That was my first moment where I knew that that's where I wanted to be and that's what I wanted to do."[10]

Storytelling also contributes to a second organizational goal: situating identity in relation to the collectivity. In some organizations, this occurs through a structured exercise in interpretation, which may be part of training for a particular action or campaign. Participants first learn to construct and share a "story of self," an individual narrative that highlights experiences of being undocumented. These stories are then connected to a "story of us"—a narrative about the struggles, triumphs, and needs of the group as a whole—and a "story of now"—an account of what these needs demand, usually in the form of collective action, from members of the group.[11] These aspects of storytelling help individuals identify themselves as members of a group. By embracing movement-specific labels—such as "DREAMers," "undocumented activists," or the "most directly affected"—they build a shared sense of identity. These labels foster bonds among participants and confer a new, affirmative sense of identity, one that is explicitly associated with specific kinds of emotional tendencies, performances, or stances. The DREAMer identity, for example, is often defined in terms of academic or professional striving, but also in terms of persistence, hope, and resilience.

Youth organizations also embrace concrete practices that foster this sense of collectivity, forging and strengthening emotional bonds among activists. For example, civic engagement organizations make a point of recruiting at high schools, where they encourage young people to bring their entire friendship groups to the organization. Those who have deep friendships in an organization are more likely to stay or undertake risky actions with it (McAdam 1988). Civic engagement organizations also offer lunches before afternoon canvassing sessions and hold evening "debriefings" after canvassing is done. Talking over food or unwinding together at the end of a long day helps strengthen bonds among activists and deepens their commitment to the movement. "They're your friends," said one teenage voter engagement participant. "You're pretty much doing it . . . not [so] much for yourself but for them as well, in honor of the friendship."[12]

The Emotion Cultures of Community-Based Organizations

In community-based organizations that focus on undocumented adults and families, socialization into the collectivity is even more important. Undocumented adults are often less prepared to engage in activism than their youth counterparts (Abrego 2011). Not only are they more likely to be targeted by immigration authorities, giving rise to legitimate fears about being publicly visible, but they have not experienced a K–12 education that provides them with a sense of cultural belonging. They are less likely to have secondary or higher education, or to be confident English speakers, and they are more likely to work in jobs that are low paid and subject to exploitation. These experiences can lead them to engage in self-isolating routines—sociologist Greg Prieto (2018) calls them "shells"—designed to protect themselves and their families from official encounters and minimize chances of immigration enforcement. Self-isolation also makes undocumented adults reluctant to engage in collective action or resistance.

One of the most important goals of organizations that aim to mobilize adults is to shift these perceptions and responses. Organizations seek to persuade new participants that they are members of a community that will nurture and support them as they respond to the state's hostility; they also aim to show new participants that they have a place in this fight. Whatever their employment, educational experience, or English proficiency, they show that they can make a difference by engaging collectively.

The message of solidarity and support is the first priority. Without this emotional grounding, it may seem too fearsome or difficult for many adults to participate. Prospective participants draw this message from their first contact with the organization—the general, or "community," meeting. Such meetings may be less professionalized, and less directed toward training or transformation. They may feel more like a neighborhood block party or potluck. One organization in Phoenix, for example, shares a meal at the beginning of every general meeting: people greet each other, visit over food, hold each other's new babies, and watch their children race around the meeting hall. This meal also offers the opportunity for community members to welcome newcomers to the organization. The group begins its meetings by posing a question to everyone assembled—about their observance of a holiday or festive occasion, or about their goals for the organization in the coming year—and every person shares an answer. Even if it takes half an hour or more, people listen carefully and nod, chuckle, or even applaud each other's answers. These practices show new members that they are part of a group in which they are seen, valued, and supported—which breaks down isolation and stigma. Celebrating festivals from their countries of origin and sharing traditions involving music, food, or visual arts also fosters bonds between community members.

Although storytelling may not be an explicit part of organizational meetings involving adults, these meetings nonetheless begin to modify participants' conceptions of who undocumented people are, and what they can bring to activism. Meetings often involve updates on recently completed campaigns or upcoming actions. These updates are partly informational: they alert new members to the activities and longer-term projects of the organization. But they also showcase the organizing skills and political courage of some of those who are the most affected. Those new to the community learn that even adult activists who are the most consistently targeted by the state, who may have little formal education or English proficiency, can be savvy organizers and relentless fighters for their families and communities. As in youth organizations, admiration for the knowledge, skill, and daring of more active members not only creates a bond of collectivity between activists; it also shapes their conception of what they are capable of achieving when they are supported by a strong, organized community.

Shared Elements of Emotion Culture and
Outward-Facing Activism

Activists learn to turn outward through training that fosters a sense of competence. Members are instructed, drilled, and mentored in the skills that they will use in approaching others. Voter engagement canvassers, for example, learn about the institutions whose members are up for election; they are taught how to read a district map, given strategies for engaging prospective voters, and perform role-plays before heading into their territories. Adult organizations also build confidence by meeting activists "where they are" and providing a "menu of options" for participation.[13] If adults feel most comfortable writing a letter to someone in detention or circulating a petition online, they are encouraged to do so. As they master these tasks, they may develop a sense of capacity and value that enables them to undertake more visible, public action. But encouraging outward-facing action is not simply a matter of supporting the development of skills: activists must come to feel that their contribution adds value and that they can be comfortable engaging others.

Storytelling can be an important vehicle in this regard. The comment I frequently heard in undocumented organizations, that "everyone has a story, and you can use it to change people's minds," is an instruction about how to persuade. It is also a phrase aimed at instilling confidence in undocumented people and convincing them that they can contribute tangibly to the movement simply by sharing their experience. Many organizations for the undocumented reinforce this valuation of experience, arguing that the perspectives of those most affected by immigration enforcement are a vital resource that should be represented not only in public persuasion but also in formal immigration policymaking.

In President Obama's second term, undocumented protesters pressured him to review his administration's deportation policies. Undocumented organizations created a (self-appointed) "blue ribbon commission," consisting entirely of activists who were or had been undocumented, to advise the president on this effort (Latino Rebels 2014). The use of a blue ribbon commission—generally a body of academic and policy experts appointed by government actors to counsel them about reform efforts—was a symbolic and practical statement about the value of undocumented immigrants' lived experiences in policymaking. It served to foster confidence and pride among participants at all levels of movement activity, establishing undocumented immigrants as experts with a role to play in the formation of immigration enforcement policy, regardless of their level of formal education, or their extent of cultural integration.

The emotion cultures of undocumented organizations also help activists manage emotions that might impede or discourage ongoing movement activity. Drawing on language, emotionally infused practices, and self-aware role modeling, organizations ease the fears of immigration enforcement that arise with public visibility or police encounters at organized protests, counter the stress or fatigue that can arise from a steep learning curve, and allay the frustrations produced by governmental delays, hypocrisy, or failures of recognition. One young participant, who became a leader in voter engagement campaigns, described how she learned from a fellow activist old enough to be her mother. "[She] was a really experienced canvasser," the youth campaigner observed, explaining why she kept her eyes on her colleague, and "if I ever—which I did at times—fe[lt] frustrated for whatever reason, she encourage[d] me."[14]

Peer modeling is central in all organizations for signaling those emotional stances that serve ongoing activism.

Prospective activists learn this within organizations, as well as by watching their fellows in outward-facing actions. In youth organizations, for example, leaders model confidence and competence, while keeping their emotions close to the surface. As they speak at general meetings or with newer participants, they are not shy about sharing feelings of excitement, nervousness, concern, or even pain for threatened loved ones, and more. This combination of demonstrated competence and emotional accessibility can have powerful effects on newer activists. As one participant related: "At my very first meeting, I ended up telling my story and bawling my eyes out in front of these strangers. And it just felt amazing being able to talk about the kind of struggles that you're going through to a group of people that know exactly what you're feeling."[15] The practice of combining competence with emotional vulnerability also lays a foundation for activists who must be able to take part in logistically challenging actions, while sharing stories with emotional immediacy. In community-based organizations, adults who have learned to manifest leadership by undertaking visible, sometimes risky, public actions may share their feelings of pride in their hard-won skills and accomplishments. Many activists see the process of sharing as a means to explain their role and accomplishments to newer participants. An activist mother in her forties sought to inspire others: "I want to be that motivation that if I can do it with no education, with no resources," she declared, "then so can someone who has an education, who is in a better position, and [has] a better, promising future."[16]

Language is also vital for communicating the emotional dispositions or responses that are normative for undocumented activists. Organizations may use aphorisms—familiar expressions that encompass desired emotion states—to communicate this message.[17] Some of them, such as "DREAMers never quit," achieve their effects by connecting normative emotion states with aspects of identity that are valued, or salient, for undocumented activists. Others, such as "being out of our comfort zone is the way we grow," encourage new participants to reinterpret uncomfortable or unpleasant feelings as signs of progress in their new, activist role. The statement "we thrive on adversity," which I sometimes heard in Phoenix organizations, appears to be a simple description; although it is not fully accurate (adversity can be difficult, even for those who are familiar with it), it is important in establishing the expectation that movement participants will demonstrate emotional resilience. The same is true of the best-known aphorism of this movement: "we are undocumented and unafraid."

"Undocumented and unafraid" is a self-characterization that originated as DREAMers became impatient with government inaction and began to utilize contentious, direct action tactics to rally public support and place pressure on government actors.[18] The declaration was a tactic in and of itself: making undocumented immigrants visible while knowingly exposing them to the risks of detention and deportation, and rallying public support as it created dilemmas of enforcement for Immigration and Customs Enforcement (ICE) and executive branch officials. But it is also an emotional stance: It evokes a fearlessness or defiance that signals participants' courage and reveals to public officials that they face a more determined and empowered adversary than they may have anticipated. This defiance has sometimes had a performative dimension. Activists outwardly embrace an affective stance they do not fully inhabit in the expectation—or the hope—that it will make an impression on others as they gradually come to feel it internally. One youth explained the performative effect of being "undocumented and unafraid" in this way:

> [It began] . . . I guess, like an empowerment phrase . . . even if [you] were still afraid, [you] didn't have to show [you] were afraid to the public . . . even if [you] were dying inside . . . you had to put that face on where it was—you know what? I'm not afraid. . . . As people started telling their stories and started coming out, they started noticing that it really wasn't something to be afraid of, that it was something you could live with, that you were okay with; and when you sa[id] so, certainly people believe[d] you . . . so even if it started as . . . an empowerment phrase, it became true over the years.[19]

Through this phrase, activists not only invoke the selves that they want the public and the government to see; they invoke the selves that they aim to become—and help others to become—through their ongoing activism.

Beyond modeling and language, organizations also engage in specific practices and reminders to manage the kinds of emotions that can thwart public action, even among established activists, in a high-risk, high-frustration movement. Fear—which is ubiquitous in those families and communities facing ongoing concern about deportation—is eased through various forms of solidarity. Organizations reassure individual activists, and activists reassure each other, that the community "has their back" and will advocate for them if they are arrested or detained. Frustration—another emotion prevalent among activists who are often disappointed by legislators or policymakers—is met with a variety of cognitive and affective strategies. Organizers encourage participants to shift their time horizon: to think about what will be true for their children or grandchildren rather than themselves, or to remember how long other social movements, such as the civil rights movement, have taken to bring about social change.[20] They encourage activists to celebrate small victories, particularly when achieving the ultimate goal will likely require a protracted fight. Following the 2012 "Adios Arpaio" campaign—a Latino voter registration effort focused on the defeat of the virulently anti-immigrant sheriff of Maricopa County—organizers planned a large rally. An event that might have been sober, as Arpaio was narrowly reelected and removing him would require another four years, became buoyant and festive as organizers celebrated the 50,000 new voters added to the rolls and envisioned the long-term effects on Arizona's politics.

Organizers also foster emotions, such as joy, countering the painful emotions that often derail activism. They punctuate difficult actions or protests with musical interludes, chants, or even dancing—to reduce tension and to remind people of why they are sustaining particular risks. For instance, at the end of a sixty-mile walk to end immigrant detention, Phoenix activists held a vigil outside Eloy, a notorious private prison in the Arizona desert. After an emotionally wrenching session in which activists used a public address system to call out messages to detained loved ones, organizers suddenly turned on a boom box and dance music flooded the plaza where the vigil was being held. Activists, exhausted by the emotional intensity of the morning's activities, slowly began to dance in place. Several detained men began moving white placards—which they were holding to signal their solidarity with those outside—in time to the music.

Emotion Cultures and Movement-Based Change

A final goal of emotion cultures moves beyond the goal of movement persistence, to enable adaptation over time.

Emotion cultures have proven vital to helping organizers and participants respond to changes in the external environment or government decision making and develop new strategies and tactics. In *Moving Politics* (2009), Deborah Gould describes a period in the struggle against AIDS in which LGBT activists moved from an "emotional habitus" that emphasized compassion and community-based responsibility for those suffering from the disease, to one that emphasized anger at government inaction and used innovative direct action to challenge that response. The shift in emotion cultures among undocumented organizations has been more gradual and less dramatic than this. Yet in the latter part of the Obama administration, undocumented organizers and activists began to manifest a new sense that it was acceptable, and indeed necessary, to express a broader range of emotions than they had previously exhibited, including anguish and anger.

In Arizona, this shift was less a response to the actions of state officials—whose rapid and full-blown implementation of the hostile SB 1070 took many immigrants by surprise and provoked a determined, but not overtly angry, response[21]— than to the federal government. In the 2000s, the then-small cadre of DREAM activists seemed conspicuously to avoid accusing the government of injustice or using contentious tactics to disrupt institutional processes. They treated the government's failure to create a path to citizenship for undocumented youth as a kind of remediable error, displaying confidence that Congress, having glimpsed their character, would make it right. As the administration's first push for comprehensive immigration reform stalled in Congress in early 2010, undocumented youth began to press for a standalone DREAM Act. They set aside the cheerful optimism of early DREAMer narratives to acknowledge feelings of frustration and grievance against the government. Activists began to "come out" as "undocumented and unafraid," approaching the government in a posture of demand.

The "coming out" speeches of activists at the first "Coming Out of the Shadows" event in the spring of 2010 are peppered with grievance, frustration, and impatience. Co-organizer Tania Unzueta remarked: "Every time I take a step forward in my life, I have to consider that my options are limited, because in this country, I am not free. We are not free. I believe that this is the only life that I get to live, and I am tired of hiding. My name is Tania and I'm undocumented" (Holderness 2016, 5:39). Another activist's "coming out" speech reflected similar emotions: "I refuse to think about what another ten years of not knowing whether I will be able to come home to my mother and brother will feel like. I refuse to think about what another ten years of dreams shut down will feel like: dreams of a good education, dreams of a normal life without fear. I am undocumented. I am not afraid. I will not hide any longer. I will come out of the shadows every day if I have to. I'm a human being. I deserve to be happy" (Holderness 2016). These emotions were not simply the expression of individual activists; they reflected a new understanding among organizers about what emotions and tactics were required when the federal government failed to respond. As one Arizona youth leader explained following the first act of civil disobedience by DREAMers in late spring 2010,

> People are angry that nothing has been done. . . . When we have been working for this issue for so long and we know that we have done it the "right" way, and not . . . ruffled anyone's feathers, and not done anything that's given us a bad image, six years, seven years, eight years, nine years, and we still don't see any change . . . [protesters] just think, I need to put myself out there, I need to be the

catalyst for this change, in order for me to motivate other students. (Cruz 2010, 2:44)

A combination of publicly manifested anger and more contentious forms of protest continued through the failure of the DREAM Act in December 2010; they fueled the ultimately successful campaign for Deferred Action for Childhood Arrivals (DACA) in 2011–2012.

Another emotional transition occurred in 2013–2014, after a second push for comprehensive immigration reform sputtered to a halt in the House of Representatives. Arizona activists played a central role in a national campaign called Not1More Deportation, aimed at securing families who no longer had the prospect of a path to citizenship from being separated through detention and deportation. Activists shifted from anger to outrage as they accused Obama of inhumanity in his deportation policy. They expressed anguish at being separated from their loved ones. Shortly after leading Arizona youth activist Erika Andiola's mother and brother were taken into ICE custody in January 2013, she recorded a video urging supporters to help her fight her family's deportation. The video shows Andiola, distraught and weeping, as she says:

> Hello, my name is Erika . . . my mother and my brother were just taken by Immigration. They just came to my house, they knocked on my door. . . . My mom came outside and they took her, for no reason. And then . . . they just took [my brother]—they didn't want to tell me why. They just said that they needed to go because they were here illegally, and that they shouldn't be here.
>
> This needs to stop. We need to do something. . . . We need to stop separating families. This is real, this is so real. This is not just happening to me, this is happening to

families everywhere. We cannot let this happen anymore. *I need everybody to stop pretending like nothing is wrong, to stop pretending that we're just living normal lives, because we're not. This could happen to any of us at any time.* (DreamActivist.org 2013, 1:58)

Andiola's decision to film herself at the moment of greatest impact, before she had the opportunity to assimilate her fear, anger, and grief, vividly conveyed the costs of government policies. Her decision to film her unprocessed fear, anger, and grief struck an immediate chord with viewers; as the video went viral, it brought her effort to save her mother national support and visibility. Andiola's willingness to leverage the power not only of social media but also of unfiltered emotion to amplify an anti-deportation message became a model for future efforts.

Another Phoenix organization, for example, mounted an ongoing campaign to prevent deportations, often circulating videos on social media that featured emotional encounters with the families of those detained. The campaign's lead organizer carefully explained the rationale for this strategy:

[E]very day, we['d] have these people come into our space or we'd be outside the jail and we'd run into these people. . . . They're just [crying] to us, we would swallow it and then we would go into this mechanism and come up with a strategy to fight it. [Finally, we said] *we need to share that. We can't be swallowing it and making these political arguments. We needed to put that [pain] out there.* And we also put it back on the people, that this is going to help your loved ones get out. People need to see what you're going through. That's how we're going to get the people engaged and involved in fighting for this.[22]

By explaining that the public communication of private suffering was the best way to help fight deportation, organizers helped people to assume the burden of this more demanding form of self-disclosure.

Activists' willingness to judge and condemn also reflected their growing political confidence. "Undocumented people feel that it's not okay to express your outrage," one Arizona youth leader explained. "It's not okay to express how things are not right, because *you're not supposed to have rights*, right?"[23] Yet as undocumented youth became increasingly empowered, they gradually shed such inhibitions and began to conduct themselves more like those with a formal stake in American politics, expressing a range of emotions in response to ongoing government-inflicted injury. Organizers endorsed these emotions as a legitimate response to the inhumanity of family separation. They explained the necessity of manifesting these emotions tactically, in political action, and supported activists as they brought these difficult feelings into public view.

Conclusion

Undocumented immigrants, in Arizona and elsewhere, have begun to create distinctive, dynamic emotion cultures that motivate and support activism. New activists are taught to be resourceful, to manage their fears, to be resilient in the face of disappointment or frustration, and to be unafraid of vulnerability. They learn to see themselves as interdependent and to share their apprehension, loss, or pain, with neighbors and strangers. This complex emotion culture has enabled undocumented activism to emerge and thrive under conditions that would seem likely to thwart its existence. Yet the emotions cultivated by undocumented activists are not simply a vehicle for fueling and sustaining political engagement.

These emotions also reflect and animate undocumented people's changing political consciousness, and their growing sense of authorization and belonging, despite the fact that the civic realm tends formally to exclude them.

There is a lesson in these developments that is both chastening and challenging. Many Americans understand, correctly, that legal status[24] is vital to the aspirations of undocumented migrants. Legal status creates opportunities for secure employment, limits the possibility of family separation through detention and deportation, allows people to plan long-term futures, and in many cases offers a first step toward formal citizenship. But many people also assume that legal status is the sine qua non of formal membership in economic institutions and ultimately in the polity—and is key to subjective belonging in social and political communities. The experience of undocumented activists suggests, however, that there are more routes to such belonging than we have previously understood.[25]

Robust political participation—whether or not it culminates in the casting of a vote—may fuel an understanding of, affinity for, and sense of investment in political institutions. For undocumented immigrants, this sense of affinity and investment accrues over time, even without the grant of formal membership. Undocumented immigrants develop a sense of social belonging through a deep connection with preexisting immigrant communities and with social activists who have struggled for a more just and inclusive United States in the past. The experience of undocumented immigrants suggests that voice and agency are not solely a product of formal status; those who mobilize for their political rights make their road to political membership, in part, by walking it.

The experience of immigrant activists in Arizona and elsewhere offers a challenge to the tenuous relationship between formal citizenship and democratic engagement that is common in the United States. Many activists I encountered in Arizona expressed the view that their extended—and sometimes adversarial—engagement with political institutions actually demonstrates a commitment that *should* be associated with citizenship. Some expressed frustration that many, if not most, of those who enjoy the privilege of citizenship do not share this sense of responsibility. Their example, fueled by the cognitive and emotional practices that have animated this movement, promises not only to energize the local and national political communities of which they are a part. It can also show those who may take their formal citizenship for granted that another path is possible.

Notes

1. McAdam responded to a theoretical tradition in which most scholars emphasized either the institutional openness of a political system to the claims of an emerging movement (Meyer 2004), or the financial, networking, and media resources that were available to it through the support of well-endowed, external organizations and donors (McCarthy and Zald 1977). McAdam's signal contributions included a recognition of the "indigenous"—or community-based—resources that an emerging movement might be able to mobilize, a focus on the sense of possibility and efficacy he described as "cognitive liberation," and the melding of opportunity, resources, and consciousness to produce a more holistic theory of social movement emergence, that he referred to as the "political process model."

2. Undocumented immigrants and their allies have mobilized for more than a decade against hostile legislation and enforcement in Arizona. This movement is the subject of my book *Open Hand, Closed Fist: Practices of Undocumented Organizing in a*

Hostile State (University of California Press, 2022). The book draws on several years of empirical research with undocumented activists and their allies in Phoenix, Arizona.

3. Law professor and former Kansas secretary of state Kris Kobach was the architect of this program. See Kobach (2008).

4. It also cut a bizarre swath through mixed-status families: if a citizen drove his undocumented grandfather to the grocery store or church, he could technically be charged—which is why activists and others in immigrant communities sometimes referred to it as the "grandfather provision."

5. Menjívar and Abrego describe an undocumented worker seized in a federal immigration raid on a workplace in Postville, Iowa, who—despite the explanations of an attorney—declared repeatedly, "I'm illegal. I have no rights. I'm nobody in this country. Just do what you want with me" (2012, 1404).

6. The DREAM Act is a federal bill that provides a path to citizenship for (some) undocumented youth brought to the United States as children; it has been introduced in various forms since 2001. The 2010 DREAM Act was the version that came closest to becoming law: it passed in the House of Representatives but failed by five votes in the Senate.

7. For a thoughtful discussion of the role of storytelling in early DREAM activism, see Nichols (2013).

8. This particular narrative is taken from a story offered publicly by an Arizona activist (Montoya 2019). But it replicates many of the features of stories shared within organizations.

9. DM, Interview with author, July 2014.

10. DV, interview with author, April 2013.

11. This framework is based on an approach to storytelling formu-lated by sociologist Marshall Ganz (2009), drawing on his experience with the Farmworkers Union. Some organizations in Phoenix have cited Ganz's approach specifically in their training materials, or used variants of it in organizing meetings for new participants.

12. D, M, and K, interview with author, August 2012.

13. Carlos Garcia (director and lead organizer of Puente-Arizona), interview with author, March 2015.

14. KI, interview with author, January 2015.

15. DV, Interview with author, April 2013.

16. MCR, interview with author, April 2015.

17. Many of these statements function as what anthropologist William Reddy called "emotives"—terms that sound descriptive, but actually convey a normative view of an optimal or valued emotional stance (Reddy 1999, 1997).

18. See generally Beltran (2015).

19. CC, interview with author, July 2013.

20. For a discussion of lessons learned about the civil rights movement among undocumented activists traveling on a nationwide "Freedom Ride" to protest state immigration enforcement and influence the Obama administration, see Ramirez Jimenez (2012).

21. As I note in the introduction to my book, anger was not conspicuous in the protests that initially sought to respond to SB 1070. The denial of rights was so comprehensive that activists may have felt more fearful than angry, or may have concluded that, in that political environment determination and resolve were more likely to create a resonant public impression than anger or outrage. See Abrams (2022).

22. Carlos Garcia, interview with author, March 2015.

23. RM, interview with author, August 2014.

24. Some of these benefits, including the ability to work legally and relief from deportation, may be available on a temporary basis to those who enjoy forms of legal presence without formal legal status, such as Deferred Action for Childhood Arrivals (DACA).

25. I offer a version of this argument, grounded in my empirical research, in chapter 6 of Abrams (2022).

References

Abrams, Kathryn. 2022. *Open Hand, Closed Fist: Practices of Undocumented Organizing in a Hostile State.* Berkeley: University of California Press.

Abrego, Leisy. 2011. "Legal Consciousness of Undocumented Latinos: Fear and Stigma as Barriers to Claims Making for First Generation and 1.5 Generation Immigrants." *Law and Society Review* 45, no. 2: 337–369.

Almeida, Paul. 2019. "The Role of Threat in Collective Action." In *Wiley-Blackwell Companion to Social Movements*, 2nd ed., edited by David A. Snow, Sara A. Soule, Hanspeter Kriesi, and Holly McCammon, 43–62. Oxford: John Wiley & Sons.

Alonzo, Monica. 2012. "SB 1070 Fuels a Movement of New Voters." *Phoenix New Times*, July 5. https://www.phoenixnewtimes.com/news/sb-1070-fuels-a-movement-of-new-voters-6454767.

Arizona State Senate. 2010. "Fact Sheet for SB 1070," 49 A.Z. 2d, January 15, 2010.

Beltran, Cristina. 2015. "'Undocumented, Unafraid, and Unapologetic': DREAM Activists, Immigrant Politics and the Queering of Democracy." In *From Voice to Influence: Understanding Citizenship in a Digital Age*, edited by Danielle Allen and Jennifer Light, 80–104. Chicago: University of Chicago Press.

Chua, Lynette. 2018. *The Politics of Love in Myanmar: LGBT Mobilization and Human Rights as a Way of Life.* Stanford, CA: Stanford University Press.

Cruz, Gabriel. 2010. "Daniel Rodriguez Speaks about 'Dream Act 5' outside McCain's Phoenix Office." *YouTube*, May 18. www.youtube.com/watch?v=fviT-u7DMSQ.

DreamActivist.org. 2013. "Arizona Activist Erika Andiola's Home Was Raided; Her Mother and Her Brother Taken!" *YouTube*, January 11. https://www.youtube.com/watch?v=nMPWhn8HEJk.

Ganz, Marshall. 2009. "Why Stories Matter: The Art and Craft of Social Change." *Sojourner*, March. https://sojo.net/magazine /march-2009/why-stories-matter?action=magazine .article&issue=sojo903&article=why-stories-matter.

Goodwin, Jeff, James Jasper, and Francesca Polletta, eds. 2001. *Passionate Politics: Emotions and Social Movements*. Chicago: University of Chicago Press.

Gould, Deborah. 2009. *Moving Politics: Emotion and ACT UP's Fight against AIDS*. Chicago: University of Chicago Press.

Hochschild, Arlie. 1979. "Work, Feeling Rules, and Social Structure." *American Journal of Sociology* 85, no. 3: 551–575.

———. 1983. *The Managed Heart: Commercialization of Human Feeling*. Berkeley: University of California Press.

Holderness, Peter. 2016. "Immigrant Youth Justice League—2010 Coming Out." *YouTube*, April 12. https://www.youtube.com /watch?v=Sv6d7TEeCGY.

Jasper, James. 2008. *The Emotions of Protest*. Chicago: University of Chicago Press.

Kobach, Kris. 2008. "Reinforcing the Rule of Law: What States Can and Should Do to Reduce Illegal Immigration." *Georgetown Immigration Law Journal* 22: 459–483.

Latino Rebels. 2014. "NDLON Publishes Blue Ribbon Immigration Recommendations for President." *Latino Rebels*, April 10. https://www.latinorebels.com/2014/04/10/ndlon-publishes-blue -ribbon-immigration-recommendations-for-president/.

McAdam, Doug. 1988. *Freedom Summer*. Oxford: Oxford University Press.

McCarthy, John, and Mayer Zald. 1977. "Resource Mobilization and Social Movements: A Partial Theory." *American Journal of Sociology* 82, no. 6: 1212–1241.

Menjivar, Cecilia, and Leisy Abrego. 2012. "Legal Violence: Immigration Law and the Lives of Central American Immigrants." *American Journal of Sociology* 117, no. 5: 1380–1421.

Meyer, David. 2004. "Protest and Political Opportunities." *Annual Review of Sociology* 30: 125–145.

Meyer, Rachel, and Janice Fine. 2017. "Grassroots Citizenship at Multiple Scales: Rethinking Immigrant Civic Participation." *International Journal of Politics, Culture, and Society* 30, no. 4: 323–348.

Montoya, Reyna. 2019. "Aliento: Transforming Trauma into Hope and Activism." *YouTube*, August 27. https://www.youtube.com /watch?v=WLshXBW9L3o.

NDLONvideos. 2014. "The Most Passionate Speech You Have Ever Heard." *YouTube*, April 17. www.youtube.com/watch?v =lSStVYqxcno.

Nichols, Walter. 2013. *The Dreamers*. Stanford, CA: Stanford University Press.

Prieto, Greg. 2018. *Immigrants under Threat: Risk and Resistance in Deportation Nation*. New York: New York University Press.

Ramirez Jimenez, Mari Cruz. 2012. "In Admiration: Learning about the Civil Rights Movement." *No Papers, No Fear: Ride for Justice*, August 16. http://nopapersnofear.org/blog/post.php?s =2012-08-16-in-admiration-learning-about-the-civil-rights -movement.

Reddy, William. 1997. "Against Constructionism: The Historical Ethnography of Emotions." *Current Anthropology* 38, no. 3: 327–351.

———. 1999. "Emotional Liberty, Politics and History in the Anthropology of Emotions." *Cultural Anthropology* 14, no. 2: 256–288.

Zepeda-Millan, Chris. 2016. "Weapons of the (Not So) Weak: Immigrant Mass Mobilization in the U.S. South." *Critical Sociology* 42, no. 2: 269–287.

2

"The Women of Egypt Are a Red Line"

Anger and Women's Collective Action

NERMIN ALLAM

The image of an Egyptian woman dragged, beaten, and stripped down to her jeans and bright blue bra by an army solider on December 17, 2011, signified the violence and brutality of Egypt's military government against women protesters.[1] The anonymous woman became known as "Sitt el-Banāt" (The Lady of All Ladies) in Egypt, or the "girl in the blue bra" in Western media. In response to the army's brutal attack on Sitt el-Banāt and the subsequent media campaign against her, Egyptian women participated in a massive demonstration on December 20, 2011. They demanded the end of interim rule by the Supreme Council of the Armed Forces (SCAF) and a halt to violence against women. Local and international media described the protest as the largest women's march in Egyptian history, with an estimated 10,000 participants (National Post 2011a). The protest came to be known as "Sitt El-Banāt's

March" (The Lady of All Ladies' March) in honor of the brutalized young woman.

Media coverage of the march described an "outpouring of anger" (National Post 2011a) and quoted "angry female protesters" criticizing the army for its use of violence against women (Al-Ahram 2011). Marchers expressed their anger through chants, slogans, and graffiti. They chanted "Banāt Miṣr khat aḥmr" (The women of Egypt are a red line), and this became the slogan of the march and its rallying cry. They displayed the iconic blue bra on banners, signs, and graffiti-clad walls. In a show of solidarity with the victim, some women stenciled drawings of bras on their plain white shirts and paraded them throughout the march (Invicta 2011). The women's anger shifted blame from the victim to the army and created moral outrage over the latter's transgression.

In this chapter, I examine the expression of anger during the 2011 women's march, highlighting its productive role in mobilizing collective action and political change. My overarching argument is that the protesters' expression of anger successfully secured recognition for the victim, created moral outrage against the army, and brought attention to women's bodily rights. In line with the rich tradition of feminist scholarship on rage,[2] I argue that anger can be productive in politics (Rich 1973; Lorde 1981; Frye 1983; Narayan 1988; Jaggar 1989; Gilmore 1993). Anger is not only a means for revenge but also to secure recognition (Srinivasan 2018). This recognition is an important prerequisite for focusing on broad issues of welfare.

In making this argument, I challenge Martha Nussbaum's account of the relationship between ordinary, "garden-variety anger," and what she terms "Transition-Anger," a forward-looking emotion that abandons obsessions over status and retribution, and rather focuses from the start on broad issues of welfare (Nussbaum 2016, 6).

Nussbaum views ordinary anger as senseless and unproductive, and Transition-Anger as proper and unusual in its unadulterated form. Contrary to Nussbaum, I do not view "garden-variety anger" or "status-focused anger" as always futile or inappropriate. In the case of the Egyptian women's march, I argue that anger, expressed through protests, was important to secure recognition. Women later channeled their expression of anger over the army's violence into different initiatives and campaigns, embodying a form of Transition-Anger. Transition-Anger was therefore the culmination of the anger expressed by activists against the army's violence.

My examination of the 2011 Egyptian women's march also challenges the normative claims implicit in Nussbaum's argument. Nussbaum briefly acknowledges that "it is much more common to get angry first and then head to the Transition, than to be there already, focused on social welfare" (2016, 36). However, she asserts that this is not how circumstances *ought* to be, because ordinary forms of anger are senseless and wrong, and they often fail to evolve into Transition-Anger. As someone who studies, works, and lived under an authoritarian regime for the majority of my life, the idea that we ought to start from Transition-Anger completely overlooks the complexities of feminist activism under autocratic regimes.

In the Middle East and North Africa (MENA), patriarchy intersects with authoritarianism. The regime's viewpoints are positioned as beyond scrutiny, and individuals who express dissenting perspectives are subject to moral condemnation and marginalization. Within this hypermasculinized, paternal framework, women who dissent against the regime are particularly targeted, their rights undermined, and their voices suppressed. The patriarchal authoritarian character of many regimes in the region curbs the expression of certain subjectivities, silences certain conversations, affects and shapes the very nature of gender politics. In these closed political and social structures, getting angry and securing recognition are necessary stepping stones for achieving "general social concern" (Nussbaum 2016, 53). By acknowledging the complexity of activism outside of liberal democracies, researchers stay true to their subjects and their stories, and avoid producing extraverted knowledge—knowledge that is only directed toward Western academia and irrelevant to the societies we are studying (Jackson and Kelly 2019; Joseph, Meari, and Zaatari 2022).

Theoretical Framework: Anger in Philosophy and Politics

Anger is a complex feeling and a contentious force. Its critics associate it with populism and far-right politics in Western societies. The negative view of anger in political and social life can be traced back to ancient Western philosophy. Aristotle, for instance, defined anger as normatively wrong, describing it as a "desire, accompanied by [mental and physical] distress, for conspicuous retaliation because of a conspicuous slight that was directed, without justification, against oneself or those near to one" (Aristotle 1991, 124).

Contemporary philosophers reiterate Aristotle's claim that anger intrinsically includes a desire for revenge. In line with this definition, Nussbaum argues that what distinguishes anger from other similar emotions such as grief is the focus on payback, on retribution (2016, 18). The element of retribution that is so intrinsic and distinct to the emotion of anger is normatively problematic, and thus so is anger (Nussbaum 2016, 15–18). It is problematic because of its retaliatory tendency as well as its futility; anger is futile since retaliation does not restore what is lost (Nussbaum 2016,

15–16). According to Nussbaum, anger is therefore never apt, as it either focuses narrowly on relative status—one's injured pride—or on the injury itself (2016, 15–16). "Transition-Anger" or "anger leading toward the Transition" is distinct from ordinary anger—sometimes described by Nussbaum as "garden-variety anger" or "status-focused anger"—that wishes the offender ill. Nussbaum conceptualizes Transition-Anger as a forward-looking emotion that ought to focus, from its inception, on broader welfare (2016, 35–36). It does not even briefly focus on retribution, diminishing the transgressor, or elevating the status of the victim. She views anger that focuses on retribution, status, or recognition as counterproductive; it hinders our move away "from excessive ego-involvement" and obscures our transition toward "general social concern" (Nussbaum 2016, 53).

Debates surrounding women's anger in politics have often reproduced the same view of anger as antithetical to critical thinking and productive political engagement. In Western societies, women have been criticized for expressing their anger and encouraged to silence it in social, political, and even academic contexts. In the Middle East, those in the women's movement grapple further with cultural norms that expect them to mute angry emotions and public displays of anger. A saying attributed to Mohamed, the Prophet of Islam, describes women as lacking in intellectual capacity and religious faith. The saying is often used in Muslim majority society to suggest that women are temperamental and have clouded judgment compared to men. Public outbursts of anger by women are used as evidence of "their lack of mental capacity" and to declare them unfit for leadership.

In Egyptian society, women encounter a range of patriarchal narratives that reinforce gender inequalities. One pervasive narrative is the primacy of male authority, whereby the society positions men as the primary decision makers and leaders within both familial and societal contexts. This view of male superiority undermines women's agency and participation in decision-making processes. Dominant patriarchal norms propagating the notion that women's primary role is confined to the domestic sphere further limit women's economic, educational, and political opportunities. Additionally, inheritance laws, influenced by patriarchal values, perpetuate the unequal distribution of assets, with women receiving a smaller share compared to men, thus reinforcing economic disparities. Traditional gendered, moral discourses seek to control women's bodies and sexuality and impose strict codes of modesty and chastity. Cultural expectations of marriage and motherhood further reinforce these traditional gender roles and structures, discouraging alternative paths or the prioritization of personal aspirations beyond these realms. Women's voices and experiences are thus often marginalized or silenced within public discourse, perpetuating a lack of representation and participation in decision-making processes. Women's activism in Egypt exposes and challenges these entrenched patriarchal strictures to foster a more equitable and inclusive society that upholds the rights of all individuals, irrespective of gender.

The display of anger by women's groups in the Middle East generally, and in Egypt specifically, is thus situated within a complex web of social, religious, and cultural networks. These networks are imbued with local but also global meanings. Globally, critics of women's anger have used the derogatory "angry feminist" label to discredit activists and their demands. As Sara Ahmed elucidates in her analysis of emotions in neoliberal societies, anger is often used to label women as angry "killjoys" (Ahmed 2004, 177). Indeed, the dreaded "angry feminist" is a powerful social trope that, as Barbara Tomlinson rightly argues, is increasingly used to "delegitimize feminist argument even before it begins, to undermine feminist politics by making its costs personal, and to foreclose feminist futures by making feminism seem repulsive to young women" (Tomlinson 2010, 102).

Feminist theorists, however, reframe anger as a legitimate response against injustice and a tool to expose oppressive structures (Lorde 1981; Frye 1983; Narayan 1988; Jaggar 1989; Gilmore 1993). In "The Uses of Anger: Women Responding to Racism," Audre Lorde famously describes the significance of anger in developing political consciousness and building the strength necessary to foreground structural oppression (1981, 124). Women's "well-stocked arsenal of anger," she argues, is "potentially useful against those oppressions, personal and institutional, which brought that anger into being" (Lorde 1981, 122). Anger that is channeled into actions, she adds, can become a mobilizing source for change (Lorde 1981, 122). Anger can thus be productive for women's collective action and political engagement; it is epistemically necessary to expose gender hierarchies, and to challenge them in public and political debates. This view of anger as a productive force has been increasingly gaining resonance with the advent of the #MeToo movement. Feminists have been emphasizing the epistemic significance of anger and its important emotive energy in mobilizing the movement and framing its feminist demands (Blair 2018; Orgad and Gill 2019; Kay 2019; Wood 2019).

My work expands discussions surrounding the expression of anger in women's collective action and puts forward a nuanced reading of this complex emotional response. By examining Egyptian women's anger during the 2011 women's march, I illuminate the dynamics of feminist activism during and after the 2011 Egyptian uprising and how anger was central in sustaining engagement. In the next section, I provide an overview of the violence committed by state and non-state actors against women protesters in Egypt during the transitional period between the 2011 uprising that ousted Egyptian President Hosni Mubarak and the 2012 election of Mohamed Morsi to the presidency. During this time, the Supreme Council of the Armed Forces (SCAF) ruled the country. The overview provides important background information about the status of women under the interim presidency of SCAF, and about women's collective action during Egypt's transitional period.

State Violence and Women's Political Participation

The agenda of women's rights in Egypt suffered major blows and setbacks after the 2011 uprising that led to the ousting of Egypt's former President Hosni Mubarak. During the transitional period following the uprising, SCAF held the interim presidency and Islamist political parties held the legislative power. The transitional period ended with the election of Muslim Brotherhood–affiliated Islamist candidate Mohamed Morsi as president of Egypt in 2012. Morsi's victory was short-lived and soon came to an end with the ousting of his regime in 2013 and the election of the military-backed regime of Abdel Fattah el-Sisi in 2014.

On March 8, 2011, less than one month after Mubarak's ousting, Egyptian women marked International Women's Day by taking to the streets to advocate for gender equality and representation during the transitional period. It was already evident that women's rights were being pushed aside. For instance, the transitional government under the interim presidency of SCAF did not include any women. When women went out to march on International Women's Day, they were beaten, accused of betraying the revolution, and even told they were "not Egyptians" by an angry mob (Coleman 2011).

In the 2011–2012 parliamentary election that brought the Muslim Brotherhood's Freedom and Justice Party (FJP) to power following the fall of Mubarak, women secured only eight elected seats in parliament. SCAF appointed an additional ten members, two of whom were women ("National Election Authority Official Site" 2012). Women thus secured only 2 percent of the seats in parliament, and those who won were mostly candidates of the Freedom and Justice Party. Candidates belonging to Islamist parties won the overall majority of parliamentary seats, with the Muslim Brotherhood leading the polls, followed by the al-Nour Party—the political party of the Salafi group.

While a number of studies document the underrepresentation of women in Islamist political parties (Sika and Khodary 2012; National Council for Women and Dokhan 2015; Shalaby 2016; Kato 2017), it is worth noting that the representation of women in liberal and left-leaning parties, which paid lip service to women's participation and meaningful incorporation in party politics, was also problematic (Kamal 2015; McLarney 2016). As Nadine Sika and Yasmin Khodary (2012) rightly argue in their study of the evolution and decline of women's organizations in Egypt, the limited representation of women following the uprising underscores the absence of women's rights and gender equality from the legislative agendas of Islamist parties in power. They add that it also emphasizes the absence of women's rights from the agenda of SCAF, which held executive power in the immediate period after the uprising.[3]

Women were not only marginalized in formal politics; they were also targeted during their participation in collective action. In the period following the uprising, women suffered a series of violent attacks and sexual assaults at the hands of security forces. The attacks started soon after the uprising, on March 19, 2011, with virginity tests conducted by an army doctor on women who took part in ongoing protests in the aftermath of the uprising that ousted Mubarak (Amnesty International 2011). The military justified its actions by attacking the women protesters and their presence in public space and by othering them, emphasizing that they "[w]ere not like your daughter or mine. These were girls who had camped out in tents with male protesters" (Coleman 2011). By describing how the women shamelessly spent nights on the street and slept next to men during sit-ins, the army challenged their chastity and morals.

The pinnacle of SCAF's violence against women activists was the brutal beating and stripping of the "girl in the blue bra" during Aḥdath Maglis al-Wuzara' on December 17, 2011 (Zayed 2011). The Aḥdath Maglis al-Wuzara' was a massive sit-in in front of the cabinet building. Activists demanded the transfer of power to a civilian government and protested the appointment of Kamal al-Ganzouri, who served as prime minister during the 1990s under the ousted Mubarak regime (Al-Ahram 2011). A video recording of the attack shows the woman fleeing as security forces chase protesters away from Qasr al 'īny street, where the demonstration took place. The woman stumbles and falls to the ground. A young man, also a protester, stops to help her. Soldiers advance on them, separate the two, and beat them violently. The woman's body goes limp as soldiers drag her by her abaya—the long black dress that covers her whole body—and tear it open, exposing her. She lies on the ground, naked except for her jeans and bright blue bra, as one soldier brutally kicks her breasts and bare abdomen, and another solider pulls the abaya to cover her body.

National and international newspapers ran the image of the girl in the blue bra on their front pages to highlight the degradation of women's rights in Egypt. The then U.S. secretary of state, Hillary Clinton, expressed her outrage and described the attack as a disgrace to the state and the army (National Post 2011b). While some mainstream commentators in Egypt expressed sympathy with the protester, many others squarely placed the blame on the woman. A number of analysts and political commentators claimed that the video and the images were fabricated and meant to tarnish the army's reputation (Al Arabiya 2011). Even when the army General Adel Amara confirmed the authenticity of the recording in a press conference on December 19, 2011, and promised to investigate the attack, a number of media analysts and commentators continued to reproduce conspiracy theories around the intentions and motives of Sitt el-Banāt (Al Wafd 2011). As Sherien Hafez rightly notes, these conspiracy theories pinned the blame on the victim and deflected it away from the army.[4] Islamist political parties also attacked women protesters and later criticized the women's march.[5] A political analyst claimed that the whole incident was a setup, that the victim deliberately posed with her bra and body exposed to embarrass the army (Al Arabiya 2011). Some online news sites later ran stories alleging that the victim's male colleague stripped her to portray the army in a negative light (Misr Al-Arabiya 2014). Others cast doubt on the identity of the solider who attacked the woman; they claimed that he probably did not belong to the army because he was wearing shoes instead of army boots (Al Arabiya 2011). A controversial TV host asked why the victim did not wear an extra layer of clothing under her abaya, and used the absence of an undergarment as evidence to implicate her ("Tawfīq ʿukasha Yatahakm ʿala Al-Fatah al-Shugaʿa" 2011).

Several commentators, including Islamist television host Sheikh Khaled Abdellah, asked why the young woman put herself in harm's way by participating in the protests ("Al-Sheikh Khaled Abdellah Yaskhar Men Taʿryat al-Fattah al-Muntaqibah" 2011; Kirkpatrick 2011). The underlying objective of this question, Shereen Abouelnaga rightly notes, was to delegitimize women's participation in the protests (Abouelnaga 2015; see also Al-Najjar and Abusalim 2015; El Said 2015). More squarely, the question reproduced the view that "respectable" women do not protest, do not get angry, and do not participate in collective action. This view also functioned to exclude women participating in protests from state protection and restraint, thus effectively justifying violence against them and precluding moral outrage in response. To further lend accusations against Sitt el-Banāt an aura of legitimacy, media coverage of the incident often included quotes from women who criticized her by casting aspersions about her intentions (Al Arabiya 2011).

In response to the army's brutal attack on female protesters and the subsequent media campaign against the victim, women marched in a massive demonstration on December 20, 2011, demanding the end of the army's brutality and SCAF's interim presidency. During the march, women expressed their anger through their chants, slogans, and graffiti. Egyptian women's expression of anger served to shift blame away from the victim and toward the army and create moral outrage and shock over its transgression.

While women have participated in past protests against the army, women's participation in the Sitt el-Banāt march was distinct from earlier engagements. Not only was the Sitt el-Banāt march the largest women's demonstration in terms of numbers; it was also squarely intended both to defend women's rights to protest and to reclaim the dignity of the protester beaten and stripped by the army. In the Sitt el-Banāt march, women protesters were not simply among the players, they were *the* players challenging the military institution, in direct confrontation with the army. Women's bodies, Sherine Hafez rightly notes, "emerge as sites of resistance and transformation that both mediate and stabilize violence and disciplinary power" (Hafez 2014, 22). By describing the young woman in the blue bra as Sitt el-Banāt (a woman of absolute moral integrity), and naming the march in solidarity with her, protesters defied the army's ascribed gendered norms and expectations and asserted that women protesters should be treated with moral restraint.

During the march, women chanted "Banāt Miṣr khat aḥmr" (The women of Egypt are a red line). The chant was the march's slogan and its rallying cry (Zayed 2011). A red line is a metaphorical boundary. To cross a red line is to carry out a transgression, to trespass the boundaries of accepted norms and expected behaviors. Crossing a red line carries a threat of possible retaliation, a reminder of negative consequences. In the period following the uprising, SCAF generals reiterated the statement "the army is a red line" to challenge those who criticized the military or condemned its actions against protesters (Al-Dangalāwī 2011). By appropriating the slogan and turning it against the military, women protesters stripped the army of its claimed moral superiority and self-ascribed sacred status in society. The red line, the mark in the sand, was now drawn by the women, not the army, and women protesters, rather than the military institution, firmly dictated its location.

In addition to the slogan's tone, women communicated their anger through the aesthetics of their banners. They wrote "Banāt Miṣr khat aḥmr" in bold red ink on a contrasting white background. Tom Nyamache and Ruth Nyambura

(2012) remind us in their study of color symbolism in African societies that red signals fury and outrage. These banners also resembled the red card, a penalty given to players who cross the line in sporting arenas. Frederic Volpi and James Jasper argue that contentious episodes in such arenas occur when players and actors attempt to make strategic decisions, renegotiate rules, and achieve their preferred outcomes (2018, 15). Within such arenas, players carry out different—and shifting—roles and display a variety of skills and capacities; sometimes players act as bystanders, while at other times they are active participants (Volpi and Jasper 2018, 15). In the Sitt el-Banāt march, women were active participants in direct confrontation with the army.

Protesters also held banners showing an angry woman frowning at the sight of a hand attempting to touch her. On the edge of the drawing a hand can be seen lurking at the side, emerging from an army uniform, and attempting to touch the woman (National Post 2011b). Under the drawing, protesters wrote "Qd' Īdk." The expression "Qd' Īdk" loosely translates to "hands off" in English, but literally translates to threatening to "cut off" the predator's hand in punishment for the latter's transgression. The drawing and its angry message displayed a warning to the army. The army's violation of the protester's rights and their assault on her dignity were presented as an afront to the rights and dignity of all Egyptian women.

Protesters also held giant posters displaying the blue bra, an icon that was drawn on banners and signs. Graffiti artist Bahia Shehab later stenciled the blue bra on Cairo's walls (Shehab 2012). By proudly displaying this image, protesters emphasized that the exposed woman's body and her blue bra brought shame to the army, not to her. Protesters chanted that the violence exposed the army and the deceit of its generals. Indeed, one of the prominent chants and slogans of the march was calling the army "Kāzbuon" (liars) and using the derogative "'askr" (mercenaries) to describe the soldiers (Amaria 2011). The term 'askr is a derogatory term in Egypt that is meant to degrade the army from its status by drawing a parallel between the army and the mercenary soldiers of the Mamluk era. Displaying the blue bra icon and using it to symbolize the army's—rather than the female protester's—shame shifts the blame away from the victim and places it on the army. Shame is a strong emotive punishment; its danger lies in its tendency to turn into a "stigma"—that is, "to become permanent" (Jasper 2018, 50). Shame becomes permanent when the victim internalizes the aggressor's discourse. James Jasper rightly argues that "whether or not the victims of moral shame internalize it depends on whether they share the value of their oppressors" (2018, 49). By communicating their anger over the army's transgression, female protesters forcefully rejected and challenged the army's values and placed shame on the army.

Transition-Anger and Women's Anti-Sexual Violence Campaigns

On the day of the women's march, SCAF issued a statement expressing its "regret" over the attack and promising to pursue "all legal measures to hold accountable the people responsible for these violations" (Akhbar el-Youm 2011). Women's groups, however, refused the army's apology and criticized the vocabulary used by SCAF in its statement. "Expressing their regret is different than apologizing and acknowledging their mistake," they argued (activists quoted in Al-Ahram 2011). Activists expressed their anger over the army's delay in issuing an apology and emphasized that it only happened as a result of women's mobilization. They noted that the army chose not to apologize during an earlier press conference. In fact, during this earlier press conference on December 19, 2011, General Amara defended the army, commending officers on their "self-restraint" and thanking them for their service to the country (CBC Egypt 2011). By contrast, SCAF's later statement, issued on December 20, 2011, demonstrated a change in tone, describing the army's utmost respect for the "great women of Egypt" (Akhbar el-Youm 2011) and acknowledging their right to protest. While SACF's statement was viewed by activists as too little too late, it was a move toward recognizing female activists and their right to protest.

It is true that the recognition would not right the wrong, but in the case of Sitt el-Banāt it was necessary to alleviate the moral shame that both the army and the media inscribed on her. When moral shame is based on skewed and gendered values it drags us downward and destroys our sense of self, it does not "goad us onward" (Nussbaum 2009, 206). Under such circumstances, groups and individuals often find it challenging to recover. This is because, as Amélie Rorty points out, shame "tends to involve obsessive imagistic replays of the moment of exposure," which makes time feels frozen and "arrested" (1980, 498). It is because of this obsessive quality that social movements across history mobilize to defend those who are shamed and to shift the blame to the aggressor (Jasper 2018, 50).

While women protesters' anger initially focused on recognition, by demanding an apology for the victim, and retaliation, by demanding that the army generals step down, it gave way to Transition-Anger. In response to the violence carried out against female protesters by state and non-state actors, a number of anti-sexual violence and harassment groups emerged in 2012 to protect women's political participation in the public sphere. Groups such as Operation Anti-Sexual Harassment and Tahrir Bodyguard carried out important awareness campaigns, ran self-defense workshops and hotlines, and documented cases of harassment and sexual violence.[6] In my work, I illuminate the dynamics of feminist activism during and after the 2011 Egyptian uprising and how emotions were central in sustaining hope and engagement following contention and defeat (Allam 2018, 2020).

Women's firsthand experiences of gender violence in public spaces informed their priorities. This gender awareness, Vickie Langohr astutely notes, spread among women as well as among some male volunteers and members in anti–sexual harassment campaigns (Langohr 2013, 2015). Langohr rightly observes that unlike the experience of women's mobilization during political transition in Latin America, anti-harassment groups in Egypt included large numbers of young men and did not mobilize around issues "in which motherhood is salient" (Langohr 2015, 133). Through their engagement, activists developed a better understanding of gender issues and refashioned their understanding of power and hierarchy. The discussions and the initiatives inspired by them, Hala Kamal argues in her study of the feminist movement in Egypt, mark the emergence of fourth-wave feminism, with a focus on woman's body, gender violence, and sexuality (Kamal 2015).

Women's anger did not, thus, turn melancholic or become futile. Melancholia, according to Sigmund Freud, arises when we cling to our pain and refuse to express or relinquish it (Freud 1989). By expressing their pain and anger over the army's transgression, women's groups raised awareness, which resulted in diverse segments of society joining their collective activism, including men. They communicated agency and displayed power, which made certain forms of action possible, such as the rise in the number of anti-sexual violence groups. Even though women protesters' anger initially focused on recognition and status, it gave way to Transition-Anger.

Nussbaum's distinction between "status-focused anger" or "garden-variety anger" (Nussbaum 2016, 37) and Transition-Anger remains useful for analyzing political life. I argue that both forms of anger are productive and complement each other. For Nussbaum, we ought to start from Transition-Anger to avoid "the errors of payback fantasy and/ or status-obsession" that can hinder social welfare (2016, 52). I do not think that we ought to start from Transition-Anger; starting from "status-focused anger" or "garden-variety anger" is not always futile. A status-focused anger is not necessarily associated with retaliation as Nussbaum suggests, but rather seeks recognition. A desire for recognition, Srinivasan (2018) rightly argues, is not the same as a desire for revenge. Recognition is a powerful status that challenges and deters further transgression. It forms the moral basis for future projects that focus on broader welfare.

By analyzing the relationship between women's initiatives and Transition-Anger, I do not intend to downplay the influence of the structure—represented in the regime and its oppressive policies—on activism. While challenging the structure can open up spaces for possibility and change, these efforts will not yield transition if the structure is completely closed off. Melancholia may be inevitable as a result of closing the political space. In Egypt, following the elections of current President Abdel Fattah el-Sisi, the new regime closed off the political landscape and restricted independent activism against sexual violence. Women's activism against sexual violence, however, continued online. Through online platforms, survivors of sexual violence share their stories, steering anger and moral outrage against prevalent gender norms and differential structures of moral accountability (Allam 2023). Their activism reflects the continued significance of anger in women's collective action on the ground and online and its productive function in mobilizing bystanders, securing recognition, and transitioning to broader reform, even in the face of a restricted political landscape.

Conclusion

In 2012, renowned Brazilian cartoonist Carlos Latuff published the "Masked Avenger" in solidarity with Sitt el-Banāt ("The 'Blue Bra Girl' Comes Back as a Masked Avenger" 2012). Latuff's cartoon re-creates the scene of the attack, transforming the woman protester into an avenger. Rather than lying limply on the ground, Sitt el-Banāt is portrayed as flying in the air, with a furious face partly masked by her black abaya. She kicks the soldier's face, knocking out his teeth and causing blood to splatter from his mouth. The solider cringes in pain while the woman looks strong and assertive. Through role reversal, the cartoon thus attempts to reclaim the victim's agency. As Arne Johan Vetlesen reminds us, reclaiming the victim's agency is powerful, as "the shame of passivity, the passivity of shame" is often simply "intolerable" (2005, 204). Shame closes off possibilities for action, change, and redemption.

My analysis in this chapter highlights the productive element of anger and its function in mobilizing immediate collective action and future change. Women's expression of anger following the attack on Sitt el-Banāt, I argue, succeeded in securing recognition for the victim, brought attention to women's bodily rights, and created moral outrage toward the army. While women's anger initially focused on recognition and status, it gave way to Transition-Anger and was channeled into projects, initiatives, and campaigns to raise awareness and push for reform.

The analysis underscores how anger is a complex and complicated emotional response that cannot be reduced to an unproductive fleeting emotion or a futile melancholic mood. When leveraged into collective action, anger paves the way for projects that focus on broader welfare. The work of social change is indeed a work of emotional change. We abide by certain norms because we often feel strongly about them or are ashamed to deviate from them. To change gender norms and attitudes toward gender-based violence is thus to change how we feel about them.

Despite anger's disruptive potential, anger is a significant motivator to question and subvert gendered norms and inequalities. Displays of anger in women's collective action communicate a powerful message to society and affect its members' moral intuitions and principles. Angry feminists thus force society to reevaluate its existing moral emotions and articulate new affects and gender commitments. The flip side of "not getting angry" or calling out evil is cementing the norms that enabled transgression in the first place, and normalizing them in society. Under these conditions, we just cannot move on.

Notes

1. A recording of the attack can be found at RT (2011).
2. In this chapter, I use rage and anger interchangeably. While some philosophical traditions distinguish between the two, feminists have traditionally used the two terms interchangeably to describe the same emotional response.
3. See Allam's article "Smoke and Mirrors" (2019) for a detailed discussion of the status of women's rights in the period following the uprisings.
4. See Abdalla F. Hassan's book *Media, Revolution and Politics in Egypt* (2015) for a discussion of media in Egypt before and after

the uprisings and how state-owned and some private media reproduced counterrevolutionary discourses.

5. Manal Abul Hasan, the Freedom and Justice Party (FJP) women's secretary, accused female protesters of carrying out foreign agendas and described the march as an "affront to women's dignity" (Abou Al-Hasan 2012).

6. For a discussion of the rise of anti-sexual violence initiatives and campaigns following the uprisings, please see Vickie Langohr's article: "Women's Rights Movements during Political Transitions" (2015).

References

Abou Al-Hasan, Manal. 2012. "Aminat al-Marʾah fī ḥizb al-Akhwan." *Donia Al-Watan*. January 14. https://www.alwatanvoice.com/arabic/news/2012/01/14/237751.html.

Abouelnaga, Shereen. 2015. "Reconstructing Gender in Post-Revolution Egypt." In *Rethinking Gender in Revolutions and Resistance: Lessons from the Arab World*, edited by Maha El Said, Lena Meari, and Nicola Pratt, 35–58. London: Zed Books.

Ahmed, Sara. 2004. *The Cultural Politics of Emotion*. Edinburgh: Edinburgh University Press.

Akhbar el-Youm. 2011. "Al-Maglis al-ʿskarī Yaʿtadhr Le-Sydāt Maṣr" [The Supreme Council of the Armed Forces apologies to Egyptian women]. Akhbar El-Youm Gate, December 23. https://m.akhbarelyom.com/news/newdetails/359540/1/المجلس-العسكري-يعتذر-لسيدات-مصر.

Al-Ahram. 2011. "Nashiṭat Radan ʿala Bayan Al-Maglis Al-ʿaskary" [Female activists responding to SCAF's statement]. *Al-Ahram*, December 12. http://gate.ahram.org.eg/News/151242.aspx.

Al Arabiya. 2011. "Gadl fī Maṣr ḥawl siḥat fiduw saḥl wa taʿryat fatāt Maglis al-Wuzaraʾ" [Debate around the authenticity of the video of the beating and stripping of the Maglis al-Wuzaraʾ

girl]. *Al Arabiya*, December 21. https://www.alarabiya.net
/articles/2011%2F12%2F21%2F183779.html.

Al-Dangalāwī, Osman. 2011. *2011: ʿam Al-thawrah* [2011: The year of
the revolution]. Cairo: Ktab.

Allam, Nermin. 2018. "Activism amid Disappointment: Women's
Groups and the Politics of Hope in Egypt." *Middle East Law
and Governance* 10, no. 3: 291–316. https://doi.org/10.1163/18763375
-01003004.

———. 2019. "Smoke and Mirrors: State-Sponsored Feminism in
Post-Uprising Egypt." *Social Research: An International Quarterly*
86, no. 1: 365–86.

———. 2020. "Affective Encounters: Women, Hope, and Activism
in Egypt." In *Arab Spring: Modernity, Identity and Change*, edited
by Eid Mohamed and Dalia Fahmy, 135–155. Cham, Switzerland:
Springer. https://doi.org/10.1007/978-3-030-24758-4_8.

———. 2023. "The Role of Emotions in Anti-Sexual Violence
Groups in Egypt." *Mobilization: An International Quarterly* 28,
no. 2: 189–208. https://doi.org/10.17813/1086-671X-28-2-189.

Al-Najjar, Abeer, and Anoud Abusalim. 2015. "Framing the Female
Body: Beyond Morality and Pathology?" In *Rethinking Gender
in Revolutions and Resistance: Lessons from the Arab World*, edited
by Maha El Said, Lena Meari, and Nicola Pratt, 135–154.
London: Zed Books.

"Al-Sheikh Khaled Abdellah Yaskhar Men Taʿryat al-Fattah
al-Muntaqibah" [Al-Sheikh Khaled Abdellah mocking the
stripping of the veiled girl at Tahrir]. 2011. *YouTube*, December 18. https://www.youtube.com/watch?app=desktop&v
=gskGjtZMC_s.

Al Wafd. 2011. "Al-ʿaskarī: Saḥl al-Fatah Ḥaqiqī Wa Sanuḥaqiq
Fīh" [SCAF: Dragging the girl did happen and we will
investigate the incident]. https://bit.ly/3nnkm8Q.

Amaria, Kainaz. 2011. "'Girl in the Blue Bra' Symbol of Egypt's
Ongoing Strife." *NPR*, December 21. https://www.npr.org

/sections/pictureshow/2011/12/21/144098384/the-girl-in-the-blue
-bra.

Amnesty International. 2011. "Egyptian Women Protesters Forced
to Take 'Virginity Tests.'" March 23. https://www.amnesty.org
/en/press-releases/2011/03/egyptian-women-protesters-forced
-take-e28098virginity-testse28099/.

Aristotle. 1991. *On Rhetoric: A Theory of Civic Discourse*. Translated
by George Alexander Kennedy. New York: Oxford University
Press. https://catalog.hathitrust.org/Record/002497339.

BBC News. 2011. "Egypt Violence: PM Ganzouri Blames 'Counter-
Revolution.'" *BBC*, December 17. https://www.bbc.com/news
/world-africa-16229863.

Blair, Elaine. 2018. "The Power of Enraged Women." *New York
Times*, September 27. https://www.nytimes.com/2018/09/27
/books/review/rebecca-traister-good-and-mad-soraya-chemaly
-rage-becomes-her.html.

"The 'Blue Bra Girl' Comes Back as a Masked Avenger." 2012.
EastWestWestEast, January 11. https://eastwestwesteast.wordpress
.com/2012/01/11/566/.

CBC Egypt. 2011. "Mo'tamar Al-Maglis al-'askarī Bisha'n Aḥdāth
Maglis al-Wuzara" [The Supreme Council of the Armed Forces'
press conference in relation to the events on Maglis al-Wuzara'].
YouTube, December 19. https://www.youtube.com/watch?v
=GTyjBmdlZPo.

Coleman, Isobel. 2011. "'Blue Bra Girl' Rallies Egypt's Women vs.
Oppression." *CNN*, December 22. https://www.cnn.com/2011/12
/22/opinion/coleman-women-egypt-protest/index.html.

El Said, Maha. 2015. "She Resists: Body Politics between Radical
and Subaltern." In *Rethinking Gender in Revolutions and
Resistance: Lessons from the Arab World*, edited by Maha El Said,
Lena Meari, and Nicola Pratt, 109–134. London: Zed Books.
http://ebookcentral.proquest.com/lib/rutgers-ebooks/detail
.action?docID=2041742.

Freud, Sigmund. 1989. *The Freud Reader.* Edited by Peter Gay. New York: W. W. Norton.

Frye, Marilyn. 1983. *Politics of Reality: Essays in Feminist Theory.* Berkeley, CA: Crossing Press.

Gilmore, Ruth Wilson. 1993. "Public Enemies and Private Intellectuals: Apartheid USA." *Race & Class* 35, no. 1: 69–78. https://doi.org/10.1177/030639689303500107.

Hafez, Sherine. 2014. "Bodies That Protest: The Girl in the Blue Bra, Sexuality, and State Violence in Revolutionary Egypt." *Signs: Journal of Women in Culture and Society* 40, no. 1: 20–28. https://doi.org/10.1086/676977.

Hassan, Abdalla F. 2015. *Media, Revolution and Politics in Egypt: The Story of an Uprising.* London: I. B. Tauris.

Invicta, Femina. 2011. "Women Protest." Femina Invicta, December 26. https://feminainvicta.com/tag/women-protest/.

Jackson, Ruth, and Max Kelly. 2019. *Women Researching in Africa: The Impact of Gender.* Cham, Switzerland: Palgrave Macmillan. https://doi.org/10.1007/978-3-319-94502-6.

Jaggar, Alison M. 1989. "Love and Knowledge: Emotion in Feminist Epistemology." *Inquiry* 32, no. 2: 151–176. https://doi.org/10.1080/00201748908602185.

Jasper, James M. 2018. *The Emotions of Protest.* Chicago: University of Chicago Press.

Joseph, Suad, Lena Meari, and Zeina Zaatari. 2022. *The Politics of Engaged Gender Research in the Arab Region: Feminist Fieldwork and the Production of Knowledge.* New York: Bloomsbury Academic.

Kamal, Hala. 2015. "Inserting Women's Rights in the Egyptian Constitution: Personal Reflections." *Journal for Cultural Research* 19, no. 2: 150–161. https://doi.org/10.1080/14797585.2014.982919.

Kato, Miwa. 2017. "Women of Egypt." *The Cairo Review of Global Affairs*, January 10. https://www.thecairoreview.com/essays/women-of-egypt/.

Kay, Jilly Boyce. 2019. "Introduction: Anger, Media, and Feminism: The Gender Politics of Mediated Rage." *Feminist Media Studies* 19, no. 4: 591–615. https://doi.org/10.1080/14680777.2019.1609197.

Kirkpatrick, David D. 2011. "Mass March by Cairo Women in Protest over Abuse by Soldiers." *New York Times*, December 20. https://www.nytimes.com/2011/12/21/world/middleeast/violence -enters-5th-day-as-egyptian-general-blames-protesters.html.

Langohr, Vickie. 2013. "'This Is Our Square': Fighting Sexual Assault at Cairo Protests." *Middle East Report* 268: 18–25.

———. 2015. "Women's Rights Movements during Political Transitions: Activism against Public Sexual Violence in Egypt." *International Journal of Middle East Studies* 47, no. 1: 131–135. https://doi.org/10.1017/S0020743814001482.

Lorde, Audre. 1981. "The Uses of Anger: Women Responding to Racism." In *Sister Outsider: Essays and Speeches*, 120–129. Berkeley, CA: Crossing Press.

McLarney, Ellen. 2016. "Women's Rights and Equality: Egyptian Constitutional Law." In *Women's Movements in Post-"Arab Spring" North Africa*, edited by Fatima Sadiqi, 109–126. New York: Palgrave Macmillan. https://doi.org/10.1057/978-1-137-50675 -7_8.

Misr Al-Arabiya. 2014. "Nushaṭaʾ Yatadawalun Fidiuw-l-Muḥawalat Inqadh Sitt al-Banat" [Activists share videos of attempts to save Sitt al-Banat]. *Misr Al-Arabiya*, October 23. https://m.masrala rabia.net/نشطاء-يتداولون-فيديو-لمحاولات-إنقاذ-ست-البنات/390377.ميديا.

Narayan, Uma. 1988. "Working Together across Difference: Some Considerations on Emotions and Political Practice." *Hypatia* 3, no. 2: 31–47.

National Council for Women, and Noor Labib Dokhan. 2015. "Al-Maraa Wa Al-Irhab [Women and Terrorism Concept Note]." Cairo Egypt: National Council for Women (NCW) in Egypt. https://www.google.ca/url?sa=t&rct=j&q=&esrc =s&source=web&cd=1&cad=rja&uact=8&ved=0ahUKEwiUsc 7Lo7HTAhXH7IMKHRQTDi4QFggiMAA&url=http%3

A%2F%2Fwww.ncwegypt.com%2Findex.php%2Far%2
F2013-03-06-14-17-01%2Fdoc_download%2F134-&usg
=AFQjCNHaKEF6I_eDtPqrQx8JmZC4soUgxQ.

"National Election Authority Official Site." 2012. https://www
.elections.eg/en/.

National Post. 2011a. "Police Beating of 'Girl in the Blue Bra'
Becomes New Rallying Call for Egyptians." *National Post*,
December 20. https://nationalpost.com/news/beating-of-blue
-bra-woman-reignites-egyptian-protests.

———. 2011b. "'The Girls of Egypt' Rally after Blue Bra Beating."
National Post, December 21. https://nationalpost.com/news/the
-girls-of-egypt-rally-after-blue-bra-beating.

Nussbaum, Martha C. 2009. *Hiding from Humanity: Disgust, Shame,
and the Law*. Princeton, NJ: Princeton University Press.
https://doi.org/10.1515/9781400825943.

———. 2016. *Anger and Forgiveness: Resentment, Generosity, Justice*.
New York: Oxford University Press.

Nyamache, Tom, and Ruth Nyambura. 2012. "Colour Symbolism
in Africa: A Historical Perspective." *Asian Journal of Research in
Business Economics and Management* 2, no. 2: 50–56.

Orgad, Shani, and Rosalind Gill. 2019. "Safety Valves for Mediated
Female Rage in the #MeToo Era." *Feminist Media Studies* 19,
no. 4: 596–603. https://doi.org/10.1080/14680777.2019.1609198.

Rich, Adrienne Cecile. 1973. "The Phenomenology of Anger." In
Diving into the Wreck, 27–28. New York: New York.

Rorty, Amélie. 1980. *Explaining Emotions*. Berkeley: University of
California Press.

RT. 2011. "Shocking Video: 'Blue Bra' Girl Brutally Beaten by Egypt
Military." *YouTube*, December 18. https://www.youtube.com
/watch?v=mnFVYewkWEY&bpctr=1609560056.

Shalaby, Marwa. 2016. "Women's Political Representation and
Authoritarianism in the Arab World—Project on Middle East
Political Science." https://pomeps.org/2016/04/14/womens-political
-representation-and-authoritarianism-in-the-arab-world/.

Shehab, Bahia. 2012. "A Thousand Times No." *TED*, June. https://www.ted.com/talks/bahia_shehab_a_thousand_times_no.

Sika, Nadine, and Yasmin Khodary. 2012. "One Step Forward, Two Steps Back? Egyptian Women within the Confines of Authoritarianism." *Journal of International Women's Studies* 13, no. 5: article 9. https://vc.bridgew.edu/cgi/viewcontent.cgi?article=1008&context=jiws.

Srinivasan, Amia. 2018. "The Aptness of Anger." *Journal of Political Philosophy* 26, no. 2: 123–144. https://doi.org/10.1111/jopp.12130.

"Tawfiq ʿukasha Yatahakm ʿala Al-Fatah al-Shugaʿa" [Tawfiq ʿukasha criticizes the brave girl]. 2011. *YouTube*, December 20. https://www.youtube.com/watch?app=desktop&v=SqdDWERqtlQ.

Tomlinson, Barbara. 2010. "Transforming the Terms of Reading: Ideologies of Argument and the 'Trope of the Angry Feminist' in Contemporary US Political and Academic Discourse." *Journal of American Studies* 44, no. 1: 101–116. https://doi.org/10.1017/S0021875809991344.

Vetlesen, Arne Johan. 2005. *Evil and Human Agency: Understanding Collective Evildoing.* Cambridge: Cambridge University Press. http://ebookcentral.proquest.com/lib/rutgers-ebooks/detail.action?docID=244083.

Volpi, Frederic, and James Jasper, eds. 2018. *Microfoundations of the Arab Uprisings: Mapping Interactions between Regimes and Protesters.* Amsterdam: Amsterdam University Press.

Wood, Helen. 2019. "Fuck the Patriarchy: Towards an Intersectional Politics of Irreverent Rage." *Feminist Media Studies* 19, no. 4: 609–615. https://doi.org/10.1080/14680777.2019.1609232.

Zayed, Dina. 2011. "Attack on Egyptian Women Protesters Spark Uproar." *Reuters*, December 21. https://www.reuters.com/article/us-egypt-protests-women-idUSTRE7BK1BX20111221.

3

Our Paranoid Politics

NOËLLE MCAFEE

Conspiracy thinking can be deeply appealing, especially
when one does not like how things are going. As I write,
Republicans in Congress and in many states across the country are disgruntled about having lost the White House and
have latched on to the conspiracy theory that the 2020 presidential election was stolen. Even with Trump out of office,
our post-truth, media-siloed, fake-news era continues. Even
when actual facts undermine widely held conspiracy
theories—such as the QAnon theory that Trump was put in
office by God to overturn the "'deep state' cabal of Satan-
worshipping pedophiles, Democratic politicians and Holly-
wood celebrities who run a global sex-trafficking ring"
(Alter 2020)—another new conspiracy pops up to take its
place. Now the reigning theory, believed by 30 percent of
those surveyed, is that Biden won the 2020 presidential
election because of election fraud. This conspiracy theory
fueled the mob that stormed the Capitol on January 6, 2021.
As of this writing, more than half of Republicans still
believe this lie and nearly all Republicans holding office
refuse to acknowledge Biden's presidency. Even without

any evidence of actual election fraud, state houses throughout the country are passing laws making it harder for people to vote.

What is behind the thrall of conspiracy theories? Many people think that if the American people had a better grasp of the facts, they'd be better able to distinguish truth from conspiracy fictions. Millions of people would not have been taken in by QAnon or dismiss the January 6, 2021, Capitol riots as the work of Antifa. As *Nature* magazine reported in relation to the spread of false information about COVID-19, "researchers hope to understand where such information comes from, how it grows and—they hope—how to elevate facts over falsehood" and thereby "come up with effective strategies to 'flatten the curve' of the infodemic, so that bad information can't spread as far and as fast" (Ball and Maxmen 2020). According to this take, the problem with politics today is rampant misinformation.[1] If people had their facts straight, they would stop believing in false conspiracy theories.

I am going to wager that the problem is not one of misinformation but of something deeper, something closer to what Richard Hofstadter in 1964 called "the paranoid style in American politics." This style encourages delusions of persecution, from the Masons to the Red Scare. It is replete, Hofstadter wrote, with "heated exaggeration, suspiciousness, and conspiratorial fantasy" (Hofstadter 1964). It is a mindset that is predisposed to latch on to the idea that the believer, or the group the believer belongs to, is being unfairly targeted. It is surely not a feature of American politics alone. The world over, as I discuss in *Fear of Breakdown* (McAfee 2019), social and political bodies easily succumb to what Melanie Klein saw as persecutory anxieties and their concomitant defenses: splitting, projection, and denial (Klein 1986).[2] Now, as I survey the lure of conspiracy theories during the treacherous year 2020 through a psychoanalytic prism, I see that the problem lies in the mindset and the internal anxieties of those perpetuating and harboring conspiracy theories, in their fragile and anxious identities. Conspiracy theories posit an external enemy not because there really *is* one, but because anxious individuals *need* one.

To make my case, in this chapter I begin with an overview of some elements of conspiracy theories, mainly political ones at work in large-group identities. I then turn to the fundamental anxieties that motivate them and to the defense mechanisms that arise: misrecognition, positing of a phobic object, splitting, projection, and displacement. I close with a discussion of the pernicious consequences of these phenomena.

QAnon and Company

Conspiracy theories have taken many different forms over the centuries. They might be fully articulated and elaborate narratives, or they might be just a cluster of hunches. The bad guys might be Jews or communists or Masons, varying according to the worries and fears that are driving the theory. Regardless, as I argue in this chapter, conspiracy theories always come down to this: They form in relation to the subject's (or the subject's group's) anxious identity. They might originate in an unconscious fantasy, or they might be deliberately foisted on a people. But even if they are purposely targeted, they operate and spread largely unconsciously, rippling out across linkages of individual and shared identities. They feed on insecurities, making them contagious and difficult to corral. Though they might show up in a particular individual's delusions, the root problem is often collective, deriving from the anxious identity of the group itself.

What better sign of this anxiety than the slogan "Make America Great Again"? This slogan exhibits an anxiety about America's large-group identity, its lost and supposed greatness, perhaps even more a worry that its greatness was really nothing at all, and that whatever is left will fall by the wayside as its enemies encroach.

These are the unconscious anxieties I see at work underneath the rampant conspiracy theories of our day. They might show up with just one person encountering numerous accounts of a conspiracy and then acting on it alone, such as in "Pizzagate," the conspiracy theory that a pedophile sex ring backed by the Clinton Foundation was operating out of a small pizza parlor in northwest Washington, DC. As Volney Gay writes, "That induced one man to rush into a DC pizza parlor on December 4, 2016, the site of the imagined sex ring debauchery. Assault rifle in hand, he was there to save the children from Hillary Clinton" (Gay 2018, 257). While he acted alone, he imagined himself acting on behalf of a larger group of good people being attacked by demonic people (Haag and Salam 2017).

The Pizzagate theory continued to proliferate, taking in other people who seemed to think that depraved predators were attacking "civilized" society. In 2019 another person set fire to the same pizza restaurant, apparently motivated by the same conspiracy theory (ABC7 2019). Perhaps unconsciously, the Pizzagate conspiracy theory that there were such depraved people taking advantage of innocent children served to shore up the identity of those doing the imagining. Anyone holding the theory could feel righteous and good.

Pizzagate later morphed into the conspiracy theory of QAnon, where the Satan-loving pedophiles were not just a feature of a small little pizza joint in DC but part of a global conspiracy aimed at destroying America and instituting a global world order. As Ethan Zuckerman explains,

QAnon is a big tent conspiracy theory, a meta narrative that knits together contemporary politics and hoary racist tropes with centuries of history behind them. At its core is the idea that all American presidents between John F. Kennedy and Donald Trump have been working with a cabal of globalist elites called "The Cabal" to undermine American democracy and forward their own nefarious agenda. . . . In all versions of the mythos, The Cabal seeks to destroy American freedom and subjugate the nation to the wills of a world government. In some versions of the mythos, the agenda also includes pedo-philia, blood sacrifice, Satanism and other attention-getting transgressions. (Zuckerman 2019)

The conspiracy theory also holds out hope, namely that Donald Trump has been sent to earth, part of "the Storm" that is coming, to vanquish The Cabal.

QAnon has proven to be extraordinarily contagious, per-haps because it taps into so many archaic anxieties as well as dreams of overcoming. Consider the case of Michael Caputo, who in September 2020 took a leave of absence from his posi-tion at the Department of Health and Human Services after posting a half-hour rant on Facebook complaining of long shadows on his wall, as well as sedition within the Centers for Disease Control and Prevention, where scientists were sup-posedly withholding COVID-19 treatment from the public in order to hurt Donald Trump politically. Caputo urged Trump supporters to stock up on ammunition to stave off a violent left-wing rebellion should Trump win reelection. CBS News reported, "At one point during the Facebook Live session in which Caputo made the comments, he said that 'there are hit squads being trained all over this country' to prevent a second term for Mr. Trump. When he added, 'You understand that they're going to have to kill me—unfortunately, I think that's where this is going,' Caputo claimed he was reacting in real time to a man driving by his house screaming, 'You're a dead man, Caputo'" (Jiang 2020). Shortly thereafter, Caputo resigned to seek treatment for a medical condition he had learned about earlier that day.

Was this the case of one person who happened to be a Trump loyalist experiencing paranoia—or a symptom of a larger paranoid politics where otherwise stable people get swept up in a collective delusion?[3] Caputo is hardly alone in these delusions. U.S. Attorney General William Barr, according the *New York Times*, warned "that the United States would be on the brink of destruction if Mr. Trump lost." Under such circumstances, "the nation could find itself 'irrevocably committed to the socialist path' ... and that the country faced 'a clear fork in the road'" (Benner 2020). And now, as I write, several months after the election in which Donald Trump did indeed lose, 30 percent of the nation believes that the system is "rigged," that Republican votes were destroyed and Democratic ones fabricated (SSRS Research 2021). Two days after the election, as the results were still being tabulated, Trump addressed the nation about how he had won but "they," meaning Democrats, were trying to steal the election. The worst perpetrators, Trump claimed, were Detroit and Philadelphia, "known as two of the most corrupt political places anywhere in our country," which "cannot be responsible for engineering the outcome of a presidential race, a very important presidential race" (Heer 2020).

Many networks cut away before Trump concluded his remarks. But he had already thrown enough gas on the fire of right-wing discontent to plunge the nation into further turmoil, with right-wing protesters showing up at vote-counting sites brandishing assault rifles, the Republican establishment in lockstep denouncing supposed rampant election fraud, and then on January 6 an attempted insurrection at the U.S. Capitol.

Large-Group Archaic Fantasies

How do we make sense of Trump, Caputo, Barr, and the 55 percent of Republicans who think that that the election was stolen? What binds them together? Some of the most prevalent accounts point to social and economic factors, such as globalization, that have left many U.S. citizens feeling alienated and left behind (Pettigrew 2017; Rodríguez-Pose 2022). While these accounts contribute to our understanding, their explanatory value is limited, for not all those economically left behind turn to conspiracy thinking, and many who engage in conspiracy thinking have hardly been left behind at all. Moreover, socioeconomic accounts often lead to paradoxes, for example, that those harmed by the exploits of capitalism are often fervently pro-market, that populist anti-elitism is often embedded in very elite networks (Öniş and Kutlay 2020). Whatever value these accounts have, I believe they need to be, at the very least, supplemented by accounts of the underlying psychological dynamics that lead people to coalesce around shared delusions. For this, I turn to a psychoanalytic account, which makes it possible to diagnose political maladies, to identify the ways of thinking that lead to dysfunctional politics.

From this psychoanalytic perspective, the first element to understand is the phenomenon of "large-group" identity and what happens to it in certain moments. Vamik Volkan defines large-group identity as a persistent and subjective sense of sameness shared by thousands or millions of people who may not even know each other (Volkan 2019). The identification may be national, ethnic, religious, or otherwise. Large-group identification is a part of early development. "Children assimilate their core large-group identities and prejudices against the Other by identifying with parents and other important people in their environments," Volkan writes. "Furthermore, parents and other important people 'deposit' images of past historical events, heroes and martyrs into their children's minds. . . . When thousands or millions of children become receivers of the same or a similar deposited item, they begin to share 'psychological DNA' linked to large-group identity" (Volkan 2019, 141).

These identifications emerge very early in development, as the child identifies with its caregivers and their extended networks. It is the process by which the child develops social, religious, national, and other identifications. But it is also how they begin to identify who is other to their own group. "After age two, children begin mending their 'good' (libidinally invested) and 'bad' (aggressively invested) images of important objects and corresponding self-images," Volkan writes. And they begin investing both these kinds of images into what Volkan calls "suitable reservoirs of externalization": good things go in one's own group, bad things in the other group.

Volkan notes that large-group identities can also form in adulthood, ranging benignly from membership in a profession to, problematically, membership in a cult or militant organization. In the more problematic kinds of identifications, "these individuals exaggerate selected aspects of their childhood large-group identities by holding on to a restricted special religious or nationalistic belief" (Volkan 2019, 143). Volkan emphasizes that large-group identities acquired in adulthood can drastically alter an earlier large-group identity. There are indeed such cases (think of the Midwestern nineteen-year-old who signs up to go fight for ISIS), but quite often these new identities exaggerate aspects that were there all along.

Whether formed in childhood or adulthood, innocent or malignant, large-group identifications bind people together and demarcate them from others. Volkan describes large-group identification as being like a tent. He suggests visualizing the classical Freudian theory of large groups as "people arranged around a gigantic maypole representing the group leader." He writes: "Individuals in the large group dance around the pole/leader, identifying with each other. I have expanded this maypole metaphor by imagining a canvas extending from the pole out over the people, forming a huge tent. This canvas represents the large-group identity—whether it is evolved in childhood or adulthood—and provides a psychological border for those living under it, including the leader" (Volkan 2019, 143).

Volkan extends the analogy with an image of symbols of the group's identity stitched on the canvas. These can include what he calls chosen traumas and chosen glories, events that happened many generations, perhaps hundreds of years, earlier that are fixed as points of shared pain or pride. A chosen trauma "refers to the shared mental image of a very traumatic event at the hand of an enemy" (Volkan 2019, 144). For the modern Greek people, for example, a chosen trauma is the fall of Constantinople. A chosen glory is "the shared image of an ancestor's great accomplishments in dealing with another large group" (Volkan 2019, 144). For some descendants of settler colonialists, a chosen glory might be the conquest of another people/land.

Under duress, says Volkan, those who share a large-group identity can succumb to archaic fantasies, such as paranoid delusions, splitting, and denial. I will explain this all in due course, but the fundamental idea is that when an anxiety is too much, the people may resort to defense mechanisms to ward it off, just as a child may hide under the covers to keep the monsters away. Defense mechanisms are not in and of themselves pathological, but if clung to, they can become maladaptive and dysfunctional. We can understand a three-year-old hiding under the covers, but we'd hope that a thirty-five-year-old will have found more mature ways to cope.

What is the large group that Donald Trump, Michael Caputo, William Barr, and QAnon followers belong to? At the very least they are Trump loyalists. But beyond that, what is their fundamental core identification? To track that, I identify their favorite stereotypes. Where Freud noted that dreams are the royal road to an individual's unconscious, David Marriott suggests that stereotypes are the royal road to the cultural unconscious (Marriott 2018, 151). The stereotypes a group holds of others are the key to understanding their unconscious world.

We need not look far to identify all the stereotypes that Trump and his surrogates invoke: Mexicans as criminals and rapists, women as pussies waiting to be grabbed, Black Lives Matter protesters as violent hooligans, Detroit and Michigan (with their sizable minority populations) as the most corrupt cities in the country. During the 2020 election season, every single time Trump or one of his surrogates was asked about racial injustice and the largely peaceful protests that swept the country (and indeed the world) in the wake of the killing of George Floyd by police, they immediately brought up Antifa. But what they were pointing to was not the actual Antifa (or anti-fascist) movement, which is a loose and diverse group of activists opposed to fascism—but a largely imaginary violent and monolithic organization. In interview after interview, speech after speech, Trump and company invariably linked anti-racist movements with violence. Apparently, the image of people asking for justice conjures up images of angry Black people, violent agitators, looters, and arsonists. The cultural unconscious of Caputo, Barr, and

Trump consistently links calls for racial equality to terror and violent destruction.

We can identify this association as a symptom, an instinctual representative, a sign of the large-group identification and its archaic defenses. Out of fear of being destroyed by the other, members of the group mount a defense of self-holding, that is, holding their group to be a solid entity, even the most supreme and best ever. This fantasy is illusory and fragile, calling for vigilance at every turn, namely a concomitant fantasy of the other as a threat, something to be abjected and torn away in order to protect the large-group identification. In short, because of their existential anxieties and fantastical delusions of greatness, their primary large-group identification is as white—not whiteness as one of many racial identifications, but whiteness as normal and normative. This is a largely unconscious fantasy of white supremacy, a defense that emerges with the historical creation of whiteness, which only developed in the context of colonialism. It took centuries of European colonial powers vying for authority all over the world before "white" would be an identity at all. Through the colonial era—that is, through the rise of modernity from the sixteenth through eighteenth centuries—the only way that colonial powers could begin to justify colonialism was to say that there were two kinds of people: those equipped to rule and those needing to be ruled. And this dichotomy mapped neatly onto Europeans (the landed men, in particular) and everyone else. The Europeans competed among themselves furiously—the French, the Dutch, the Portuguese, the British—in planting their flags all over the world. The main thing they shared was the hue of their skin, close enough to being white to call it so, especially in comparison to the darker peoples all over the rest of the world.

As a product of colonialism, whiteness is guilt-ridden and fragile to its core. Though it's really not a tangible thing at all, throughout American history whiteness has been a ticket to membership, inclusion, and citizenship. Now, in the second decade of the twenty-first century, that ticket is being called out for being a fraud. It will no longer get you to the front of the line. You will need to wait your turn like everyone else. Maybe right now it is not your turn. No wonder so many "white" people are so anxious.

What Motivates Conspiracy Thinking

I am suggesting that the root of the conspiracy theory phenomenon is not bravado but a deep insecurity, a fragile and anxious identity. As Marriott puts it, "most people are antiblack not because they are avowedly racist but because such is the insecure being of their world" (2018, xi). As I see it, what is at the root of any large-group identification is a deep insecurity that it may fall apart at any moment. This operates at the level of the individual and the social unit.

Individually, this insecurity is an existential crisis for any mammal possessing language, because development involves moving from speechlessness to the world of words, thing presentations to representations (to cope with absences), and relations with others—identifications that give us a footing in an otherwise perplexing world.

Ideally, the environment would help the child develop the capacity to tarry with indeterminacy so that it would not have to cling to idealized notions of the group. Children would be able, as Volkan puts it, "to separate realistic dangers from fantasized ones" and be more "willing to open the metaphorical large-group tent's gate and accept newcomers without experiencing much anxiety" (Volkan 2019, 147–148).

It is also a social phenomenon. Affects are contagious, and when many in the group feel secure in their identities, then others will tend to as well. So it is not just a matter of what happens developmentally to each member of a group, but the ways that a sense of security can be transmitted and reproduced over generations.

But development is often far from ideal. As D. W. Winnicott noted, sometimes our environments fail and the self may carry on with life with an ongoing, underlying fear that something terrible will happen (Winnicott 1974). Borrowing from Winnicott, I have called this a fear of breakdown (McAfee 2019). As a result of it, many of us, at one moment or another, may cling to large-group identifications as a form of security, sometimes demanding their reality, insisting on excluding, abjecting, or destroying those who are not part of the group. Unlike those who can tarry with indeterminacy, those caught in the grip of a fear of breakdown defend themselves against this anxiety by developing an idealized notion of their own group (evidenced in the slogan "Make America Great Again"), and they "defensively perceive the huge immigrant population as a threat" that is "tearing a hole in the group's canvas" (Volkan 2019, 147–148).

In addition to the fear of breakdown, there is another key force behind conspiracy theorizing. It is what, drawing from Lacanian theory, we can call an "impossible desire" for an ultimate truth, perhaps a truth that will quell one's deep anxieties. At the risk of oversimplifying Lacan, the root of longing is to be the object of the Other's desire, to be the apple of their eye, to be their one and only. So one goes spinning about, trying to be what the other (other people) or the Other (the system) wants. Hence the desire to conform. But that doesn't really work out well because one never knows what the Other wants, does one? One might begin to suspect that the Other/the System robbed us of something very important (the Thing) and the pleasure that would go with it (*jouissance*). Hence that terrible insecurity. As Mari Ruti puts it, "The Other blocks our direct access to jouissance so that it can only be approached in [a] roundabout way . . . through (more or less) socially recognizable objects of desire" (Ruti 2012, 19). But none of these objects are really satisfying; they are never the "real," sublime Thing, which might at any rate be quite overwhelming. "The task of desire, then, is to keep us at a reassuring distance from the Thing while at the same time allowing us to *fantasize* about attaining it" (Ruti 2012, 19).

It seems to me that this is the very structure of conspiracy theories: a *fantasy* that there is an ultimate Truth or answer to be had, but a Truth that is always safely deferred. As a result, conspiracy theories are often unsatisfiable and unresolvable. Hence they keep desire, the motive force of life itself, alive. To remain unsatisfiable, they often involve deep contradictions, impossible truths—for example, that Trump should have remained in power regardless of the democratic process in order to save American democracy. But when the democratic process bounced him out of office, then that process must have been flawed. There is a deeper meaning of events yet to be uncovered.

There is another, even weirder permutation of this logic. If the system (big Other) seems to be what is robbing me of enjoyment, then maybe what is called for is someone to be the other to the big Other. And if the Deep State is a manifestation of the big Other, then maybe someone like Trump can recuperate what has been robbed. Maybe someone like Trump can be the other to the big Other.

This may sound strange, but it is really familiar. It's all about jealousy. Subjects want their own pleasure but become suspicious that they are being robbed, that others are stealing it from them. But this is a delusion. No one is actually stealing anything, but the fragile identity at issue can't help but think so.

A conspiracy theory allows its adherents to maintain a delusion of rightful ownership of identity, one that is being robbed. The fragility of the identity is externalized so that the fragility isn't inherent but an effect of there being enemies. Conspiracy theories allow subjects to maintain and keep up the fight, endlessly, without resolution, without ever winning, without losing, and without having to admit that it is all an illusion.

How Conspiracy Theories Operate

Perhaps by the time this chapter makes its way to publication, some of the conspiracy theories I've mentioned will have passed into oblivion. But the motive forces I've just discussed—a deep anxiety and a fantasy that assuages it—will unfortunately still be with us. And so other conspiracy theories will arise. Just as Pizzagate gave way to QAnon, and QAnon lost steam in the aftermath of the Trump administration (since Trump could no longer fight the Deep State), new conspiracy theories are likely to take shape, perhaps fueled by #StopTheSteal, the notion that "they" are stealing the election from "the People."

Though I don't know what will be next, I wager that it will largely operate according to familiar mechanisms: misrecognition, the creation of phobic objects, splitting, projection, and displacement. Not coincidentally, some of these mechanisms are also recognized as very early defenses that an infant deploys before it is mature enough to use more developed ones, such as rationalization or sublimation. I say it is not coincidental because conspiracy theorizing is something that members of large groups do under stress, regressing to earlier forms of feeling and thinking. We might even say they've gone a little mad.

By mad I mean that they have begun to lose their tether to "the real world," insofar as they are more prone to unconscious processes, what Freud called primary processes as distinguished from secondary processes. Before we become skilled in using language, our ideas are in the form of pictures and images, "thing presentations" rather than "word presentations." But even the most developed person has regular moments of regression to primary processes, including when we dream and are bombarded with images that have a logic to them when we are asleep but make hardly any sense upon waking, when we return from primary process thinking to secondary process thinking. Upon waking, we might try to put those images into words; but they often quickly slip away.

Our dreams do have a grammar, but not a linguistic one. They operate through chains of associations, displacements, and condensations. One image can stand for many things (condensation) or be a way of disavowing something else (displacement). The most we can do to uncover the meaning of a dream is to trace these chains of associations to get to the ultimate (latent) meaning. When people(s) regress, they go back to these more primary ways of thinking, including the various phenomena of conspiracy thinking that I will describe below. Though these mechanisms overlap, I will explain them one by one.

MISRECOGNITION

Madness is fundamentally a matter of misrecognition, not being able to recognize or care about reality or how one fits into the web of the world. The ultimate misrecognition is to misrecognize oneself. "Assuredly," Lacan writes, "one can say that the madman believes he is different than he is" (Lacan

2006, 139). To explain, Lacan offers this cryptic example: "If a man who thinks he is a king is mad, a king who thinks he is a king is no less so" (2006, 139). If the king were sane, he would know that, really, he is only a man, that only the pomp and circumstance surrounding his office has afforded him the role of king.

One who mistakes oneself for something else can engage in a further misrecognition, one that becomes trouble for everyone else when "the madman seeks to impose the law of his heart onto what seems to him to be the havoc of the world. This is an 'insane' enterprise," Lacan writes, not just because it is maladaptive, but because "the subject does not recognize in this havoc the very manifestation of his actual being, or that what he experiences as the law of his heart is but the inverted and virtual image of that same being" (Lacan 2006, 140). So there is a double misrecognition: first of who they are, and second that the havoc that appears to be out there in the world is not there but residing in their own being. In other words, they project their own chaos onto the world. If they act on the notion that there is havoc in the world, if they try to set it straight, Lacan says, they will likely face social repercussions from their mad actions.

Consider how misrecognition fuels conspiracy theories. In the QAnon fantasy, Trump and his followers think he is the president who *really is* the president, regardless of how the vote turned out—because any vote that turns out otherwise is proof that the vote was rigged. The second misrecognition is thinking that the system is rigged, that there is a cabal creating havoc in the world. The fact that so many people sent in absentee ballots is "evidence" of a rigged system—when in fact people voted absentee because of the pandemic, which had reached such dangerous proportions due to the havoc of this president. He had projected his own internal havoc onto the world.

Many conspiracy theories trade in stereotypes, and these stereotypes typically result from the group's shared phobias becoming phobic objects. Stereotypes are more than ill-informed mental constructs. They are phobic objects that are, as Frantz Fanon pointed out, overdetermined. "This object does not come at random out of the void of nothingness," Fanon writes (quoted in Marriott 2018, 139). As Marriott explains, "The myth of the Negro that organizes negrophobic identity appears to be *needed*" (2018, 139).

The phobic person needs a phobic object, largely, I think, to concretize and contain *elsewhere than within oneself* the anxiety or "radical destitution" (Marriott 2018, 140) that the phobic person is experiencing. Hence the object becomes, as Fanon puts it, "endowed with evil intentions and with all the attributes of a malefic power" (Marriott 2018, 139). Anxiety leads to fear, fear to the need for a phobic object, an obsession with it, and then that object becomes endowed with outsized malevolent power. This is all in the service of getting rid of anxiety, putting it into something that is not the real source of anxiety but an external substitute—a fetish—of it.

By "fetish," following Freud, Fanon, and Marriott, I mean something that stands for something else. Fetishes help those who cannot bear castration (that is, the fact of one not being all that big a deal, of being "cut down" to size) to disavow their castration (I really am large and powerful). In other words, fetishes help us to avoid acknowledging that one is not all-powerful and virile. A person is phobic when the thought of being "not a big deal," or even worse truly vulnerable, is intolerable. (Hence Trump's bragging that he could grab any women's pussy exhibited his own anxiety over being cut down to size.) As opposed to the normal neurotic who accepts but largely represses their castration, this person becomes a pervert, to use Freud's terminology, insisting on satisfaction of their drives rather than repressing them. Instead of renouncing drives, they get off through fetishistic substitutions. The racialized other to "white civilization" becomes a phobic object not because it actually poses any real threat but because it fits a handy stereotype and is a tolerable substitute for the anxiety.[4] As Marriott puts it, "If it is true that the phobic object forms itself *out of* the stereotype (with the ambiguity that that implies—the stereotype as the material from which desire is built, and the stereotype as the disfiguring of desire by culture), only to find the stereotype returning to haunt this fantasy of the black object at its root—then it is reasonable to suppose that the stereotype, the one that returns to the ego its own murderous-shameful attachment, is in fact *standing for* a fear of disintegration that is the originary trace of the other within us" (2018, 141). Again, the source of the anxiety is not the racialized other but the phobic's own ego "and its fetishistic attachments" (Marriott 2018, 141). And it is not just the phobic's ego but its larger culture, the large-group identification to which it belongs. Bringing together Volkan and Marriott, we can see that the stereotype of the dangerous, racialized other is a sign on the royal road to the cultural unconscious and its large-group identification. Trump loyalists, and white supremacists more generally, position themselves as the guardians of "civilization" against arsonists, looters, hooligans, and thugs—Black folks and their allies.

SPLITTING

One of the most primordial defense mechanisms, especially according to Melanie Klein, is splitting. It is one of the first ways that an infant can try to make sense of the flurry of sounds, sights, and other sensations it experiences, basically by splitting them into two groups, good objects and bad objects. (In psychoanalytic parlance, "objects" means people in one's world.)

To decide whether something is good or bad, one needs to know little else than whether the experience brings pleasure or pain, comfort or anxiety. This very primordial way of distinguishing things comes back under duress in any kind of regressed state. Somewhat similarly, there can be a splitting of the self's own ego, slicing off parts that are unacceptable or intolerable onto other objects, leading to the experience that one is good and the other is bad. When Lacan was describing the madman misrecognizing his own havoc as havoc in the world, he was describing a kind of splitting. Likewise, phobic objects are the result of splitting, of the need to get rid of anxiety within the self by putting it elsewhere. (This is also at work in projection, which I'll turn to in the next section.)

Splitting anxiety off oneself and into something else feeds into the good and bad object dichotomy such that, when the bad parts of oneself are split off into something else, it comes to seem outsized and diabolical. This is another feature that shows up in conspiracy theories. The imagined enemy is not just an adversary but something malevolent, its deeds diabolical and atrocious. Volney Gay describes these as atrocity fantasies: "Atrocity allegations awaken archaic fantasies of degradation and loss that, if believed, provoke violent retaliation against the alleged perpetrators. Those archaic fantasies are that something terrible has occurred, a vicious attack on one's body or one's mind or on one's beloved child. The worst thing imaginable, an image that arose briefly and then was hurriedly repressed, has actually happened. Atrocity allegations generate revulsion, rage, and then, unless corralled by legal or cultural restraints, bloodshed" (Gay 2018, 253).

Gay argues that the very thought of an atrocity arouses universal human feelings, drawing on "primal somatic terrors" (Gay 2018, 253). The motifs of these atrocities repeat across time and cultures. Because they arouse such revulsion, propogandists and warmongers often make use of them, accusing their adversaries of these kinds of crimes in order to win support for their own causes. They have been used to conquer native peoples, to create scapegoats, and to gin up hatred. As Gay notes, taking us back to the Pizzagate conspiracy theory that I noted earlier, "atrocity fantasies about Hillary Clinton centered on her alleged sexual practices; her alleged sexual crimes; and her alleged sex trafficking of children" (Gay 2018, 257). The man with the assault rifle in the Pizzagate conspiracy seemed to be fully under the sway of the atrocity fantasy. Others have knowingly deployed such fantasies to prevail in their battles too, including an elaborate story drawn up by Kuwaitis in 1990 that their assailants, the Iraqis, were snatching babies from incubators and leaving them to die. The Kuwaitis' account tapped all the atrocity motifs that elicit outrage and sympathy, stoking war fever against the Iraqis. But it all turned out to be a complete ruse. Whether or not the authors of a conspiracy theory know their account is false matters little. The problem is that, because of the allure of splitting, broad swaths of the population easily fall prey to them.

Just as happened in early childhood development, it feels so much better to be able to split off or disavow the unsavory parts of oneself and project them—literally put them—into others. And likewise, it feels good to put what is good and valued into one's own group identity. And if the aggrieved person's group identity is regressed, this process is a perfect storm for conspiracy thinking.

A key element of atrocity fantasies and other conspiracy theories is the form of splitting known as projection. In sum, projection comes down to an unconscious formulation: I'm not bad, you're bad. As Laplanche and Pontalis define it, projection is an "operation whereby qualities, feelings, wishes or even 'objects,' which the subject refuses to recognize or rejects in himself, are expelled from the self and located in another person or thing" (1973, 349). Then this other thing, rather than oneself, becomes terrifying.

Projection is a major feature of paranoia, itself a central feature of conspiracy thinking. It can be an unconscious form of disavowal. We saw it in Trump's cries that "they" are trying to steal the election when in fact he was trying to steal the election. The political leaders egging on the "stop the steal" conspiracy were the very ones trying to suppress the vote. Again the pattern: I'm not bad, you're bad.

As a form of splitting, it is a way to get rid of intolerable affects and phenomena, like Lacan's madman putting his internal havoc into the world. Likewise, Trump's destructive internal havoc was put into the "caravan" of Mexicans coming to the border to destroy America. His havoc was also put into all of Biden's supporters, who became phobic objects, as in his tweet of November 2, 2020: "The Anti-American radicals defaming our noble history, heritage & heroes; and ANTIFA, the rioters, looters, Marxists, & left-wing extremists. THEY ALL SUPPORT BIDEN."

DISPLACEMENT

Displacement was one of the first features that social scientists trying to make sense of conspiracy theory noticed. In 1930 Harold Lasswell came up with a general theory of the political personality: a person who could displace a private motive onto a public object and then rationalize it as being in the public interest (Blanuša and Hristov 2020, 70). But Lasswell only scratched the surface of this phenomenon and how it operates in conspiracy thinking.

Displacement is the process by which affects jump from one thing to another, revealing how they are mobile and free-floating, and explaining in part how hard it is to pin down a conspiracy theorist with any facts. They take one thing to be an epiphenomenon of another thing, and do this without end. Where projection moves a cluster of phenomena, wholesale, into something external to oneself, displacement is an operation of moving the ball through chains of associations. It operates metonymically, where a part of one thing can connect with or move aside a part of something else. It is a way for an affect around one thing to detach from it and then attach itself to something else.

As we saw, this is how the phobic object is constituted. It is not because there is any particular feature in the object itself, but that the subject has an intolerable feeling that needs to be put somewhere, put in another place, *displaced*. As Laplanche and Pontalis explain, "In a phobia, for instance, displacement on to the phobic object permits the objectivation, localization and containment of anxiety" (1973, 123). But beyond the particular object, displacement will let the association continue to move: from the #BlackLivesMatter movement to the most corrupt cities of Detroit and Philadelphia to Biden to those who want to shut down the economy to who knows what next. It is ceaseless. It trades in innuendo. It runs in many, sometimes contradictory directions at once. Its aim is to confirm the sought-after "impossible truth" I discussed earlier, which, at bottom, is a revelation that I/we are beloved and powerful and will triumph over anyone who denies this.

"If the object of conspiracist desire is an impossible truth," write Blanuša and Hristov, "conspiracy theorists can sustain their desire only by displacing it onto endless further details" (2020, 74). It would seem that Trump's loss of the 2020 election would invalidate the QAnon theory that Trump really is and must be the president, but to retain the fantasy a new conspiratorial twist emerges: there was widespread voter fraud. Such a chain of responses "becomes meaningful if it is read as a symptom of [a] desire that can never fulfilled," requiring "deferring the realization of its impossibility" (Blanuša and Hristov 2020, 74).

The phenomenon of displacement helps explain how conspiracy theories are so hard to falsify. Ethan Zuckerman explains how QAnon, like any successful conspiracy theory, is "self-sealing": "Any objection or disproof can be turned into support for theory. . . . [E]vents that would seem to doom the theory . . . are turned into evidence that those behind the conspiracy . . . are clever beyond our understanding" (2019). Hence it well *could* be true, as any paranoid delusion *might* be true. In reality, these conspiracies are highly unlikely, but in the minds of peoples regressed, they explain everything.

The Aftereffects

All these defense mechanisms, from misrecognition to displacement, have had terrible political consequences, with conspiracy thinking fueling ethnic conflict, civil wars, the refugee crisis, and even refusals to wear a mask during a deadly pandemic. At bottom, for those who are most prone to the archaic defenses underlying conspiracy theories, there is fear coupled with a fantasy that there is a way out.

Through the rise of modernity in the constellation of European nations and their offshoots, large-group identification for those on the side of the colonizers has largely been founded on a delusion of (white and male) "civilization" as opposed to people who supposedly need or deserve to be colonized. There is a vast literature on this. I point to it to make the larger point that the dominant cultural imaginary of Eurocentric peoples has been that the norm is white and male, that the other includes women and people of color. But a psychoanalytic perspective adds a new dimension. The real enemy of white "civilization" is not people of color, not the colonized, not the enslaved, but the fragile and anxious identity of the colonizers themselves, their own other within. The colonized are fetishistic substitutes and targets of externalization of these intolerable anxieties.

When people's social, political, and group identities become threatened, anxieties mount and fantasized ideals lead to demonization and extremism. This is a tendency that all people have, under duress, to split the world into forces of light and forces of darkness; to project paranoid, Manichaean views onto others. People caught in the grip of a paranoid politics will gravitate to whatever "facts" fit their delusions.

No "fact-checkers" will be able to set them straight. No account of Trump's tens of thousands of lies will unsettle their certitude that Trump (or whoever comes next) is their savior. Those archaic defenses of splitting, projection, and the like kick in, all in some variation of "we are good and they are trying to destroy us." Adversaries become enemies. One's own group becomes idealized. Peaceful protesters appear as domestic terrorists trying to destroy the nation. Any disagreement is tantamount to imminent violence and destruction.

These delusions operate at a preverbal level, what Freud called primary processes. They serve unconsciously to protect the anxious body. Making others the enemy serves to split off bad feelings from ourselves and deposit them in others, who become suitable repositories for intolerable affects. Fantasies of "law and order" promise reprieve from destruction. When anxieties become intolerable, they revert to primary process, thing presentations, not word presentations. I think this is what makes political discourse in times like these difficult if not impossible.

A psychoanalytic hermeneutics points to the large-group identity of Trump, his surrogates, and his base as white-identified coupled with a fantasy of "Western/white civilization." But one doesn't need psychoanalysis to confirm that. The key point here is how this identification and its anxieties operate: finding enemies not because they are any real threat, but because the anxiety at work in the large-group identification *needs* an enemy as a fetish surrogate for its fear of falling apart. If there wasn't a ready enemy, they would have to invent one. And often they do.

This phenomenon at the root of conspiracy thinking stands in the way of democratic practices, which, by their very nature, require people who disagree with each other to decide together matters of common concern. Yet if we demonize our adversaries, we endlessly defer the hard work of democratic deliberation, choice, and action. It may be that the root of paranoid politics is the fantasy that one might have it all, that there will be no need for making hard choices, that if we could just vanquish our enemies we could have everything we desire, even if the object of that desire will be always deferred.

Notes

1. For an overview of various conspiracy theories, especially those that claim the problem is a lack of information coupled with others intentionally out to deceive people, see Cassam (2021).
2. In chapter 12 of *Fear of Breakdown*, I show how a fear of breakdown may also underlie anxieties over female sexuality.

Perhaps the seeming danger of the enemy group is really a projection or displacement of men's anxieties regarding their capacity to satisfy their own women (McAfee 2019, 225–227).

3. In this chapter, I use the term *paranoia* intentionally in order to psychodynamically diagnose how it operates in individuals and large groups. On paranoia as a diagnostic category, see Kendler (2017).

4. As Katie Howard pointed out in conversation with the author, this logic is also at work in the demonization of women as witches during the Middle Ages.

References

ABC7. 2019. "Man Arrested in Arson at Comet Ping Pong, D.C. Restaurant Associated with 'Pizzagate.'" February 14. https://wjla.com/news/local/man-arrested-arson-comet-ping-pong-dc-pizzagate.

Alter, Charlotte. 2020. "How Conspiracy Theories Are Shaping the 2020 Election—and Shaking the Foundation of American Democracy." *Time*, September 20. https://time.com/5887437/conspiracy-theories-2020-election/.

Ball, Philip, and Amy Maxmen. 2020. "The Epic Battle against Coronavirus Misinformation and Conspiracy Theories." *Nature*, May 27. https://www.nature.com/articles/d41586-020-01452-z.

Benner, Katie. 2020. "Barr Told Prosecutors to Consider Sedition Charges for Protest Violence." *New York Times*, September 22. https://www.nytimes.com/2020/09/16/us/politics/william-barr-sedition.html.

Blanuša, Nebojša, and Todor Hristov. 2020. "Psychoanalysis, Critical Theory, and Conspiracy Theories." In *Routledge Handbook of Conspiracy Theories*, edited by Michael Butter and Peter Knight, 67–80. Abingdon, UK: Routledge.

Cassam, Quassim. 2021. *Conspiracy Theories*. Cambridge: Polity Press.

Gay, Volney P. 2018. "Atrocity Fantasies and Atrocity Allegations." *International Journal of Applied Psychoanalytic Studies* 15, no. 4: 253–263.

Haag, Mathew, and Maya Salam. 2017. "Gunman in 'Pizzagate' Shooting Is Sentenced to 4 Years in Prison." *New York Times*, June 22. https://www.nytimes.com/2017/06/22/us/pizzagate-attack-sentence.html.

Heer, Jet. 2020. "Trump's Dangerous End Game." *The Nation*, November 6. https://www.thenation.com/article/politics/trump-election-fraud-biden/.

Hofstadter, Richard. 1964. "The Paranoid Style in American Politics." *Harper's Magazine*, November. https://harpers.org/archive/1964/11/the-paranoid-style-in-american-politics/.

Jiang, Weija. 2020. "HHS Spokesman Michael Caputo Claims He Received Death Threat during Facebook Live Session." *CBS News*, September 15. https://www.cbsnews.com/news/michael-caputo-hhs-facebook-live-video-death-threat-claims/.

Kendler, Kenneth. S. 2017. "The Clinical Features of Paranoia in the 20th Century and Their Representation in Diagnostic Criteria From DSM-III through DSM-5." *Schizophrenia Bulletin* 43, no. 2: 332–343. https://doi.org/10.1093/schbul/sbw161.

Klein, Melanie. 1986. *The Selected Melanie Klein*. Edited by Juliet Mitchell. New York: Free Press.

Lacan, Jacques. 2006. *Ecrits: The First Complete Edition in English*. Translated by Bruce Fink. New York: W. W. Norton.

Laplanche, Jean, and Jean-Bertrand Pontalis. 1973. *The Language of Psychoanalysis*. Translated by Donald Nicholson-Smith. New York: W. W. Norton.

Marriott, David. 2018. *Whither Fanon: Studies in the Blackness of Being*. Stanford, CA: Stanford University Press.

McAfee, Noëlle. 2019. *Fear of Breakdown: Politics and Psychoanalysis*. New York: Columbia University Press.

Öniş, Ziya, and Mustafa Kutlay. 2020. "The Global Political Economy of Right-Wing Populism: Deconstructing the

Paradox." *International Spectator* 55, no. 2: 108–126. https://doi.org/10.1080/03932729.2020.1731168.

Pettigrew, Thomas F. 2017. "Social Psychological Perspectives on Trump Supporters." *Journal of Social and Political Psychology* 5, no. 1: 107–116. https:doi.org/10.5964/jspp.v5i1.750.

Rodríguez-Pose, Andrés. 2022. "The Rise of Populism and the Revenge of the Places That Don't Matter." In *Populism: Origins and Alternative Policy Responses*, edited by Andrés Velasco and Irene Bucelli, 79–103. London: LSE Press. https://doi.org/10.31389/lsepress.pop.

Ruti, Mari. 2012. *The Singularity of Being*. New York: Fordham University Press.

SSRS Research. 2021. https://cdn.cnn.com/cnn/2021/images/04/30/rel3e.-.voting.and.elections.pdf.

Volkan, Vamik D. 2019. "Large-Group Identity, Who Are We Now? Leader-Follower Relationships and Societal-Political Divisions." *American Journal of Psychoanalysis* 79, no. 2: 139–155.

Winnicott, D. W. 1974. "Fear of Breakdown." *International Review of Psychoanalysis* 1: 103–107.

Zuckerman, Ethan. 2019."QAnon and the Emergence of the Unreal." *Journal of Design and Science*, July 15. https://doi.org/10.21428/7808da6b.6b8a82b9.

4

The Political Branding of COVID-19

CIARA TORRES-SPELLISCY

Eleven months into the COVID-19 pandemic, the president of the United States, Donald Trump, caught the virus and was hospitalized. Figuring out exactly where Trump contracted this virus is difficult. Throughout his reelection campaign in 2020, he attended in-person rallies and in-person fundraisers in defiance of the best public health advice. He accepted his nomination from the Republican Party in front of a large crowd on the White House grounds. Shortly before falling ill, he held a huge in-person event to celebrate conservative Judge Amy Coney Barrett's nomination to fill the late Justice Ruth Bader Ginsberg's Supreme Court seat. This ceremony, held in the White House's Rose Garden, is now considered a "super-spreader event" because several attendees later tested positive for COVID-19 (Clark 2020). Video footage of Judge Barrett's nomination gathering shows many in the crowd, who included political and financial elites, not wearing masks, not social distancing, fist bumping, and hugging. Nearly everyone in the crowd was a Republican (Buchanan et al. 2020). By September 26, 2020, when the Rose Garden ceremony took place, Trump had politicized the virus, made wearing masks a partisan matter, and consistently failed to practice social distancing. He used the bully pulpit to downplay the dangers of COVID-19 while blaming China for the pandemic (Hamblin 2020). In short, the president played a key role in creating the conditions that led to his own illness.

On Election Day 2020, there were 11 million cases of COVID-19 in the United States, the most of any nation in the world at the time (Johns Hopkins 2020). At the heart of this calamity was the partisan branding of the disease (Torres-Spelliscy 2019a). The American public processed COVID-19 via the different information silos they inhabited (Lasco 2021). These were the same information silos that for years had facilitated partisan differences of opinion on the presidency of Donald Trump, the legality of his actions, and the appropriateness of his first impeachment (Pew Research Center 2019a; Baker 2019).

What propelled the partisan perception of the pandemic? President Trump's view that the COVID-19 pandemic weakened his chance of winning the 2020 presidential election led him to convey misinformation about the disease (Brennen et al. 2020). His fabrications were spread by social media platforms that allowed misinformation to travel with great alacrity, along with traditional brick-and-mortar media that amplified Trump's messages. As Laurie Garrett explained, "[i]n a world of polarizing distrust . . . , the spread of . . . COVID-19 . . . both within nations and internationally, is aided and abetted by misinformation that circumnavigates the planet in microseconds" (Garrett 2020). A congressional committee investigating Trump's COVID-19 response in 2021 "uncover[ed] evidence of the Trump Administration's deliberate efforts to undermine the nation's coronavirus response for political purposes" (Select Subcommittee on the Coronavirus Crisis 2021).

This chapter will argue that the United States' failure to address COVID-19 can be laid at the feet of President Trump. His mendacity in branding the virus a "hoax," and at times as China's fault, exacerbated preexisting partisan divides (Levinson 2018). After discussing how political branding works and the problem of partisan information silos, this chapter will examine President Trump's shifting emotional discourse about the pandemic, using Elizabeth Kübler-Ross's five stages of grief as a narrative structure. As *Washington Post* columnist Eugene Robinson noted, "[i]t was as if he had to go through the five stages of grief—denial, anger, bargaining, depression and acceptance, to mourn the economic growth and stock market gains he believed could win him reelection" (Robinson 2020). I will show that Trump used denial, anger, and bargaining to manipulate his supporters and brand COVID-19, ensuring that the American response to COVID-19 became a partisan disaster. The fact that Trump hid any depression while in power and only revealed his acceptance of COVID's dangers when he was out of power both had lasting impacts on how his political followers perceived COVID-19.

How Branding Works

Branding is the practice of purposefully repeating a word, phrase, or image until its intended audience absorbs it (Torres-Spelliscy 2019a, 1). Branding is most effective when delivered through a trusted network (Holt 2016). A trusted network might include friends or family, a social media feed, or a media source like a newspaper or television channel (Grabner-Kräuter and Bitter 2015). The key is that the intended audience member assigns a level of credibility to the information because of the presumed integrity of the messenger.

Businesses develop commercial branding to sell merchandise and use paid advertising to repeat key claims about their products. Advertising has evolved in terms of both how it is presented to an audience, and the message it carries. During the American Civil War, advertising included leaflets and newspaper advertisements, as well as paintings on the sides of buildings. As one study of *Harper's Weekly* showed, at the start of the Civil War, ads for everyday ailments proliferated, but later advertisements for bullets, guns, and artificial limbs became common. In the South in the midst of the Civil War, there were still ads for the sale of slaves ("Ad: Slaves for Sale, Tennessee 1863" n.d.).

Advertising was frequently a financial driver of communication technologies. Radio stations ran advertisements soon after radio arrived in the United States in the 1920s (Campaign Live 2016). Particular brands sponsored certain radio dramas (Levine 2020). Even quiz shows had brand-name sponsors. Reynolds Tobacco sponsored a radio quiz show called *Information Please* and tried to get contestants to smoke its brand of cigarettes (PBS 2020).

Advertisers moved seamlessly from radio into television in 1941 (Marketing Wit 2020). TV ads in the 1950s placed "a salesman in every living room," and corporations often monopolized the sponsorship of shows like "*Kraft Music Hall, Hallmark Hall of Fame, The Kelvinator Kitchen*, [and] *Gillette Cavalcade of Sports*" (O'Barr 2010). Once the internet expanded, advertisers found ways to insinuate themselves into content-based ads, pop-up ads, ads that interrupted content, and ads that completely obscured content until clicked away. By 2019, $60.5 billion was spent on television advertising, an eight-year low, but in 2018, approximately $100 billion was spent on digital ads in the United States (Marketing

Charts 2020; Guttmann 2020). In 2020, $63.4 billion was spent on TV ads and $139.8 billion was spent on digital ads (Lafayette 2021; Graham 2021). In other words, during the 2020 election, advertisers, including political advertisers, bet that they could reach more people through their computers and phones than through their TVs.

Branding builds awareness of a product. Repetition breeds familiarity, and familiarity breeds trust. The more a person sees an ad for a given product, the more trustworthy that product seems to them. This is why commercial sellers pay so much to advertise a product repeatedly.

Political branding uses the same techniques and modalities as commercial branding, but the source and content of the message are political. If commercial branding aims to sell products, political branding aims to sell politicians, ideas, and ideals through any available media that reaches a target audience (Torres-Spelliscy 2019a). Consequently, as Robert Spero warns, "[t]he political television commercial . . . is a dangerous weapon in the hands of the unscrupulous" (Spero 1980).

As a businessman, Donald Trump was a master of branding. He brought this acumen to politics. He used branding techniques to get elected in 2016. He manipulated the emotions of his followers by painting a dark picture of outside threats. He claimed that he alone could fix the grave problems confronting the country. In this fashion, he constructed a psychological system threat and offered himself as the solution to that threat. Gina Roussos posits that a "[s]ystem threat occurs when people's belief that society is fair and stable is challenged; they are persuaded to believe that the nation's future is dark and uncertain. This manipulation induces fear and uncertainty and has many influences on behavior—in this case, voting behavior" (Roussos 2016).

Once elected, President Trump continued to deploy branding techniques. He regularly repeated emotionally laden words, phrases, or slogans to hammer home points to his followers. As Elliot Benjamin notes, "[t]hrough his barrage of daily tweets, Trump sow[ed] confusion and distort[ed] reality, and has ultimately called into question the foundations of national institutions. . . . [He does this because he knows to] 'repeat [his] message over and over and over again. Repetition makes the heart grow fonder and fiction, if heard frequently enough, can come to sound like fact'" (Benjamin 2021, quoting Pratkanis and Aronson 1992). Using branding techniques in politics can pathologize or normalize nearly any topic—even a deadly contagion. Because the press provides almost continuous coverage of a president's every move and utterance, the president has the capacity to brand things, people, or concepts simply by repeating a (mis)characterization. Then the press amplifies this (mis)characterization—or brand—far and wide. The more the public hears a message, even a regurgitated lie, the more normalized it becomes.

When a charismatic political leader like Trump repeats a message, especially a seductive and pleasing lie, it can also have a psychological effect on listeners. As George Hagman and Harry Paul explain: "[i]n regards to Trump's relationship to his base the technique is simple: tell yourself what you need to hear: tell them what they want to hear, be relentless, keep doing it until the intersubjective becomes an hypnotic cryptopsychotic echo chamber" (Hagman and Paul 2020). Thus, by repeating what his audience wanted to hear—that COVID-19 was not that serious or that the pandemic would vanish quickly—Trump created a soothing myth that was emotionally attractive to his followers. The myth was seductive as Americans had to simultaneously deal with the disorientating reality of COVID-19, including life disruptions, closed offices, remote schooling, a shuttered Broadway, a tanking economy, and never-ending reports of death. Trump told these comforting lies about the pandemic in a bid to retain power through reelection in 2020. As Hagman and Paul argue, "[w]ith Donald Trump, truth is fair game, any lie, no matter how grotesque can be a tactic to manipulate the public into doubting their own perception of reality—to protect his hold on power, and his hunger for success" (Hagman and Paul 2020). Why would intelligent voters fall for these lies? There is often a chasm between facts and voting preferences, because "facts matter surprisingly little in elections, in part because many voters are voting for emotional instinctual reasons" (Torres-Spelliscy 2019a, citing Westen 2007).

Commercial brands "allow businesses to reach consumers directly with messages regarding emotion, identity, and self-worth" (Desai and Waller 2010). Branding often plays on the public's emotions and tries to fill deep psychological needs like wanting to be accepted (Packard 1957). Emotionally evocative branding is more likely to leave a lasting imprint on viewers (Rapaille 2007). The same is doubly true with political brands. In other words, if a politician can scare a voter into voting for him, he will. If a politician can seduce a voter into voting for her, she will.

Partisan Information Silos

Some scholars have argued that partisan echo chambers are not a real threat. For instance, Dubois and Blank claim that "[w]hatever may be happening on any single social media platform, when we look at the entire media environment, there is little apparent echo chamber." Their research found that "[p]eople regularly encounter things that they disagree with. People check multiple sources. People try to confirm information using search. Possibly most important, people discover things that change their political opinions" (Dubois and Blank 2018). Yet the experience of COVID-19 in the United States challenges these assumptions. COVID-19 physically pushed many individuals out of their normal workplaces and educational environments and onto online platforms, changing their susceptibility to echo chambers and previous models of online behavior in ways that were more extreme than the pre-pandemic baseline, as this chapter explores.

At the end of 2019, Pew Research, which has been tracking partisanship in the United States for decades, reported that "[p]artisanship continues to be *the* dividing line in the American public's political attitudes, far surpassing differences by age, race and ethnicity, gender, educational attainment, religious affiliation or other factors." This Pew study found that "the differences *between* the two parties are starker than those *within* the two parties. Across 30 political values—encompassing attitudes about guns, race, immigration, foreign policy and other realms—the average partisan gap is 39 percentage points" (Pew Research Center 2019b). This comports with findings that marriages across the Democrat/Republican partisan line were exceedingly rare, at 4 percent in 2020 (Wang 2020).

"Partisan information silos," in which conservatives only read conservative-slanted news and liberals only read liberal-slanted news, hardened during the Trump presidency. The negative consequences of partisan information silos are often self-inflicted, as Americans seek out news that reaffirms what they already believe politically. As Justin de Benedictis-Kessner, Baum, and Berinsky (2020) note, "[w]hen looking for political news, people will often seek out media that reduces their cognitive dissonance and agrees with their political beliefs and identification. Much research has shown that Democrats and Republicans prefer to consume news that supports their pre-existing beliefs while avoiding news that challenges those beliefs" (de Benedictis-Kessner et al., citing Arceneaux et al. 2012; Iyengar and Hahn 2009; Stroud 2011). In other words, Americans typically seek out media that reconfirms their preexisting biases, thereby deepening their partisan views.

Sometimes information silos are reinforced by external factors like the algorithms running social media sites and search engines. As Eli Pariser writes in his book *The Filter Bubble*, each time individuals use a search engine to look for information, it filters away facts that could challenge a cherished belief—because of the search engine's algorithms. "Since December 2009," Pariser observes, "you get the result that Google's algorithm suggests is best for you in particular—and someone else may see something entirely different. In other words, there is no standard Google anymore" (Pariser 2011). Google builds a profile for its users based on their past searches. This profile includes the algorithm's predictions about the user's age, gender, marital status, income, and personal interests (Holmes 2020). Republicans and Democrats seeking similar information are both offered search results skewed to whoever Google thinks they are.

Information silos are easier to build now that television offers over a hundred channels instead of just three networks. And online sources of information are even more numerous. This variety of information sources allows people to pick and choose, mix and match, filter and block what sources of information they will see, read, and believe. As de Benedictis-Kessner, Baum, and Berinsky (2020) describe, "[t]he typical U.S. household now receives about 190 television channels. . . . This explosion of media outlets has . . . allowed for the development of ideological 'niche' news programming . . . made up of largely partisan media sources. . . . If people can choose to watch or read exclusively ideologically extreme news sources, they may only be exposed to one side of political debates." The risk with a partisan information silo, as de Benedictis-Kessner, Baum, and Berinsky describe, is that "[b]y consuming only these slanted news sources, individuals might come to believe that the particular one-sided version of issues they consume represents the unvarnished truth" (de Benedictis-Kessner, Baum, and Berinsky 2020).

Media is also likely to give audiences a distorted view of what members of the opposing political party are really like. As Douglas Ahler and Gaurav Sood note, "perceptions about party composition . . . [become] less accurate as interest in political news increases." Ironically, the more a person consumes political news, the more distorted a view she may have of her ideological opposites. Ahler and Sood also observe that "[t]he most voracious news consumers . . . are . . . most liable to hold skewed perceptions about party composition." Living in a partisan bubble makes perceptions more rigid, as "partisans are less likely to have personal information about the out-party, rendering impersonal information—e.g., media portrayals of the parties—more meaningful" (Ahler and Sood 2018). Indeed, as Cinelli and colleagues find, "users online tend to prefer information adhering to their worldviews, ignore dissenting information, and form polarized groups around shared narratives. Furthermore, when polarization is high, misinformation quickly proliferates" (Cinelli et al. 2021). If one really lives in a partisan bubble, one may never run into a political opposite in real life.

Now that the reader understands the basics of how branding works, as well as the dangers of information silos, understanding how a contagious disease became partisan in 2020 is considerably easier. Trump's emotionally laden rhetoric about COVID-19 was a display of political branding.

President Trump's Emotional Rhetoric
and the COVID-19 Pandemic

DENIAL

President Trump's first reaction to the COVID-19 virus, which originally appeared in China in late 2019 and then quickly traveled throughout the globe, was denial. He used the bully pulpit of his presidency to spread lies about COVID-19, refusing to acknowledge that it posed an existential threat. On January 22, 2020, the president claimed that the coronavirus was under control (Belvedere 2020). On February 27, 2020, Trump said, "[i]t's going to disappear. One day—it's like a miracle—it will disappear" (Trump 2020b). On March 11, 2020, he added that "[for] [t]he vast majority of Americans: The risk is very, very low" (Trump 2020a). Later congressional investigations would find that in March 2020, "then-President Trump continued to downplay the virus and refused to mobilize a coordinated response to procure supplies, even as the nation faced overrun hospitals and critical shortages" (Select Committee on the Coronavirus Crisis 2021).

This misleading framing of the novel coronavirus has led some academics to call COVID-19 not just a pandemic, passing quickly from person to person, but also an infodemic, in which misinformation about the disease spread just as hurriedly (Brennen et al. 2020). And because there was a torrent of information about COVID, both true and false, many in the public were cognitively overwhelmed and unable to distinguish the truth from the lies (Pan American Health Organization 2020). An Oxford University study about the COVID-19 infodemic notes that, "Mis- and disinformation about science, technology, and health is neither new nor unique to COVID-19" (Brennen et al. 2020). However, COVID-19 is "the biggest challenge fact-checkers have ever faced" (Cristina Tardáguila, quoted in Brennen et al. 2020). Some commentators argue that Trump used the same emotional appeals that any quack healer uses to manipulate others. As James Hamblin writes in *The Atlantic*, "[t]he narratives and tactics Trump used to persuade people to trust him as a sole beacon of truth—amid a sea of corrupt, lying scientists and doctors—draw on those of cult leaders, self-proclaimed healers, and wellness charlatans as much as those of authoritarian demagogues" (Hamblin 2020).

Another key pathway for disinformation about the pandemic was the world's biggest social media company, Facebook. A poll of journalists covering the pandemic revealed that "[t]he majority . . . say Facebook is the biggest spreader of disinformation, outstripping elect[ed] officials who are also a top source" (Meade 2020). According to Facebook itself, at least 140 million users visited its platform during the 2020 American election season, and by their own calculation they placed disinformation warnings on 180 million posts (Facebook 2020). The disinformation in this case was about the election itself. But there were only approximately 160 million Americans who voted in the 2020 presidential election (Lindsay 2020). Thus, any disinformation about COVID-19 traveling over Facebook in 2020 would have reached millions living in the United States, including many voters.

During the 2020 election, Twitter, a social media platform that allows individuals to post 280 character–long posts (or tweets), as well as pictures and videos, had 353 million users (Iqbal 2021). President Trump was a frequent Twitter user until he was barred from the platform in January 2021 (Crichton 2021). Trump was also a very adept Twitter user. As Ott and Dickinson note, "[w]hether employing Twitter to brand his products and properties, to define 'Make America Great Again,' or to dissemble reality, Trump has mastered the art of the short, simple message" (Ott and Dickinson 2020).

Did it matter that Donald Trump tweeted inaccurate myths about COVID-19? Indeed, it did. When famous people post, they are likely to generate engagements with the public, even when what they post is a lie (Brennen et al. 2020). A study of Trump's tweets about COVID-19 found that they were aimed at persuading his political followers. It analyzed almost 400 COVID-19–related tweets made by President Trump in the first half of 2020, and revealed that "Donald Trump's tweets . . . [exemplify] simplicity, [and] brevity, ensuring they can stand alone." In this way, Trump employs "(political) marketing principles" designed to persuade an audience (Maierová 2020). In other words, Trump used classic branding techniques in his tweets about COVID-19.

Many of President Trump's lies about COVID-19 manipulated the emotions of his followers who trusted him. George Hagman and Harry Paul wrote that Trump deployed gaslighting techniques during the pandemic. They compared the president to an abuser who "manipulates the victim into questioning reality, and substitutes a set of alternate truths, e.g. false beliefs (a type of induced cryptopsychosis), and then by means of this newly acquired authority . . . manipulates the victim[']s vulnerabilities, seeking to control their mood and self-state for the abuser's own interests" (Hagman and Paul 2020).

Trump followers have been noted for their cult-like devotion to him (Benjamin 2021). This also has a psychological explanation. Alexandra Homolar and Ronny Scholz argue that "if we look at the 'grip' of Trump's communication style . . . through a socio-cognitive lens, a picture emerges not only of clear linguistic patterns, but also of a decidedly populist crisis rhetoric that relies on the activation of cognitive biases to generate electoral support" (Homolar and Scholz 2019). They maintain that "political agents choose how they discursively legitimate their leadership claims in order to manipulate individuals' psychological traits and fuel pre-existing socio-economic grievances for short-term political gain" (Homolar and Scholz 2019). Trump's populist rhetoric, they argue, was politically motivated and designed to shore up support from his base.

Early in 2020, there were likely to be mistakes and misstatements about the novel coronavirus since it really was *novel*. At first, even medical experts did not know for sure how deadly or contagious the disease was (National Institutes of Health 2020). But as scientists provided a clearer picture of contagion and morbidity, the president of the United States ignored the science and acted like a political animal (Paz 2020). Critically, during the key month of February 2020, with Democratic presidential primaries under way and the election season beginning in earnest, President Trump called the coronavirus a "Democratic hoax" (quoted in Choi 2020).[1] This rhetorical move helped push the pandemic into partisan information silos. For those who already believed Trump's myths, this was just another "alternative fact" that they were already conditioned to accept (Bierman and Stokols 2020).

Ever the master political brander, the president constantly repeated the word "hoax" when referencing the novel coronavirus, and refused to back off. At a February 29, 2020, press conference he said that he used the term "hoax" to refer not to coronavirus itself, but to Democrats' criticism of his response to it. Asked if he regretted using that particular word, he replied "No. No. No. Hoax referring to the action that they take to try and pin this on somebody because we've done such a good job. The hoax is on them ... I'm talking what they're doing. That's the hoax. That's just a continuation of the hoax, whether it's the impeachment hoax or the Russia, Russia, Russia hoax" (Trump 2020c).

Indeed, a quantitative study by Cornell University researchers found the use of the phrase "'Democratic Party hoax' began to build strongly in the second week of February [2020], continuing with minor peaks and troughs up until the end of [the] data sample in May [2020]" (Evanega et al. 2020). By calling COVID-19 a "hoax," Trump followed a familiar rhetorical pattern. He had previously used the terms "hoax" and "witch hunt" to describe both the Robert Mueller investigation into his 2016 campaign and the first impeachment investigation of his dealings with Ukraine (Torres-Spelliscy 2019b). In this way, Trump could blunt criticism from his base by placing a real problem into a dismissible category of fake problems (Egan 2020).

Early in the pandemic, on March 3, 2020, polling showed that few Americans believed the president's claim that COVID-19 was a Democratic hoax (Jensen 2020). The polling found that "[v]oters take the virus a lot more seriously than the president does. Only 8% of voters agree with Trump's claim that the virus is a Democratic hoax, while 82% think the virus is real. Only 16% of Trump's own voters agree with him that the virus is a hoax" (Jensen 2020). At this point, Trump's messaging had only had days to sink in.

This rare near-unanimity among the American electorate about the pandemic would be evanescent, however. In subsequent months, Americans in the Fox News bubble were repeatedly told that the risks of COVID-19 were overblown (Peters 2020). Republican Congressman Matt Gaetz belittled the risk by wearing a huge World War I–style gas mask on the floor of Congress (Noor 2020). Thanks to reporter Bob Woodward, the public now knows that Trump's attempts to downplay the risks of COVID-19 were a deliberate political gambit. Yet publicly, Trump told stadiums of supporters standing cheek to cheek that the virus was a hoax, and a partisan one at that. As Elliott Detjen argues, "Trump's use of explicit and implicit rhetoric is driven by political objectives—desire to set aside public health protocols in favor of intertwined economic and electoral aims—ultimately placing the American people in a distortion of reality in the midst of an unprecedented pandemic" (Detjen 2020).

A 2020 Cornell University study found that President Trump was the source of most misinformation about COVID-19 in the English-speaking world (Evanega et al. 2020). As the authors of the study bluntly state, "[w]e conclude . . . that the President of the United States was likely the largest driver of the COVID-19 misinformation 'infodemic'" (Evanega et al. 2020). This is remarkable for a number of reasons. First, as president, Trump had access to the best information about the virus. Second, the president could have risen to the occasion because of the stakes of mismanaging a deadly pandemic. He did not. Top scientists tried to brief him about best practices, and still he ignored their advice and continued to act recklessly with his own health and the health of the nation.

Over time, the result of Trump's denial had a distinct impact on Republicans who trusted him as a primary source of pandemic information. A study by Pew Research found that these Republicans underestimated the seriousness of the problem. The Pew study concluded that "Republicans who turn to Trump for coronavirus news are . . . more likely than other Republicans to say the pandemic has been overblown, that Trump is getting the facts about the outbreak right and that public health organizations are *not* getting the facts right" (Jurkowitz and Mitchell 2020).

Denial was Trump's most long-lasting response to the COVID-19 pandemic, and it became the leitmotif of his final year in office. On October 23, 2020, a day when over 85,000 Americans were diagnosed with COVID, he told a Florida Republican crowd, "All he [Biden, his political opponent for the presidency] talks about is COVID, COVID, COVID because they want to scare people. And we've done so well with it. . . . I mean, you look at what's going on and we're rounding the turn. . . . We're rounding the corner beautifully" (Trump 2020d). By the time Trump left office, 400,000 Americans had succumbed to the disease (Stone 2021).

BARGAINING

In the classic Kübler-Ross taxonomy, patients try to bargain their way out of terminal illnesses. One can no more bargain their way out of a pandemic than one can bargain their way out of personal mortality. The problem in both cases is that diseases lack sentience and therefore cannot negotiate. During the spring of 2020, President Trump began holding daily White House briefings on the pandemic, accompanied by members of his Coronavirus Task Force. Many networks broadcast these briefings live in their entirety—thereby spreading misinformation far and wide. This period of briefings could be seen as Trump's bargaining phase, and it was as futile as any individual patient trying to bargain his way out of dying.

Trump tried to strike a bargain between shutting down the economy to curb the virus and revving it up to help his reelection. The dilemma was that if a shutdown was too short or incomplete, then the virus would boom and the economy would take an even greater hit in the long run. The president chose to ignore the risk, and to speed reopening. To bolster the case for reopening, he argued that there were miracle cures for COVID-19, and therefore that the economy could safely return to pre-pandemic levels of activity. Needless to say, there was no miracle cure for COVID-19 in 2020, and the premature economic reopening allowed COVID-19 to spread state to state unchecked.

Trump's desire to reopen the economy was motivated by self-interest, since his business was in hospitality and recreation. During the first year of the pandemic in 2020, many cities and states put strict limits on how many people could gather in restaurants, ballrooms, and other public places (Bunis and Rough 2021). Several businesses shut down temporarily because of COVID-19 mitigation restrictions. In mid-2020, the consulting firm McKinsey and Company predicted that hospitality businesses, one of the hardest-hit industry sectors, would take years to recover to their pre-pandemic levels (McKinsey 2020). According to McKinsey, the only business hit harder by the pandemic was recreation. Trump had businesses in both sectors (golf clubs and hotels). Thus, reopening the economy sooner by dropping COVID restrictions would be beneficial to Trump's personal bottom line as a businessman.[2]

The topics raised during White House COVID briefings during spring 2020 swung wildly, sometimes providing sober advice from health care professionals who urged coronavirus testing, mask wearing, hand washing, and social distancing, and at other times highlighting statements from the president, who downplayed the seriousness of the disease (O'Kane 2020). Trump also made a number of false statements about the pandemic that kept fact-checkers on their toes. As the *Washington Post*'s chief fact-checker noted, "Trump keeps exaggerating the statistics or making claims that turned out to be incorrect. 'Anyone who wants a test can get a test,' he declared March 6, a statement so false it needed to be corrected the next day by Health and Human Services Secretary Alex Azar" (Kessler 2020).

Then in a truly bizarre moment at the White House on April 24, 2020, President Trump seemed to encourage people to drink or inject bleach to prevent COVID-19 (Mackey 2020).

According to the Cornell study of the COVID-19 infodemic:

> [m]ultiple different misinformation themes converged around the idea of a 'miracle cure' for coronavirus. . . . President Trump began to advocate for the use of hydroxychloroquine and chloroquine (already in use as anti-malarial drugs) as treatments or cures for COVID-19 from March 19, though there was no peer-reviewed clinical data showing that these drugs had any efficacy for treating those suffering from the disease. This sparked a substantial amount of media coverage regarding his announcement, the subsequent shortage of these drugs, and later the finding that they were not effective in treating COVID-19 and might indeed be harmful. Coverage received another boost when President Trump claimed on May 20 to be taking hydroxychloroquine as a preventative, keeping this issue in the limelight longer. (Evanega et al. 2020)

The public digested this chloroquine myth. In a particularly tragic case, after hearing the president tout these unproven drugs, a man died after taking a form of chloroquine made for cleaning fish tanks; his wife also ingested the substance and was hospitalized (Neuman 2020). The White House COVID briefings were suspended after that.

Conservative media played a key role in broadcasting and reinforcing misinformation about COVID-19 from Trump. A Pew study found that Republicans who relied on Fox News were as misled as those who relied on Trump as their primary source of information on the pandemic (Jurkowitz and Mitchell 2020). Pollsters at Gallup found confirming data that "an individual with a conservative news diet is 10 percentage points more likely to say the media is giving the coronavirus too much attention than a similar individual with a liberal news diet" (Ritter 2020). Consequently, which information silo Americans occupied during 2020 shaped how they viewed the COVID-19 pandemic and its attendant dangers.

Telling the public that there were miracle cures for COVID-19 also allowed Trump to bond emotionally with those who believed him. After all, what he was saying was more comforting than the day-to-day reality of illness and death from an invisible pathogen. According to James Hamblin, "Trump's primary approach to the pandemic has been to tell people what they would like to be true. He has promised, repeatedly: Everything will go back to normal; everyone will have amazing treatments; there will be a vaccine very soon; the disease isn't that serious, anyway" (Hamblin 2020).

Trump rewarded Republican governors who followed his lead in touting reopening (or in some cases never closing down) with key roles at the 2020 Republican National Convention. For example, the Republican governor of South Dakota, Kristi Noem, who never issued a stay-at-home order, was given a prime-time speaking role at the convention (Dakota News Now 2020). By the fall of 2020, South Dakota had one of the highest per capita rates of COVID-19 in the nation (Associated Press 2020).

The 2020 Republican convention culminated on the White House grounds, putting every participating federal employee except for the president and vice president in violation of the Hatch Act (Lee and Dawsey 2020). Trump bragged about how well he had handled the pandemic in his speech accepting the Republican nomination, even as evidence to the contrary piled up (CNN 2020). By

September 1, 2020, 6 million Americans had tested positive for COVID-19. A month, later 7 million Americans had tested positive. By November 11, 10 million had tested positive (New York Times 2020). His bargain did not work for the health of the nation.

ANGER

China was a frequent object of President Trump's anger during the pandemic. He called COVID-19, the "China Virus," or the "Chinese Virus," and used other deliberately racist invective aimed at China. These characterizations coincided with increased anti-Asian violence in the United States (Reja 2021) and drew on old Sinophobic tropes (Sheng-mei 2020). Picking on China reinforced Trump's habit of invoking "us versus them" rhetoric to great political effect. As Homolar and Scholz postulate, even before the pandemic, "rational arguments or detailed policy proposals . . . [paled for many Trump voters] in comparison with the emotive pull and self-affirmation of an us-versus-them crisis narrative." This narrative created "a cognitive feedback loop between individuals' ontological insecurity, their preferences for restorative policy, and strongmen candidate options" (Homolar and Scholz 2019).

In addition to expressing anger at China for, in his view, unleashing the virus on the world, Trump reserved a particularly vitriolic form of anger for governors—mostly Democrats, but a few Republicans—whose messaging on COVID-19 undermined his own laissez-faire approach (Frum 2020). America's constitutional structure of dual sovereignty, where the president only has control of the federal government and individual governors have independent control of their respective states, leaves the nation vulnerable to any attack that exacerbates federal/state tensions. Far more Republican than Democratic governors followed Trump's example on lack of COVID mitigation measures. As of October 2020, "16 states [had] yet to enact mask mandates for the general public—all of them . . . [were] run by Republican governors" (Weber and Houghton 2020).

Several Democratic governors issued stay-at-home orders in March and April 2020; meanwhile, the president wanted to reopen the economy quickly, which ran counter to public health advice (Yamey 2021). Using Twitter, Trump egged on his supporters to protest COVID-19 restrictions in blue states, tweeting "'LIBERATE MICHIGAN!' and 'LIBERATE MINNESOTA!'" to challenge the social distancing measures imposed by the Democratic governors of these two states. An April 2020 *New York Times* article explained that "[b]y embracing the backlash to the coronavirus restrictions, Mr. Trump is tapping into a powerful well of political energy as he seeks re-election this year" (Shear and Mervosh 2020). Put another way, Trump's anger had a political end goal: win the election by stoking rage at health restrictions among his political base. Two months later, in June 2020, polls showed that differences of opinion about the shutdowns were beginning to deepen along partisan lines. "[S]ince April, . . . nearly 9 in 10 Democrats (87%) say their greater concern is that states will lift restrictions too quickly," a Pew study observed. By contrast, "Republicans are closely divided between concern that restrictions will be lifted too quickly or not quickly enough (47% to 53%)" (Funk and Tyson 2020).

President Trump used anger to bully most Republican governors, mayors, and members of Congress to downplay the risks of COVID-19 and push for more in-person commercial transactions and in-person political rallies. At these huge political gatherings, Trump held psychological sway over his followers. Matthew M. Yalch observes that "Trump project[ed] a grandiose and omnipotent self-image during press conferences and rallies, and his followers at these events often respond[ed] with both effusive admiration and an inflated sense of their own self regard, all of which are aspects of narcissism" (Yalch 2021). On July 4, 2020, Trump hosted a mass and maskless gathering at the White House, which, according to Maeve Reston, was tantamount to "[p]laying with fire at a time when experts say the spread of the virus appears to be spiraling out of control." During this event, Reston describes how "Trump continued gaslighting Americans about the threat to their health. . . . [H]e minimized the dangers of Covid-19 with a baseless statement that 99% of coronavirus cases are 'harmless,' a claim his Food and Drug Administration chief could not back up" (Reston 2020).

But there was a limit to the reach of Trump's anger. It could not convince many Democratic elected officials to discount the dangers of the coronavirus. Whether Democratic elected officials did not believe Trump for partisan or factual reasons, they did not follow his lead on COVID-19 (Schwartz 2020).

During the 2020 presidential race, face masks became a political flash point for the president's anger. When the CDC said that wearing facial coverings could lessen the spread of the virus, the president undercut this message by refusing to wear one (Dwyer and Aubrey 2020). The eventual Democratic nominee, Joe Biden, on the other hand, made a point of wearing a face mask during public appearances, which ranged from Memorial Day events to church services and political speeches (Cadelago and Korecki 2020). The candidate's campaign web page featured "Biden"-branded face masks for sale.

According to Pew Research, Democrats worried that their fellow Americans were not using masks to mitigate COVID-19. Democrats had reason to be concerned as "Republicans accounted for 92% of those expressing skepticism or opposition to masks" (Van Kessel and Quinn 2020).

Mask wearing became a proxy for partisan affiliation.[3] On an even more basic level, partisans had different views about whether personal actions impacted the spread of COVID-19. "Nearly three-quarters of Democrats (73%) say that the actions of ordinary Americans affect how the coronavirus spreads in the U.S. a great deal . . . fewer than half [of Republicans] (44%) say that this affects the spread of the virus a great deal" (Pew Research Center 2020).

At the first presidential debate between Trump and Biden in 2020, Trump's anger flashed when he mocked Joe Biden for wearing masks regularly. "I don't wear masks like him," the president said of Biden. "Every time you see him, he's got a mask. He could be speaking 200 feet away and he shows up with the biggest mask I've ever seen" (quoted in Givhan 2020). President Trump almost never wore a mask in public during 2020 until he got COVID-19 himself (Briskey 2020). Indeed, even when the rules of a particular place he visited required masks, he would thwart those rules.

Views about masks filtered down to the quotidian Democrats (largely pro-mask) and Republicans (largely anti-mask). As the Kaiser Family Foundation found, "Democrats are almost twice as likely as Republicans (70% vs. 37%) to say they wear a mask 'every time' they leave their house and while most people (72%) think President Trump should wear a mask when meeting with other people, only about half of Republicans (48%) agree" (Brodie 2020). Mask wearers/anti-maskers became a proxy for Democrat/Republican voting preferences. In April 2020, "Joe Biden, the presumptive Democratic nominee, leads President Trump by 40 points among [mask wearing] voters: 66 percent to 26 percent." Meanwhile, "15 percent of registered voters said they don't tend to wear a mask—the president [Trump] leads Biden with those voters 83–7 percent" (Stahl 2020).

The president's anger seemed contagious among his most rabid followers. As the *Washington Post*'s Robin Givhan summed up, "Trump tried to make masks a test of machismo. He turned them into a political wedge issue and a referendum on freedom. He reveled in his boisterous, maskless rallies. Masks became something to fight about that left other countries baffled by the pettiness of it all" (Givhan 2020). Following the president's cues, certain "no-maskers" were caught on videos that went viral, angrily refusing to wear masks in businesses that required them (Frank, Vandell, and Robinson 2020). (Of course, such videos go viral for a reason—they feature outrageous behavior that individuals share on social media precisely because they are outrageous. These actions—violently protesting mask requirements—could be completely unrepresentative of the sentiments of Republicans generally or Trump supporters in particular.) Yet more menacingly, armed anti-mask militias showed up in the Michigan capitol to protest pandemic rules from the Democratic governor (Censky 2020). In October 2020, fourteen anti-mask militia members were arrested for plotting to kidnap Gretchen Whitmer, the governor of Michigan (Jones and Waldrop 2020).

Trump also lashed out at Dr. Anthony Fauci, the long-term director of the National Institute for Allergy and Infectious Diseases, calling him a "disaster." This was a reaction to press reports that Fauci wanted masks to be mailed to every American household. The White House allegedly put the kibosh on this plan (Miao 2020). No masks were mailed to American households. One of Trump's puzzling criticisms of his opponent, voiced at an October 2020 rally, was that Biden would listen to scientists about how to quell the pandemic (Folley 2020). Several commentators remarked that in making this assertion the president seemed to be endorsing his opponent, since listening to scientists would be objectively wise.

Outside of the conservative information silo, where Trump's anger had little currency, there was a different reality—a reality-based reality. Democratic governors who had been leaders in the fight against COVID-19 by imposing strict stay-at-home orders—including the governors of California, New York, New Mexico, Michigan, and Wisconsin—featured prominently during the DNC's all-remote 2020 convention. Michigan Governor Gretchen Whitmer told the Democratic convention, "from the jump, we took this pandemic seriously in Michigan. We listened to medical experts, we planned. And with a lot of work from the auto workers and too little help from the White House, we executed our plan. We saved thousands of lives" (Rev 2020). The Democrats' approach to shutdowns and bans on large gatherings had the legal support of the U.S. Supreme Court, which refused to overturn these restrictions even for religious gatherings during the early months of the pandemic.[4]

Emphasizing the importance of the pandemic, the 2020 Democratic Party platform mentioned "pandemic" eighty-three times, COVID fifty-nine times, and coronavirus five times (Democratic National Committee 2020). Speakers at the Democratic convention repeatedly underscored the importance of the pandemic and criticized the Trump administration for its mishandling of the crisis. Former First Lady Michelle Obama described the human tragedy of COVID-19, which by the time of the Democratic convention had resulted in more than 150,000 American deaths. "It has left millions of people jobless," she remarked. "Too many have lost their healthcare. Too many are struggling to take care of basic necessities like food and rent" (DNC Transcript

2020). The Democratic presidential nominee Joe Biden also emphasized the pandemic in his DNC convention remarks, stating: "No rhetoric is needed. Just judge this President on the facts. 5 million Americans infected by COVID-19, more than 170,000 Americans have died, by far the worst performance of any nation on Earth. More than 50 million people have filed for unemployment this year . . . if [Trump is] reelected, you know what will happen? Cases and deaths will remain far too high" (DNC Transcript 2020). Speaker after speaker highlighted the problems of the pandemic and how President Trump had failed to rise to the challenge. This rhetoric branded failures related to COVID-19 as partisan (Republican) and uniquely Trump's fault. Democrats offered Americans a different approach to the pandemic, one that involved following scientific and medical advice, including on masking, social distancing, and the embrace of soon to be ready COVID-19 vaccines.

DEPRESSION

In the Kübler-Ross taxonomy, patients facing their own morality often experience profound and understandable depression (Kübler-Ross 1969). The closest Trump got to depression about COVID-19 was when he contracted the disease in September 2020 and was briefly hospitalized at Walter Reed Hospital in October (Collins 2020). According to his then–Chief of Staff Mark Meadows, when Trump first tested positive on September 26, his reaction was to say "Oh shit, you've got to be f-cking kidding me" (Stableford and Dickson 2021, quoting Trump). Glimmers of unease peeked through his public statement from Walter Reed. As he said in a video from the hospital, "I came here [to Walter Reed], [I] wasn't feeling so well" (Trump 2020e). His niece psychologist, Mary Trump, later wrote of her uncle's return to the

White House from the hospital: "Doing his best Mussolini imitation, he took off his mask in a macho display of invulnerability. He clenched his teeth and jutted out his jaw, just as my grandmother did when she was biting back anger or clamping down on her pain. In Donald, I saw the latter." She adds: "He was in pain, he was afraid, but he would never admit that to anybody—not even himself—because, as always, the consequences of admitting vulnerability were much more frightening to him than being honest" (Smith 2021, quoting Mary Trump). Mary Trump's insights both as someone who knew the president personally and as a trained psychologist reveal why even if President Trump was feeling depressed, he would not show such emotion publicly—because to admit depression would be to show weakness.

Perhaps because his own brush with mortality was fleeting, Trump showed little empathy for fellow patients or for families who had lost loved ones to the disease (Godfrey 2020). Rather than experience personal growth, he was back to propaganda mode. He claimed that COVID-19 made him feel better and younger (Helmore 2020). Trump hosted large events even while he was likely still contagious, including one at the White House with MAGA hat–wearing supporters gathered on the lawn (BBC 2020). Instead of changing his perspective, Trump repeated his messaging from months before: COVID-19 was not a serious disease (BBC 2020). He stuck to his branding of COVID. Later news stories indicated that Trump was more ill than was reported in real time (Stieb 2021). Indeed, Trump's oxygen levels dipped dangerously into the 80s, whereas the normal level is in the 95–100 range (Saletan 2021). By not sharing the gravity of his illness, or revealing anxiety or depression at getting ill, he downplayed the seriousness of COVID-19 (and his own brush with it) to the American public.

President Trump never *publicly* accepted the magnitude of the pandemic or his role in making it worse and more partisan while he was in office. There is evidence that Trump privately accepted the dangers and lethality of COVID-19 in a tape-recorded interview with reporter Bob Woodward in February 2020. "This [referring to COVID-19] is deadly stuff," Trump said to Woodward (Costa and Rucker 2020). The president explained: "It goes through air, Bob. That's always tougher than the touch. You know, the touch—you don't have to touch things, right? But the air, you just breathe the air. That's how it's passed. . . . It's also more deadly than your—you know, your—even your strenuous flus" (NPR 2020). Trump's statements to Woodward, made very early on in the pandemic, acknowledged that the virus was airborne and worse than the common flu, and suggest that he accepted, to some degree, the dangers of COVID-19. Trump did not share this acceptance with the public in real time.

Trump's decision to get the COVID-19 vaccination with the first lady in January 2021 also suggests that he accepted the danger posed by the virus (Acosta and Kelly 2021). After all, why bother with a vaccine if the disease was not that serious, especially after already recovering from it and acquiring some natural immunity? But because his vaccination was private and was not accompanied by a public statement of acceptance, I am merely offering speculation that this self-protective action indicated President Trump's acceptance of the dangers of COVID-19 and his recognition that it was an existential threat to his own health.

Around the time that Trump was getting vaccinated in private, he and his inner circle at the White House were mostly focused on contesting the results of the 2020 election and were distracted from working on public policies to address COVID-19. As the House Select Subcommittee on the Coronavirus Crisis (2021) noted, "[we] . . . uncovered evidence showing that Trump White House officials neglected the pandemic response to . . . promote the Big Lie that the election results were fraudulent."

Perhaps if Trump had made his vaccination public, more of his followers would have followed his example and gotten vaccinated too. In December 2021, long after Trump had left the White House, the Kaiser Family Foundation found that "[p]artisanship continues to play an outsized role in initial vaccination uptake as well as intention to get a booster dose. Four in ten Republicans remain unvaccinated" (Kirzinger 2021). National Public Radio (NPR) put the matter even more starkly. Their analysis of COVID death rates in 2021 revealed that "[p]eople living in counties that went 60% or higher for Trump in November 2020 had 2.73 times the death rates of those that went for Biden. Counties with an even higher share of the vote for Trump saw higher COVID-19 mortality rates" (Wood and Brumfiel 2021). NPR concluded that low vaccination rates for Republicans were at least partly attributable to misinformation and lack of facts. I would argue that this adds to the mounting pile of evidence showing the damage done by Trump's political branding of the coronavirus.

Nearly a full year after he was secretly vaccinated, Trump finally pulled back the curtain and talked publicly about his vaccination status. This was after medical experts recommended booster shots for adults to increase the effectiveness of the original vaccines (Maragakis and Kelen 2021). Trump and former Fox host Bill O'Reilly appeared together at a public event in December 2021. O'Reilly noted that both men were vaccinated against COVID-19. Then he asked Trump, "Did you get the booster?" "Yes," Trump replied, and members of the audience—presumably Trump supporters—booed the former president (Merica 2021). The fact that Trump was triple vaccinated against COVID is further evidence that he accepted the dangers of the COVID-19 pandemic and was taking medically prudent steps to protect himself (Merica 2021). The booing audience highlighted the damage that Trump had done: he had successfully branded COVID as an insignificant threat to human health for his most devoted political followers. Like the fictional Victor Frankenstein, Trump eventually lost control of the monster he had created (Shelley 1994).[5]

Conclusion

Trump alternately branded COVID-19 as a Democratic hoax, entirely China's fault, or an overblown threat. His ability to use emotional manipulation profoundly impacted many Republicans, who trusted him as a credible information source. A Pew survey released a month before the 2020 election found that "that Trump-supporting Republicans downplayed the pandemic as a voting issue while Biden supporters emphasized that the pandemic would influence their vote (Karma 2020). A study entitled "Political Ideology Predicts Perceptions of the Threat of COVID-19" confirms "the impact that political leadership and media framing can have on perceptions of threats. Once a threat becomes politicized, the polarization induced by the current political environment may shape the way it is perceived. In the case of COVID-19, conservatives with higher levels of presidential approval were less knowledgeable about the virus, less accurate in discerning real from fake news, and in turn saw it as less of a threat. These polarized perceptions may well inhibit collective action and threat responses that require significant levels of community-level coordination" (Calvillo et al. 2020).

Trump's failure to publicly accept the magnitude of the COVID-19 crisis also influenced his adherents' willingness to taking steps to stem the pandemic's tide. Polling from Gallup revealed that "Republicans are much less likely than Democrats to report isolating themselves, adhering to social distancing, avoiding public places and wearing masks. Republicans are more likely to be out and about going to stores and others' houses" (Newport 2020). Resistance to mask wearing was particularly strong among Republican men (Brodie 2020). And distressingly, polling also revealed that many Republicans put more stock in the statements of politicians like Trump than in qualified scientists (Newport 2020). Also troubling was the partisan way doctors were perceived (Funk and Tyson 2020).

With words and deeds, President Trump made the problem worse by refusing to model mask wearing and badmouthing those who did wear them (Collman 2020). By encouraging states to reopen early, reopening his own businesses, and holding in-person political events without social distancing, he exacerbated the spread of COVID-19.

Responding to COVID-19 required federal and state cooperation, yet there was no national plan to deal with the pandemic in 2020. Although the American constitutional structure does not require governors to follow the president's policy lead, federal and state governments usually work together for the good of the nation to confront a common enemy. The virus could have had less of a chance to run wild in America if the president and all fifty governors had spoken in a similar voice on pandemic prevention measures. Instead, partisan branding led Republicans in power (with a few notable exceptions such as Governor DeWine of Ohio, Governor Baker of Massachusetts, and Governor Hogan of Maryland) to act like ostriches, sticking their heads in the sand and not giving clear guidance to their constituents on how to stay safe and healthy. Meanwhile, all of the efforts by Democratic governors to mitigate the spread of coronavirus were undercut because disease from one part of the nation could hopscotch across state lines. As studies would show, a super-spreader event in one state, like the Sturgis motorcycle rally in South Dakota in August 2020, could seed outbreaks in multiple states when attendees returned home (Rapier 2020).

The tragic counterfactual is that over 400,000 people did not have to die of COVID-19 in the United States (CDC 2023). Other more competently run nations like Canada, New Zealand, and Australia had far fewer infections and deaths (WHO 2020). If the president had acted in a bipartisan fashion to mitigate the spread, fewer people would likely have contracted the coronavirus, been hospitalized, and died. But by calling the pandemic a "Democratic hoax" in the first months of 2020, President Trump changed how the virus and its seriousness would be perceived by millions of people (Ritter 2020). By lying about COVID-19, and by utilizing emotionally appealing myths, he disarmed even his own supporters and prevented them from protecting themselves. In October 2021, a congressional committee asked Dr. Deborah Birx, who had helped run President Trump's Coronavirus Task Force in the White House, "[d]o you think that President Trump did everything he could to try to mitigate the spread of the virus and save lives during the pandemic?" She answered "no" (Birx 2021). As this chapter was being written, the United States broke records for the most new COVID-19 cases in a day. This statistic was higher than the day before, which was also a record high (Miller, Flores, and Hauk 2020). It did not have to be like this. In the end, Trump could not keep himself from catching COVID-19, and his partisan branding of the disease meant that millions of Americans would needlessly catch it too (Carter 2021).

Notes

1. David Choi (2020) quotes the transcript of Trump's February 28 speech: "Now the Democrats are politicizing the coronavirus. You know that, right? *Coronavirus.* They're politicizing it. . . . One of my people came up to me and said, 'Mr. President, they tried to beat you on Russia, Russia, Russia.' That didn't work out too well. They couldn't do it. They tried the impeachment hoax. That was on a perfect conversation. . . . And *this is their new hoax.* But you know we did something that's been pretty amazing. We have 15 people in this massive country and because of the fact that we went early, we went early, we could have had a lot more than that" (emphasis in the original).

2. One explanation for Trump's push to open the economy was his financial stake in the hospitality business, a cornerstone of his financial empire. Early in the pandemic, the Trump Organization fired 1,500 employees as a result of COVID-related closures (Perrett 2020). Even his flagship property Mar-a-Lago was shuttered to prevent the spread of COVID (Arciga 2020). As a hotelier, a restaurateur, and the owner of golf clubs, the COVID-19 pandemic was murder on Trump's bottom line (Levin 2020). He needed his customers to think everything was back to normal so that they would travel, book his hotel rooms, eat at his restaurants, and party at his clubs.

3. Stahl reports that in April 2020, Biden led Trump "by 40 points among [mask wearing] voters: 66 percent to 26 percent." Meanwhile, "15 percent of registered voters said they don't tend to wear a mask—the president [Trump] leads Biden with those voters 83–7 percent" (Stahl 2020).

4. *South Bay United Pentecostal Church v. Newsom*, 590 U.S. ____, slip at *1 (2020) (denial of injunctive relief) (Roberts, C.J.) ("The Governor of California's Executive Order aims to limit the spread of COVID-19, a novel severe acute respiratory illness that has killed thousands of people in California and more than

100,000 nationwide. At this time, there is no known cure, no effective treatment, and no vaccine. Because people may be infected but asymptomatic, they may unwittingly infect others. The Order places temporary numerical restrictions on public gatherings to address this extraordinary health emergency."); *Calvary Chapel Dayton Valley v. Sisolak*, 591 U. S. ____, slip at *1 (2020) (denial of injunctive relief) (Alito, J. dissenting) ("[The church] plans to require six feet of separation between families seated in the pews, to prohibit items from being passed among the congregation, to guide congregants to designated doorways along one-way paths, and to leave sufficient time between services so that the church can be sanitized. According to an infectious disease expert, these measures are 'equal to or more extensive than those recommended by the CDC.'")

5. According to a 2022 survey, the partisan divide on COVID-19 vaccines persists (Pew Research Center 2022). See also Clinton et al. (2021) on partisanship as a public health threat.

References

Acosta, Jim, and Caroline Kelly. 2021. "Donald and Melania Trump Received Covid Vaccine at the White House in January." *CNN*, March 1. https://www.cnn.com/2021/03/01/politics/trump -melania-vaccinated-white-house/index.html.

"Ad: Slaves for Sale, Tennessee 1863." n.d. *Newspapers.com*. https:// www.newspapers.com/clip/5594118/ad-slaves-for-sale-tennessee -1863/.

Ahler, Douglas, and Gaurav Sood. 2018. "The Parties in Our Heads: Misperceptions about Party Composition and Their Consequences." *Journal of Politics* 80 no. 3: 964–965. http://dx.doi.org /10.1086/697253.

Arciga, Julia. 2020. "Coronavirus Petri Dish Mar-a-Lago Shutters as Florida Governor Orders Palm Beach Businesses to Close." *Daily Beast*, March 20. https://www.thedailybeast.com/mar-a

-lago-shutters-as-florida-governor-orders-palm-beach
-businesses-to-close.

Arceneaux, Kevin, Martin Johnson, and Chad Murphy. 2012.
"Polarized Political Communication, Oppositional Media
Hostility, and Selective Exposure." *Journal of Politics* 74, no. 1:
174–186.

Associated Press. 2020. "South Dakota Reports All-Time High for
New Virus Cases." November 12. https://apnews.com/article
/health-south-dakota-coronavirus-pandemic-brookings-9541408
dbb58fbe0bb458a0a2ca9e300.

Baker, Peter. 2019. "Clinton's Impeachment Was Suspenseful.
Trump's Grip on G.O.P. Means His Won't Be." *New York Times,*
December 14.

BBC. 2020. "White House Rally: Trump Holds First Public Event
since Covid Diagnosis." *BBC News*, October 10. https://www
.bbc.com/news/election-us-2020-54493575.

Belvedere, Matthew J. 2020. "Trump Says He Trusts China's Xi on
Coronavirus and the US Has It 'Totally Under Control.'"
CNBC, January 22. https://www.cnbc.com/2020/01/22/trump-on
-coronavirus-from-china-we-have-it-totally-under-control.html.

Benjamin, Elliot. 2021. "Studies of Social Media Addiction, Cult
Indoctrination, and the Coronavirus Pandemic; All in Relation
to the Trump Presidency." *Selected Topics in Humanities and
Social Sciences* 5: 135–146. https://www.researchgate.net/profile
/Elliot-Benjamin-3/publication/354399767_Studies_of_Social
_Media_Addiction_Cult_Indoctrination_and_the_Coronavirus
_Pandemic_All_In_Relation_to_the_Trump_Presidency/links
/6136cb8f38818c2eaf8841a0/Studies-of-Social-Media-Addiction
-Cult-Indoctrination-and-the-Coronavirus-Pandemic-All-In
-Relation-to-the-Trump-Presidency.pdf.

Bierman, Noah, and Eli Stokols. 2020. "Trump Stokes Up his
Blame Game for the Coronavirus." *Los Angeles Times*. April 13.
https://www.latimes.com/politics/story/2020-04-13/trump
-stokes-up-his-blame-game-for-the-coronavirus.

Birx, Deborah. 2021. "Excerpts from Transcribed Interview with Dr. Deborah Birx: Former President Trump Failed to Do Everything He Could to Stop the Spread of the Coronavirus and Save American Lives." Select Subcommittee on the Coronavirus Crisis. October 12, 2021. https://coronavirus.house .gov/sites/democrats.coronavirus.house.gov/files/Birx%20 Testimony%20Excerpts10.26pdf.pdf.

Brennen, J. Scott., Felix Simon, Philip N. Howard, and Rasmus Kleis Nielsen. 2020. "Types, Sources, and Claims of COVID-19 Misinformation." Reuters Institute/Oxford Martin School, April 7. https://reutersinstitute.politics.ox.ac.uk/types-sources -and-claims-covid-19-misinformation.

Briskey, Mark F. 2020. "Protecting Political Leaders from Covid-19." Lowy Institute, October 3. https://www.lowyinstitute.org/the -interpreter/debate/good-government-bad-government-politics -public-health.

Brodie, Mollyann. 2020. "KFF Health Tracking Poll—May 2020." Kaiser Family Foundation, May 27. https://www.kff.org /coronavirus-covid-19/report/kff-health-tracking-poll-may -2020/.

Buchanan, Larry, Lazaro Gamio, Lauren Leatherby, Robin Stein, and Christiaan Triebert. 2020. Inside the White House Event Now under Covid-19 Scrutiny." *New York Times*, October 5.

Buechel, Jaime. 2018. "Changes in Advertisements during the Civil War." *New Errands: The Undergraduate Journal of American Studies* 6, no. 1. https://doi.org/10.18113/P8ne6161054.

Bunis, Dena, and Jenny Rough. 2021. "List of Coronavirus-Related Restrictions in Every State: Most States Have Dropped Covid-Related Restrictions, but Some Local Communities Are Reinstating Them." *AARP*, December 27. https://www.aarp.org /politics-society/government-elections/info-2020/coronavirus -state-restrictions.html.

Cadelago, Christopher, and Natasha Korecki. 2020. "'Keep Back!': How the Biden Campaign Obsesses over Covid." *Politico*,

September 14. https://www.politico.com/news/2020/09/14/joe
-biden-bubble-coronavirus-412306.

Calvillo, Dustin P., Bryan J. Ross, Ryan J. B. Garcia, Thomas J.
Smelter, and Abraham M. Rutchick. 2020. "Political Ideology
Predicts Perceptions of the Threat of COVID-19 (and Suscepti-
bility to Fake News about It)." *Social Psychological and Personality
Science* 11, no. 8 (November): 1119–1128. https://doi.org/10.1177
/1948550620940539.

Campaign Live. 2016. "History of Advertising: No 160: The First
Radio Commercials." January 28. https://www.campaignlive
.com/article/history-advertising-no-160-first-radio-commercials
/1381044.

Carter, David P. 2021. "Making Sense of the U.S. COVID-19
Pandemic Response: A Policy Regime Perspective." *Administrative Theory & Praxis* 42, no. 2: 265–277. https://www.tandfonline
.com/doi/full/10.1080/10841806.2020.1758991?casa_token
=QolAPR2gOdoAAAAA%3A-H97ZJVNuFsNATDVPaCFz
wsOqO2aCsqFIj1Lfw7nIqm-BGYYIlNNh6yjX2VxD1DpXFA
RWM9DU11Ggw.

Censky, Abigail. 2020. "Heavily Armed Protesters Gather Again at
Michigan Capitol to Decry Stay-at-Home Order." *NPR*,
May 14. https://www.npr.org/2020/05/14/855918852/heavily
-armed-protesters-gather-again-at-michigans-capitol
-denouncing-home-order.

Centers for Disease Control. 2020. "Deaths Involving Coronavirus
Disease 2019 (COVID-19), Pneumonia, and Influenza Reported
to NCHS by Week Ending Date, United States. Week ending
2/1/2020 to 11/7/2020." November 7. https://www.cdc.gov/nchs
/nvss/vsrr/covid19/index.htm.

———. 2023. "CDC Museum COVID-19 Timeline." https://www
.cdc.gov/museum/timeline/covid19.html.

Choi, David. 2020. "Trump's Campaign Is Trying to Remove a
Video in Which He Appears to Call the Coronavirus a 'Hoax,'
Saying It's Misleading." *Business Insider*, March 26. https://www

.businessinsider.com/trump-campaign-remove-video-saying
-coronavirus-hoax-2020-3.

Cinelli, Matteo, Gianmarco De Francisci Morales, Alessandro Galeazzi, and Michele Starnini. 2021. "The Echo Chamber Effect on Social Media." *PNAS*, February 23. https://www.pnas .org/doi/10.1073/pnas.2023301118.

Clark, Dartunorro. 2020. "Fauci Calls Amy Coney Barrett Ceremony in Rose Garden 'Superspreader Event.'" *NBC News*, October 9. https://www.nbcnews.com/politics/white-house /fauci-calls-amy-coney-barrett-ceremony-rose-garden -superspreader-event-n1242781.

Clinton, Joshua D., Jon Cohen, John Lapinski, and Marc Trussler. 2021. "Partisan Pandemic: How Partisanship and Public Health Concerns Affect Individuals' Social Mobility during COVID-19." *Science Advances*, January 6. https://www.science.org/doi/10.1126 /sciadv.abd7204.

CNN. 2020. "Transcript: Donald Trump's RNC Speech." August 28. https://www.cnn.com/2020/08/28/politics/donald -trump-speech-transcript/index.html.

Collins, Kaitlan. 2020. "President Trump Spooked by Coronavirus Diagnosis, Source Says," *CNN*, October 2.

Collman, Ashley. 2020. "2 Days Before His Coronavirus Diagnosis, Trump Mocked Biden for Wearing a Face Mask." *CBS News*, October 2. https://www.businessinsider.com/trump -coronavirus-mocked-biden-face-mask-presidential-debate -2020-10.

Costa, Robert, and Philip Rucker. 2020. "Woodward Book: Trump Says He Knew Coronavirus Was 'Deadly' and Worse Than the Flu While Intentionally Misleading Americans." *Washington Post*, September 9. https://www.washingtonpost.com/politics /bob-woodward-rage-book-trump/2020/09/09/0368fe3c-efd2 -11ea-b4bc-3a2098fc73d4_story.html.

Crichton, Danny. 2021. "The Deplatforming of President Trump—A Review of an Unprecedented and Historical Week

for the Tech Industry." *TechCrunch*, January 9. https://
techcrunch.com/2021/01/09/the-deplatforming-of-a-president/.

Dakota News Now. 2020. "Gov. Noem to Speak Wednesday Night
at Republican National Convention." *Dakota News Now*,
August 25. https://www.dakotanewsnow.com/2020/08/25/more
-details-about-gov-noems-rnc-speech-revealed/.

de Benedictis-Kessner, Justin, Matthew Baum, and Adam Berinsky.
"Polarization and Media Usage: Disentangling Causality." In
Oxford Handbook of Electoral Persuasion, edited by Bernard
Grofman, Liz Suhay, and Alex Tresche, 5–6. New York: Oxford
University Press. https://scholar.harvard.edu/files/mbaum/files
/polarizationcausality180806.pdf.

Democratic National Committee. 2020. "Democratic Party
Platform." *DNC*. https://www.demconvention.com/wp-content
/uploads/2020/08/2020-07-31-Democratic-Party-Platform-For
-Distribution.pdf.

Desai, Deven R., and Spencer Waller. 2010. "Brands, Competition,
and the Law." *B.Y.U. Law Review* 2010, no. 5: 1425–1499.

Detjen, Elliott. 2020. "Trump and COVID-19: The Fierce Interplay
of Rhetoric and Realities." *Harvard Politics*, November 2.
https://harvardpolitics.com/trump-rhetoric-and-realities/.

Dubois, Elizabeth, and Grant Blank. 2018. "The Echo Chamber Is
Overstated: The Moderating Effect of Political Interest and
Diverse Media." *Information Communication & Society*, January 29. https://www.tandfonline.com/doi/full/10.1080/1369118X
.2018.1428656.

Dwyer, Colin, and Allison Aubrey. 2020. "Twitter CDC Now
Recommends Americans Consider Wearing Cloth Face
Coverings In Public." *NPR*, April 3. https://www.npr.org
/sections/coronavirus-live-updates/2020/04/03/826219824
/president-trump-says-cdc-now-recommends-americans-wear
-cloth-masks-in-public.

Egan, Lauren. 2020. "Trump Calls Coronavirus Democrats' 'New
Hoax.'" *NBC News*, February 28. https://www.nbcnews.com

/politics/donald-trump/trump-calls-coronavirus-democrats-new
-hoax-n1145721.

Evanega, Sarah, Mark Lynas, Jordan Adams, and Karinne Smole-
nya. 2020. "Coronavirus Misinformation: Quantifying Sources
and Themes in the COVID-19 'Infodemic.'" *Cornell Alliance for
Science*. https://allianceforscience.cornell.edu/wp-content
/uploads/2020/09/Evanega-et-al-Coronavirus-misinformation
FINAL.pdf.

Facebook. 2020. "A Look at Facebook and US 2020 Elections."
https://about.fb.com/wp-content/uploads/2020/12/US-2020
-Elections-Report.pdf.

Fenster, Mark. 2021. "A 'Public' Journey through COVID-19:
Donald Trump, Twitter, and the Secrecy of U.S. Presidents'
Health." *Critical Analysis of Law* 8: 25–34.

Folley, Aris. 2020. "Trump: Biden Will 'Listen to the Scientists' if
Elected." *The Hill*, October 19. https://thehill.com/homenews
/521638-trump-biden-will-listen-to-the-scientists-if-elected.

Frank, Brie, Anna J. Perry Vandell, and KiMi Robinson. 2020.
"Viral Videos Show Anti-Mask Protest at Arizona Mall:
'They're Endangering People.'" *Arizona Republic*, December 21.
https://www.usatoday.com/story/news/nation/2020/12/21/viral
-videos-show-anti-mask-protest-christown-spectrum-mall-in
-phoenix/3990868001/.

Frum, David. 2020. "No Empathy, Only Anger." *The Atlantic*,
March 19. https://www.theatlantic.com/ideas/archive/2020/03
/trumps-dangerous-party-line/608383/.

Funk, Cary, and Alec Tyson. 2020. "Partisan Differences over the
Pandemic Response Are Growing." Pew Research Center,
June 3. https://www.pewresearch.org/science/2020/06/03
/partisan-differences-over-the-pandemic-response-are
-growing/.

Garrett, Laurie. 2020. "COVID-19: The Medium Is the Message."
The Lancet, March 11. https://www.thelancet.com/article/S0140
-6736(20)30600-0/fulltext.

Givhan, Robin. 2020. "Trump's Refusal to Wear Face Masks Turned Them into a Sad National Symbol." *Washington Post*, October 3. https://www.washingtonpost.com/nation/2020/10/03 /trumps-refusal-wear-face-masks-turned-them-into-sad -national-symbol/.

Godfrey, Elaine. 2020. "What COVID-19 Families Hear When Trump Brags about His Strength." *The Atlantic*, October 15. https://www.theatlantic.com/politics/archive/2020/10/trumps -covid-19-comments-hurt-victims-families/616715/.

Grabner-Kräuter, Sonja, and Sofie Bitter. 2015. "Trust in Online Social Networks: A Multifaceted Perspective." *Forum for Social Economics* 44, no. 1: 48–68.

Graham, Megan. 2021. "Digital Ad Spend Grew 12% in 2020 Despite Hit from Pandemic." *CNBC*, April 7. https://www.cnbc .com/2021/04/07/digital-ad-spend-grew-12percent-in-2020 -despite-hit-from-pandemic.html.

Guttmann, A. 2020. "Internet Advertising Spending Worldwide from 2007 to 2022, by Format." *Statista*, April 19. https://www .statista.com/statistics/276671/global-internet-advertising -expenditure-by-type/.

Hagman, George, and Harry Paul. 2020. "Gaslighting the Pandemic: Donald Trump, Lies, Manipulation and Power." International Association for Psychoanalytic Self Psychology. June 20. https://iapsp.org/gaslighting-the-pandemic-donald -trump-lies-manipulation-and-power/.

Hamblin, James. 2020. "How Trump Sold Failure to 70 Million People." *The Atlantic*, November 10. https://www.theatlantic.com /health/archive/2020/11/trump-voters-pandemic-failures/617051/.

Harsin, Jayson. 2020. "Toxic White Masculinity, Post-Truth Politics and the COVID-19 Infodemic." *European Journal of Cultural Studies* 23, no. 6: 1060–1068. https://doi.org/10.1177/1367549420 944934.

Helmore, Edward. 2020. "'I Feel Much Better': Trump Releases First Video Message from Hospital Room." *The Guardian*,

October 3. https://www.theguardian.com/us-news/2020/oct/04/i
-feel-much-better-trump-releases-first-video-message-from
-hospital-room.

Holmes, Aaron. 2020. "Clicking This Link Lets You See What
Google Thinks It Knows about You Based on Your Search
History—and Some of Its Predictions Are Eerily Accurate."
Business Insider, March 19. https://www.businessinsider.com/what
-does-google-know-about-me-search-history-delete-2019-10.

Holt, Douglas. 2016. "Branding in the Age of Social Media."
Harvard Business Review, March. https://hbr.org/2016/03
/branding-in-the-age-of-social-media.

Homolar, Alexandra, and Ronny Scholz. 2019. "The Power of
Trump-Speak: Populist Crisis Narratives and Ontological
Security." *Cambridge Review of International Affairs* 32: 344–364.
https://www.tandfonline.com/doi/pdf/10.1080/09557571.2019
.1575796?needAccess=true.

Iqbal, Mansoor. 2021. "Twitter Revenue and Usage Statistics."
Business of Apps, March 8. https://www.businessofapps.com/data
/twitter-statistics/.

Iyengar, Shanto and Kyu S. Hahn. 2009. "Red Media, Blue Media:
Evidence of Ideological Selectivity in Media Use." *Journal of
Communication* 59, no. 1: 19–39.

Jensen, Tom. 2020. "Americans Think Coronavirus Threat Is Very
Real; Unhappy with Trump." *Public Policy Polling,* March 3.
https://www.protectourcare.org/wp-content/uploads/2020/03
/Coronavirus-Poll-Memo-And-Results-3-20.pdf.

Johns Hopkins University. 2020. "COVID-19 Dashboard by the
Center for Systems Science and Engineering (CSSE) at Johns
Hopkins University (JHU)." Accessed November 14. https://
coronavirus.jhu.edu/map.html.

Jones, Sheena, and Theresa Waldrop. 2020. "14th Person Charged in
Alleged Plot to Kidnap Michigan Governor." *CNN,* October 16.
https://www.cnn.com/2020/10/15/us/michigan-governor-plot
-charge/index.html.

Jurkowitz, Mark, and Amy Mitchell. 2020. "Republicans Who Rely Most on Trump for COVID-19 News See the Outbreak Differently from Those Who Don't." Pew Research Center, October 12. https://www.pewresearch.org/fact-tank/2020/10/12 /republicans-who-rely-most-on-trump-for-covid-19-news-see -the-outbreak-differently-from-those-who-dont/.

Karma, Roge. 2020. "Poll: The Majority of Trump Voters Don't See Covid-19 as an Important Election Issue." *Vox*, October 25. https://www.vox.com/2020/10/25/21532166/pew -poll-republicans-democrats-coronavirus-issue-election -economy-polarization.

Kessler, Glenn. 2020. "Trump's Triumphant Rhetoric on Coronavirus Testing." *Washington Post*. April 30. https://www .washingtonpost.com/politics/2020/04/30/trumps-triumphant -rhetoric-coronavirus-testing/.

Kirzinger, Ashley, Grace Sparks, Audrey Kearney, Mellisha Stokes, Liz Hamel, and Mollyann Brodie. 2021. "KFF COVID-19 Vaccine Monitor: November 2021." Kaiser Family Foundation, December 2. https://www.kff.org/coronavirus-covid-19/poll -finding/kff-covid-19-vaccine-monitor-november-2021/.

Kübler-Ross, Elizabeth. 1969. *On Death and Dying, What the Dying Have to Teach Doctors, Nurses, Clergy and Their Own Families*. New York: Simon and Schuster.

Lafayette, Jon. 2021. "U.S. TV Ad Spending to Drop 4% in 2021 as Digital Video Booms." *AdTech Hub*, August 11. https:// adtechhub.com/u-s-tv-ad-spending-to-drop-4-in-2021-as-digital -video-booms/.

Lasco, Gideon. 2021. "Medical Populism and the COVID-19 Pandemic." *Global Public Health* 15, no. 10: 1417–1429. https:// www.tandfonline.com/doi/full/10.1080/17441692.2020.1807581 ?scroll=top&needAccess=true.

Lee, Michelle Ye Hee, and Josh Dawsey. 2020. "RNC Events at White House Raise Concerns about Violations of Hatch Act." *Washington Post*, August 26.

Levin, Bess. 2020. "Surprise: Trump Started Itching to End Social Distancing after His Six Most Profitable Clubs Closed." *Vanity Fair*, March 24. https://www.vanityfair.com/news/2020/03/trump-organization-properties-coronavirus.

Levine, Elana. 2020. *Her Stories: Daytime Soap Opera and US Television History*. Durham, NC: Duke University Press.

Levinson, Paul. 2018. "Turning the Tables: How Trump Turned Fake News from a Weapon of Deception to a Weapon of Mass Destruction of Legitimate News." In *Trump's Media War*, edited by Catherine Happer, Andrew Hoskins, and William Merrin, 33–46. New York: Palgrave Macmillan.

Lindsay, James M. 2020. "The 2020 Election by the Numbers." Council on Foreign Relations, December 15. https://www.cfr.org/blog/2020-election-numbers.

Mackey, Robert. 2020. "Quack-in-Chief Donald Trump Asks if Bleach Injections or Tanning Could Cure Covid-19." *Intercept*, April 24. https://theintercept.com/2020/04/24/quack-chief-donald-trump-asks-bleach-injections-tanning-cure-covid-19/.

Mahadevan, Alex, and Jon Greenberg. 2020. "After Contracting COVID-19, Trump Was Dinged by Platforms for Spreading Coronavirus Misinformation." *Poynter*, October 7. https://www.poynter.org/fact-checking/2020/after-contracting-covid-19-trump-dinged-by-platforms-for-spreading-coronavirus-misinformation/.

Maierová, Eva. 2020. "We Have Done a Great Job! The Coronavirus Pandemic in Donald Trump's Tweets." In *Proceedings of the 5th International Interdisciplinary Conference ON Language and Politics—Between Linguistics and Political Science*, edited by Radoslav Štefančík, 199–212. Bratislava: EKONÓM.

Maragakis, Lisa, and Gabor David Kelen. 2021. "Booster Shots and Additional Doses for COVID-19 Vaccines—What You Need to Know." *Johns Hopkins Medicine*, December 15. https://www.hopkinsmedicine.org/health/conditions-and-diseases

/coronavirus/booster-shots-and-third-doses-for-covid19
-vaccines-what-you-need-to-know.

Marketing Charts. 2020. "Online Display Estimated to Have
Overtaken TV in US Ad Spend." January 2. https://www
.marketingcharts.com/advertising-trends/spending-and
-spenders-111415.

Marketing Wit. 2020. "Television Advertising History." Accessed
May 8. https://marketingwit.com/television-advertising-history.

McKinsey and Company. 2020. "COVID-19 Recovery in Hardest-
Hit Sectors Could Take More Than 5 Years." *McKinsey.com*,
July 29. https://www.mckinsey.com/featured-insights
/coronavirus-leading-through-the-crisis/charting-the-path-to
-the-next-normal/covid-19-recovery-in-hardest-hit-sectors-could
-take-more-than-5-years.

Meade, Amanda. 2020. "Facebook Greatest Source of Covid-19
Disinformation, Journalists Say." *The Guardian*, October 13.
https://www.theguardian.com/technology/2020/oct/14/facebook
-greatest-source-of-covid-19-disinformation-journalists-say.

Merica, Dan. 2021. "Trump Met with Boos after Revealing He
Received Covid-19 Booster." *CNN*, December 21. https://www
.cnn.com/2021/12/20/politics/donald-trump-booster-shot-boos
/index.html.

Miao, Hannah. 2020. "650 Million Face Masks across the U.S. in
April, Report Says." *CNBC*, September 17. https://www.cnbc
.com/2020/09/17/white-house-abandoned-plan-to-deliver-650
-million-face-masks-across-us-report-says.html.

Miller, Ryan W., Jessica Flores, and Grace Hauck. 2020. "Coronavirus Updates: Nevada Gov. Tests Positive." *USA Today*, November 14. https://www.usatoday.com/story/news/health/2020/11/13
/covid-news-costco-ivy-league-el-paso-shutdown-california
/6271794002/.

National Institutes of Health. 2020. "NIH Officials Discuss Novel
Coronavirus That Recently Emerged in China: Research

Underway to Address Latest Viral Threat." Press Release, January 23. https://www.nih.gov/news-events/news-releases/nih -officials-discuss-novel-coronavirus-recently-emerged-china.

Neuman, Scott. 2020. "Man Dies, Woman Hospitalized after Taking Form of Chloroquine to Prevent COVID-19." *NPR*, March 24. https://www.npr.org/sections/coronavirus-live -updates/2020/03/24/820512107/man-dies-woman-hospitalized -after-taking-form-of-chloroquine-to-prevent-covid-19.

Newport, Frank. 2020. "The Partisan Gap in Views of the Corona- virus." *Gallup*, May 15. https://news.gallup.com/opinion/polling -matters/311087/partisan-gap-views-coronavirus.aspx.

New York Times. 2020. "Covid in the U.S.: Latest Map and Case Count." Accessed November 13. https://www.nytimes.com /interactive/2021/us/covid-cases.html.

Noor, Poppy. 2020. "Republican Congressman Wears Gas Mask for Coronavirus Vote." *The Guardian*, March 5. https://www .theguardian.com/world/2020/mar/05/republican-congressman -matt-gaetz-coronavirus-gas-mask.

NPR. 2020. "Trump Tells Woodward He Deliberately Downplayed Coronavirus Threat." *Morning Edition*, September 10. https:// www.npr.org/2020/09/10/911368698/trump-tells-woodward-he -deliberately-downplayed-coronavirus-threat.

O'Barr, William M. 2010. "The Rise and Fall of the TV Commer- cial." *Advertising and Society Review* 11 no. 2. https://muse.jhu .edu/article/389521.

O'Kane, Caitlin. 2020. "Trump Listens 'Even if We Disagree on Some Things,' Dr. Fauci Says in Interview about Coronavirus Task Force." *CBS News*, March 23. https://www.cbsnews.com /news/coronavirus-trump-fauci-interview-meme-listens -disagree-contradiction-white-house-task-force-press-briefings/.

Ott, Brian L., and Greg Dickinson. 2020. "The Twitter Presidency: How Donald Trump's Tweets Undermine Democracy and Threaten Us All." *Political Science Quarterly* 135, no. 4: 607–636.

Packard, Vance. 1957. *The Hidden Persuaders*. New York: D. McKay.

Pan American Health Organization. 2020. "Understanding the Infodemic and Misinformation in the Fight against COVID-19." https://iris.paho.org/bitstream/handle/10665.2/52052/Factsheet-infodemic_eng.pdf.

Pariser, Eli. 2011. *The Filter Bubble*. New York: Penguin.

Paz, Christian. 2020. "All the President's Lies about the Coronavirus." *The Atlantic*, November 2. https://www.theatlantic.com/politics/archive/2020/11/trumps-lies-about-coronavirus/608647/.

PBS. 2020. "The Rise of TV Quiz Shows." *American Experience*, accessed May 6. http://www.pbs.org/wgbh/americanexperience/features/quizshow-rise-tv-quiz-shows/.

Perrett, Connor. 2020. "The Trump Organization Laid Off 1,500 People after It Closed over a Dozen Properties Due to the Novel Coronavirus Pandemic." *Business Insider*, April 4. https://www.businessinsider.com/trump-organization-laid-off-1500-and-closed-17-properties-2020-4.

Peters, Jeremy W. 2020. "Alarm, Denial, Blame: The Pro-Trump Media's Coronavirus Distortion." *New York Times*, April 2. https://www.nytimes.com/2020/04/01/us/politics/hannity-limbaugh-trump-coronavirus.html.

Pew Research Center. 2019a. "Partisan Antipathy: More Intense, More Personal." October 10. https://www.pewresearch.org/politics/2019/10/10/partisan-antipathy-more-intense-more-personal/.

———. 2019b. "In a Politically Polarized Era, Sharp Divides in Both Partisan Coalitions." December 17. https://www.pewresearch.org/politics/2019/12/17/in-a-politically-polarized-era-sharp-divides-in-both-partisan-coalitions/.

———. 2020. "Republicans, Democrats Move Even Further Apart in Coronavirus Concerns." June 25. https://www.pewresearch.org/politics/2020/06/25/republicans-democrats-move-even-further-apart-in-coronavirus-concerns/.

———. 2022. "Partisan Differences Are Common in the Lessons Americans Take Away from COVID-19." September 6.

https://www.pewresearch.org/short-reads/2022/09/06/partisan
-differences-are-common-in-the-lessons-americans-take-away
-from-covid-19/.

Pratkanis, Anthony R., and Elliot Aronson. 1992. *Age of Propaganda:
The Everyday Use and Abuse of Persuasion*. New York: W. H.
Freeman.

Rapaille, Clotaire. 2007. *The Culture Code: An Ingenious Way to
Understand Why People around the World Live and Buy as They Do*.
New York: Broadway Books.

Rapier, Graham. 2020. "The Sturgis Motorcycle Rally That Experts
Warned Would Be a Coronavirus Superspreader Event Has
Been Linked to 100 New Cases in 8 States." *Business Insider*,
August 26. https://www.businessinsider.com/sturgis-motorcycle
-rally-spreads-coronavirus-8-states-as-experts-warned-2020-8.

Reja, Mishal. 2021. "Trump's 'Chinese Virus' Tweet Helped Lead to
Rise in Racist Anti-Asian Twitter Content: Study." *ABC News*,
March 18. https://abcnews.go.com/Health/trumps-chinese-virus
-tweet-helped-lead-rise-racist/story?id=76530148.

Republican National Committee. 2020. "Resolution Regarding
the Republican Party Platform." https://prod-cdn-static.gop
.com/docs/Resolution_Platform_2020.pdf.

Reston, Maeve. 2020. "As Trump Gaslights America about
Coronavirus, Republicans Face a Critical Choice." *WLFI.com*,
July 6. https://www.wlfi.com/content/national/571633882.html.

Rev. 2020. "Democratic National Convention (DNC) 2020 Night 1
Transcript: Speeches by Michelle Obama, Bernie Sanders, John
Kasich & more," August 17. https://www.rev.com/blog/transcripts
/democratic-national-convention-dnc-night-1-transcript.

Ritter, Zac. 2020. "Amid Pandemic, News Attention Spikes; Media
Favorability Flat." *Gallup*, April 9. https://news.gallup.com
/opinion/gallup/307934/amid-pandemic-news-attention-spikes
-media-favorability-flat.aspx.

Robinson, Eugene. 2020. "Donald Trump's Five Stages of Grief."
Washington Post, March 30. https://www.washingtonpost.com

/opinions/trump-finally-submits-to-reality/2020/03/30/512d3cca
-72c6-11ea-87da-77a8136c1a6d_story.html.

Roussos, Gina. 2016. "Donald Trump's Psychological Manipulation
of the American People." Yale Institution for Social and Policy
Studies, December 1. https://isps.yale.edu/news/blog/2016/12
/donald-trump%E2%80%99s-psychological-manipulation-of-the
-american-people.

Saletan, William. 2021 "Trump's Coronavirus Infection Was Much
Worse Than We Knew." *Slate*, June 25. https://slate.com/news
-and-politics/2021/06/trump-covid-infection-much-worse-than
-we-knew.html.

Schwartz, Matthew S. 2020. "Governors Divide by Party on
Trump Plan to Reopen Businesses Shut by Coronavirus." *NPR*,
April 17. https://www.npr.org/2020/04/17/837579713/governors
-divide-by-party-on-trump-plan-to-reopen-businesses-shut-by
-coronavirus.

Select Subcommittee on the Coronavirus Crisis. 2021. "More
Effective, More Efficient, More Equitable: Overseeing an
Improving and Ongoing Pandemic Response Year-End Staff
Report." December. https://coronavirus.house.gov/sites
/democrats.coronavirus.house.gov/files
/SSCCInterimReportDec2021V1.pdf.

Shear, Michael D., and Sarah Mervosh. 2020. "Trump Encourages
Protest against Governors Who Have Imposed Virus Restrictions." *New York Times*, April 29. https://www.nytimes.com
/2020/04/17/us/politics/trump-coronavirus-governors.html.

Shelley, Mary. 1994 (1818). *Frankenstein*. Garden City, NY: Dover
Publications.

Sheng-mei, Ma. 2020. "Kung Flu." UC Davis Clinton Institute,
May 8. https://www.ucdclinton.ie/commentary-content/kung
-flu.

Smith, David. 2021. "Trump Was 'in Pain and Afraid' during
Post-Covid Display of Bravado, Niece's Book Says." *The
Guardian*. August 10, 2021. https://www.theguardian.com/us

-news/2021/aug/09/trump-covid-coronavirus-mary-trump-book
-the-reckoning.

Spero, Robert. 1980. *Duping of the American Voter.* New York:
Lippincott & Crowell.

Spicuzza, Mary, and Oren Oppenheim. 2020. "'Holy Mackerel,
Folks!': Wisconsin Gov. Tony Evers Kicks Off the Third Night
of the 2020 DNC in Classic Fashion." *Milwaukee Journal
Sentinel*, August 20. https://www.jsonline.com/story/news
/politics/2020/08/19/wisconsin-gov-tony-evers-opens-2020-dnc
-classic-holy-mackerel/5613608002/.

Stableford, Dylan, and Caitlin Dickson. 2021. "Key Revelations from
the New Book by Trump's Former Chief of Staff Mark Meadows." *Yahoo News*, December 7. https://news.yahoo.com/mark
-meadows-trump-book-revelations-covid-bunker-204548531.html.

Stahl, Chelsea. 2020. "Mask-Wearing Habits Could Indicate How
You'll Vote." *NBC News*, April 28.

Stein, Rob. 2020. "U.S. Confirmed Coronavirus Infections Hit 10
Million." *NPR*, November 9. https://www.npr.org/sections
/coronavirus-live-updates/2020/11/09/933023659/u-s-confirmed
-coronavirus-infections-hit-10-million.

Stieb, Matt. 2021. "Trump Was More Sick with COVID Than White
House Let On: Report." *New York Magazine*, February 11.

Stone, Will. 2021. "On Trump's Last Full Day, Nation Records
400,000 Covid Deaths." *Kaiser Health News*, January 19.
https://khn.org/news/nation-records-400000-covid-deaths-on
-last-day-of-donald-trump-presidency/.

Stroud, Natalie J. 2011. *Niche News: The Politics of News Choice.* New
York: Oxford University Press.

Suess, Jeff. 2017. "Our History: P&G Put the 'Soap' in 'Soap
Opera.'" *Cincinnati Enquirer*, October 4. https://www.cincinnati
.com/story/news/2017/10/04/our-history-p-g-put-soap-soap
-opera/732149001/.

Torres-Spelliscy, Ciara. 2019a. *Political Brands.* Cheltenham:
Edward Elgar Publishing.

———. 2019b. "Trump Can Say 'Witch Hunt' as Many Times as He Wants." *The Atlantic*, January 13. https://www.theatlantic .com/politics/archive/2019/01/trump-tries-undermine-mueller -indictments-legitimacy/580081/.

Trump, Donald. 2020a. "Remarks by President Trump in Address to the Nation." White House, March 11. https://trumpwhitehouse .archives.gov/briefings-statements/remarks-president-trump -address-nation/.

———. 2020b. "Remarks by President Trump in Meeting with African American Leaders." White House, February 27. https:// trumpwhitehouse.archives.gov/briefings-statements/remarks -president-trump-meeting-african-american-leaders/.

———. 2020c. "Remarks by President Trump, Vice President Pence, and Members of the Coronavirus Task Force in Press Conference." White House. February 29. https://trump whitehouse.archives.gov/briefings-statements/remarks-president -trump-vice-president-pence-members-coronavirus-task-force -press-conference-2/.

———. 2020d. "Donald Trump Rally Speech Transcript The Villages, Florida." *Rev.com*, October 23. https://www.rev.com /blog/transcripts/donald-trump-rally-speech-transcript-the -villages-florida-october-23.

———. 2020e. "Donald Trump Video Transcript from Walter Reed Medical Center with COVID Update." *Rev.com*, October 3. https://www.rev.com/blog/transcripts/donald-trump-video -transcript-from-walter-reed-medical-center-with-covid -update.

Uscinski, Joseph E., Adam M. Enders, Casey Klofstad, Michelle Seelig, John Funchion, Caleb Everett, Stefan Wuchty, Kamal Premaratne, and Manohar Murthi. 2020. "Why Do People Believe COVID-19 Conspiracy Theories?" *Harvard Kennedy School Misinformation Review*, April 28. https://misinforeview .hks.harvard.edu/article/why-do-people-believe-covid-19 -conspiracy-theories/.

Van Kessel, Patrick, and Dennis Quinn. 2020. "Both Republicans and Democrats Cite Masks as a Negative Effect of COVID-19, but for Very Different Reasons." Pew Research Center, October 29. https://www.pewresearch.org/fact-tank/2020/10/29/both -republicans-and-democrats-cite-masks-as-a-negative-effect-of -covid-19-but-for-very-different-reasons/.

Wang, Wendy. 2020. "Marriages between Democrats and Republicans Are Extremely Rare." Institute for Family Studies, November 3. https://ifstudies.org/blog/marriages-between -democrats-and-republicans-are-extremely-rare.

Weber, Lauren, and Katheryn Houghton. "The Mask Hypocrisy: How COVID Memos Contradict the White House's Public Face." *Kaiser Health News*, October 1. https://khn.org/news /mask-wearing-hypocrisy-how-covid-white-house-memos -contradict-administration-coronavirus-defense-policy/.

Westen, Drew. 2007. *The Political Brain: The Role of Emotion in Deciding the Fate of the Nation*. New York: Public Affairs.

WHO. 2020. "Coronavirus Disease (COVID-19) Data as Received by WHO from National Authorities." October 4. https://www .who.int/docs/default-source/coronaviruse/situation-reports /20201005-weekly-epi-update-8.pdf.

Wood, Daniel, and Geoff Brumfiel. 2021. "Pro-Trump Counties Now Have Far Higher COVID Death Rates. Misinformation is to Blame." December 5. *NPR*. https://www.npr.org/sections /health-shots/2021/12/05/1059828993/data-vaccine-misinformation -trump-counties-covid-death-rate.

Yalch, Matthew M. 2021. "Dimensions of Pathological Narcissism and Intention to Vote for Donald Trump." *PLoS One*, April 15. https://journals.plos.org/plosone/article?id=10.1371/journal.pone .0249892.

Yamey, Gavin. 2020. "Donald Trump: A Political Determinant of Covid-19." *British Medical Journal* 369: m1643. https://www.bmj .com/content/bmj/369/bmj.m1643.full.pdf.

5

Toward a Decolonial Democracy

Rageful Hope in the 1961 and 1972
Afro-Asian Women's Conferences

KIRIN GUPTA

We have gathered here in answer to the call of our hearts,
the hearts of women [who] cannot be reconciled to all
this evil and injustice, in order to make our noble
struggle more active.
—Mrs. Udval (AAWC 1973, 17)

On January 14, 1961, Bahia Karam, who initiated the first
Afro-Asian Women's Conference, (AAWC), stood up in a
Cairo conference room at the outset of the event. "Our conference is meeting at a crucial time," she said, "when the
forces of imperialism and colonialism are fighting . . . [their]
last ditch battle, and when the struggle for liberation and
independence is at its [peak.] We, the women of Africa
and Asia are playing our part in that great struggle" (AAWC
1961). The feeling in the room as a group of African and

Asian women set out on a project of shaping a decolonial democracy is preserved in a slim bound volume that the conference produced.

As secretary of the Women's Committee and International Preparatory Committee to the conference, Karam had materially planned for this day for more than a year. The impetus for this conference developed out of an experience of sisterhood-solidarity at the 1959 All African People's Conference. There was a sense of momentum, coupled with a sensibility of togetherness: delegates were keen "to get together and force their way through that barrier that has stood between them and their rights for so many years" (AAWC 1960, 6–7). Karam saw her chance to lead a women's movement for decolonial democracy. The Afro-Asian Women's Conference coalesced under the umbrella of the Afro-Asian People's Solidarity Organization (AAPSO), which had organized itself in the wake of Bandung (April 18–24, 1955) (AAWC 1960, 3).

Harking to roots in Bandung's high politics of Afro-Asian solidarity, the AAPSO took shape as a masculine organization oriented toward bicontinental resistance to colonial rule (Lee 2010). It aimed to bring together both expert guidance and collective action. The AAPSO spanned horizontally across the spatial imagination of the emerging postcolonial and vertically through populations to the masses. It was articulated without sentiment but with great intent and a strong sense of righteousness.[1] The AAPSO had requisitioned country-specific reports on the political and economic status of women throughout Africa and Asia. The question of women was relegated to a committee within the AAPSO, though the inclusion of women members and the requisitioning of reports could be read as an intention to address gender more broadly.

Karam and Karima El-Said, along with a few men of "high politics" who were prominent allies in the Afro-Asian solidarity movement, advocated for a conference in which women would produce these requested recommendations themselves. Despite advocating for an international women's conference, Karam reflected, "we never pictured it to represent over 37 peoples some of them participating for the first time in an international meeting" (AAWC 1961, 1). Participant reflections echoed this sentiment of mild surprise—but far more salient was this perception of the power and presence of Afro-Asian women at the conference. There was something brand new and yet complexly inherited about this alliance between Africa and Asia in a notably decolonial moment—and the room was filled with members of a gender that had been structurally marginalized along multiple dimensions within these colonized populations (AAWC 1961, 69–74).[2] The moment of gathering produced something deeper than an exercise in report writing, recommendation making, and the production of knowledge. It produced a potent rageful hope for a decolonial democracy—a rageful hope that has left an indelible mark on intersectional movement building.

In the 1960s and 1970s, amid late twentieth-century British and French decolonization, these conferences emblematized a movement that uplifted strategies of targeted anticolonial terrorism and mourned lost martyrs who died in the name of sovereign democracy. Conference participants traded tactics and strategies of feminist anticolonial rebellion across networks of solidarity. But these conferences have been left out of feminist histories of women's conferences and anticolonial histories that focus on Afro-Asian alliances. This chapter specifically examines the 1961 and 1972 Afro-Asian Women's Conferences and the building of a movement of rageful hope that defined this era of transnational solidarity in postcolonial nations across the continents.

Histories of women's transnational solidarity have elided the democratic imaginaries produced by the anticolonial women's movements of Africa and Asia. During the 1960s and 1970s, the prospect of communist, sovereign democracies populated by people of color—and allied outside of the dominion of the capitalist West—activated the alliance of Afro-Asian "sisters." A decade after the first AAWC conference in 1961, participants in the 1972 Afro-Asian Women's Conference specifically framed anticolonial liberation, including the construction of new forms of Afro-Asian democracy, as a primary step toward gender liberation. In its twenty-first century mutations, we have come to regard the oligarchical patterns of democracy that exist in our world—and which claim themselves expressive of democratic ideals—as inextricable from capitalism and whiteness.

Today, India, governed by an authoritarian-populist regime of racial, ethnic, and caste exclusion, claims to be the world's *largest* democracy. The United States, in the midst of countrywide political polarization on almost every major constitutional issue, claims to be the world's *most powerful* democracy. The concept of "democracy" appears inevitably entwined with a self-absolving, neoliberal neocolonialism. To recover democratic possibilities beyond the current global stage, it is imperative to examine the contingent moment between 1961 and 1972: in this moment, the question of *who* would define democracy's future was openly contested. The AAWC conferences illuminate how the current state of "democracy" is not natural or inevitable. Throughout the decade between the 1961 and 1972 AAWCs, rage and hope drove an alternative imaginary of decolonial democracies rooted in women's bicontinental communist and socialist solidarity.

The 1961 Conference: From Solidarity to Sisterhood, in Rageful Hope Together

Brother, my tears have dried
I can no longer weep,
You are a young man, I know not your name . . .
You have tasted death as a free man . . .
I try to weep over you, my brother, but in vain my tears
    have dried
My heart was torn just as was your body,
Forgive me brother.
I cannot weep.

> —Poem from the speech of the Algerian
> delegation (AAWC 1961, 73)

The first AAWC in 1961 was a self-conscious coming together of women, of "sisters."[3] The conference report describes the 1961 AAWC as the making of a moment in "feminine history," when "delegates from Basutoland, Gambia[,] for example, had the chance for the first time to meet their sisters from other countries in Africa and Asia" (AAWC 1961, 1). The meeting was suffused with a sense of urgency. Many delegates arrived expecting to interrogate how solidarity would serve them in their national, regional, and overarchingly anticolonial aims.[4] But over the course of the conference, terminology shifted. While solidarity was consistently used to refer to alliances with men, sisterhood became the unexpected, resounding theme of feminine solidarity throughout the conference. Sisterhood referred to feelings of women's togetherness and the collective rage that motivated their actions.

The history of Afro-Asian solidarity has largely been a history of high politics and of a masculine, elite political imaginary. By contrast, a shared sisterhood resounded with women in the movement, representing bonds that were political, personal, and emotional. The participation records of delegates who did not figure in sweeping "Big Man" history appear instead in short paragraphs that mention thousands of women who were involved in the anticolonial struggle.[5] These histories get lost when the names and deeds of women are de facto ignored or deliberately expunged from the publicly available record.

One single report of the 1961 AAWC exists on American soil.[6] It is a unique genre of document that asserts, "We cannot claim that [this] is a complete record of the deliberations of the first Afro-Asian women's conference which took place in Cairo on 14–23 January 1961. At best it can be regarded as a roundup of the conference, the pick of the bunch." In the introduction to the report she compiled, Karam writes that it would be "almost impossible" to fully document the conference. "Though it is not the thing to say in an introduction, our finances would not permit it," she remarks pointedly (AAWC 1961, 1). Though inadequately resourced, the AAWC received piecemeal institutional support, as well as individual support from prominent figures such as Abdel Nasser, Kwame N'krumah, Ferhat Abbas, Sukarno, and Nikita Khrushchev. From this piecemeal backing, the women created a project that proclaimed coherence. "This common action will start to flow as a small brook to become a great river: the Afro-Asian Women's Solidarity Movement," read the Appeal of the conference, expressing the sense of momentum that the delegates reported feeling (AAWC 1961, 20).

National Liberation Precedes Gender Liberation

The overarching theme of the first meeting was that national liberation was the pathway to women's liberation. The Recommendations for the Struggle of National Independence and Peace, the first set of recommendations that the women offer, states: "The historic mission today of the women in Asia and Africa is mainly the final eradication of imperialism and colonialism with a view to realizing within the framework of national independence, peace and prosperity of nations and complete emancipation of women" (AAWC 1961, 19). But what does emancipation entail? For Bahia Karam and her political sisterhood, emancipation required an emancipator, the free nation-state. Women were essential to freeing the nation, and in turn would be emancipated by it. This liberatory politics posited the dangerous possibility of gender justice after decolonization. How necessary gender liberation would be for national liberation was less clear. The widely accepted take was that anticolonialism was a necessary but not sufficient condition for women's equal rights.

The AAWC's leadership consisted predominantly of African women, most prominently Bahia Karam and Karima El-Said, both North African residents of the United Arab Republic.[7] This inevitably influenced the agenda, with the emphasis on ongoing struggles for anticolonial liberation more significant than if the AAWC's leadership had been drawn from Asia, where questions of postindependence national self-definition were very much at the forefront (Finnane and McDougall 2010; Khudori 2007). However, the Resolutions section of the conference report established the official positions of Afro-Asian women on many issues worldwide. The report includes demands for: women to hold diplomatic posts at the UN (II); Algerian independence and the release of imprisoned, tortured "Algerian women patriots" (III); the end of Belgian interference in the Congo (IV); the creation of a Palestinian national entity (V); the removal of British bases in Yemen (IX); the reinstatement of the PRC (in the document, the Chinese People's Republic) at the UN and the freedom of Taiwan (XI). Further, the Resolutions condemned: U.S. action in Vietnam, Laos, and Korea (VI–VIII); French action against Guinea, "Kamerun," and Mauritania (X, XII, XXII); British action in Kenya, Rhodesia, and Zanzibar (XVI, XVIII, XIX); racist government control in South Africa (XVII); white parliamentary domination in Central Africa (XV); Dutch control of West Irian of Indonesia (XIII); the imperial severing of İskenderun (XXI); and Portuguese control of Goa and Portuguese colonies in Africa (XX). The AAWC also expressed opposition to the nuclearization of Japan (XIV) and protested atomic tests, especially in the Sahara.

"Women constitute a mighty and staunch army of peace fighters," wrote Soviet leader Nikita Khrushchev in a message to the AAWC. The conference rhetoric, however, was far less expressive of a "peace movement" than the rhetoric of liberation fighters. The women of the AAWC were quick to link their militancy for liberation to their claims for equal rights. The report praises South African women's "courageous resistance" to the pass laws: "2,000 women were imprisoned for defiance," the report proclaims. "But this did not in any way intimidate them and they continued their movement" (AAWC 1961, 44). South African women's actions justified "the boycott of commodities imported from South Africa by the people of India, Ghana, Guinea, and Malaya." The report also cites with pride instances of women's violent resistance to British rule in Kenyan concentration camps. It praises a movement in Zanzibar, where women played a key role setting up mass rallies and demonstrations against U.S. military presence. Protests led by Vietnamese and Korean women's organizations spoke directly to the warning against "neocolonialism" that echoes throughout the document, naming this capitalist cultural domination as "the most subtle and dangerous enemy of the people of the whole world" (AAWC 1961, 38).

Gender and Political-Economic Belonging in Decolonial Democracy

Directly following these accounts of solidarity and militant struggle, the report presents recommendations about women's political rights. The report insists that women deserve rights for their sacrifice. "The struggle for political rights has been an integral part of the women's movement every where [*sic*] in the world but for the women of Asia and Africa it has been closely linked with the struggle for national independence," its authors write. "Where independence is only name," no rights exist—for anyone (AAWC 1961, 49). It was especially clear that women deserved the vote where they had "participated in national movements against imperialism, fought and sacrificed together with men." These women had already shaped democracy with their actions. The demand for voting rights in the 1961 report includes a list of the countries that had endured liberation struggles and then enabled women's suffrage: the Soviet Union, Mongolia, Ceylon, Thailand, Turkey, India, Burma, Liberia, China, Pakistan, Korea, Indonesia, Lebanon, the Democratic Republic of Vietnam, UAR, Tunisia, Malaya, Nigeria, Ghana, Iraq, and Guinea. The report also calls for more political participation from all segments of society and increasing women's representation in office. It commends the "success of our sisters," Yadgar Nasridinova, the Uzbek president, and "Mrs Bandenayk," the prime minister of Ceylon, suggesting that other Afro-Asian women should aspire to hold high political office in the future (AAWC 1961, 50–52).

Economic equality was demarcated as the necessary foundation for national and gender liberation. The

Recommendations for the Economic Equality of Women is the only section of the report focused specifically on equality, making demands for "equal pay for equal work" and equal treatment under the law in a decolonial democracy. The section of the report featuring the Recommendations for the Social Rights of Women also incorporates economic provisions, including a demand for enhancing women's property rights, based on a unique argument (AAWC 1961, 56). In many of the countries that sent delegations to the AAWC, children were inherently the responsibility of the mother in cases of divorce, separation, or other family ruptures. Contrary to Western intuition, the report does not stress the importance of property to provide for the children. Instead, its authors argue that, "if we women can keep the children, surely we can keep the precious, but still less valuable land." Recognizing that "the adoption of laws alone can not free the woman from the shackles of traditions and superstition," the report's authors also call for education and the development of a shared rights discourse. The "status of women concerns not only her family but affects the status, health and happiness of the entire people," the report argues; it is simply good sense to meet these demands, the AAWC maintains, because women are in the home, on the land, and trained to fight (AAWC 1961, 58).

The conferences created space to compare the internal effectiveness and external reception of different methods for critiquing the colonizers. The topic of education is addressed in more detail in the Recommendations on Cultural Rights of Women. In this section of the report, the AAWC observes that political anti-nationalist education is central to colonial education—and progress would be made following national independence. In 1961, this prospect was reason for wild optimism: "In Guinea, where independence was only proclaimed in 1958, the number of students has doubled every year since" (AAWC 1961, 64). The radical possibilities associated with the imaginary of independence derived from the expectation that there would be grassroots organizing for educational liberation in much the same way that there had been for cultural liberation. "For strict combating of illiteracy according to the success of experiments of countries which succeeded in their struggle, we recommend: the divertion [sic] of this struggle to a large popular movement aided by popular organizations" (AAWC 1961, 67–68). The AAWC proposed a structure of "mutual cooperation," a model of community education that could emerge from grassroots organizing.

Across Two Continents: Announcing the Collective Self

After Cairo, the AAWC would not meet again for a tumultuous decade (AAWC 1972, 1973; Afro-Asian Symposium on Social Development of Women 1975).[8] But the first AAWC was a watershed moment, characterized by, "women awakening throughout both continents," according to Karima El-Said (AAWC 1961, 11). The AAWC was explicitly Afro-Asian (not African, not Asian, and not Asian-African). Its naming was "proof of the great appeal which the Afro-Asian Solidarity Movement has for women of all Afro-Asian countries" (AAWC 1961, 34). It marked this movement out as an international women's movement—one that has been left out of the history of the activism and worlds of women (Chaudhuri and Strobel 1992; Rupp 1997; Hassim 2014; Fallon 2008; Roces and Edwards 2010). The appeal of this movement spotlighted the ongoing struggle with colonialism in 1961, and women's "desire to build a new world, a world without any form of exploitation and suppression." The report highlighted the collective energies, rage, and motivation of the delegations. It spoke of the conference's role in the history of international women's movements, emphasizing that "our decisions will help in strengthening the movement of women throughout the world" (AAWC 1961, 34). This alignment with women everywhere facing gender oppression and familiar disadvantages was simultaneously a pointed jab. The AAWC was calling out the exclusionary white women's movements that had thus far defined legible feminist history. "We rejoice at the fact that women of Africa are becoming more and more [of a] decisive factor of the most urgent problems of mankind," the AAWC proclaimed of its collective self (AAWC 1961, 42). The Afro-Asian woman who claimed her significance, her share, and her sisterhood was already an essential player in the history that has so often been told without her.

The potential productivity of reading Afro-Asian women as theorizing their understandings of solidarity, sisterhood, and struggle, and their future democracies, radically transforms the grounds on which we make knowledge. A feminist pedagogy demands that we question the structures of power that delineate who gets to make theory, and when, and where.[9] A democratic feminist pedagogy mandates that we open up the canon to biography, to poetry, to storytelling, to collective manifestos, and, let us add, the praxis of conferences and resolutions, driven by mourning and hope in these moments in 1961 and 1972.

The 1972 Conference: From Decolonization as a Step toward Gender Liberation toward Decolonization as the End Itself

"To all the women in Asia and Africa, we offer this document entrusting them with the task of following up the steps taken towards putting into action all resolutions and recommendations therein," wrote Bahia Karam in 1972, introducing the report of the second Afro-Asian Women's Conference (AAWC II), which took place in Ulan-Bator, Mongolia,[10] on August 13–18, 1972. The primary stated purpose of the 1972 conference was "to discuss a broad range of problems connected with the participation of women of Asia and Africa in the national liberation movement, in the struggle for economic independence, for social and cultural progress, and with their positions in society and in the family" (AAWC 1961, 27). The first AAWC had articulated national liberation as the prerequisite for "women's emancipation." The second focused on soldiering and democratic nation construction. Both prioritized nation and race, positing a democratized racialized freedom as a necessary component of all rights and freedoms. National, racial, continental, and bicontinental identity are all layered into the ontology of Afro-Asian womanhood. The conference reports and resolutions reveal a process of self-definition as women describe themselves as soldier-builders of future socialist democracies. In their articulation of identity, they theorize themselves as synchronically multiply marked and as inherently Afro-Asian in a way that is already implicit in the form of femininity they embody.

Attending the conference were forty-five delegations from across Africa and Asia: Afghanistan, Algeria, Angola, Bahrain, Bangladesh, Burundi, Congo, Cyprus, Dahomey (modern Benin), Egypt, Gambia, Guinea, Guinea-Bissau, India, Iran, Iraq, Japan, Kenya, Korea D.R. (North Korea), Laos, Lebanon, Malaysia, Mali, Mauritania, Mongolia, Morocco, Mozambique, Nepal, Nigeria, Palestine, the Popular Front for the Liberation of Oman and the Arab Gulf, Rwanda, Senegal, Sierra Leone, Somali Coast, South Africa, Sri Lanka, Tanzania, Tchad (Chad), Uganda, USSR, Vietnam D.R. (North Vietnam), Vietnam (South), Yemen,

and Zimbabwe. Also in attendance but not technically par-
ticipating were observer nations and solidarity delegations
from across the second and third worlds.[11] These included
Bulgaria, Chile, Cuba, Czechoslovakia, France, the German
Democratic Republic, Hungary, the Philippines, Poland,
Romania, and Yugoslavia (AAWC 1972, 121–140).

Against Imperial Feminisms: The Political Is Personal

For the women who attended AAWC II, the political and
public were an innate part of their womanhood. "It would
be wrong to underestimate the danger of propagating the
purely feminist aims of the women's movement, as well as
the danger of the reactionaries' attempt to isolate this movement from the national liberation struggle in Africa and
Asia," the AAWC II said in its preliminary general report.
"Imperialist and reactionary forces" encouraged the divorce
of these issues, they argued, by "reiterat[ing] that women
have to concentrate on the solution of their own problems
instead of engaging in political and public activities." To isolate womanhood from nation and race, from political and
public, was a danger, a threat to Afro-Asian women's ontology; a way of being that feminist imperialism sought to
destroy.

In their resolutions, the women delegates attending
AAWC II claimed to create a new, more honest, expansive,
and relevant form of liberatory self-definition, a political theory that articulated a foundational feminine role in democracy:
"One of the most important tasks of our Conference . . . is to
oppose . . . propaganda and give different interpretation[s] of
the women's role and of the actual tasks facing the women's
movement in Asia and Africa today" (AAWC 1973, 32). In
articulating an ontology in which race/nation/gender were
inseparable, Afro-Asian women presented an analysis that

persists today in the theoretical work of scholars such as Lila Abu-Lughod (2013), Inderpal Grewal (2013), and Chandra Mohanty on feminist imperialism (1988, 2003), and Afsaneh Najmabadi (2005, 2006, 2014) and Saba Mahmood (2011) on the question of gendered being. Decades before these scholars began to write, the Afro-Asian women of the AAWC II shaped political theory from the praxis of their lives.

The Afro-Asian women of the AAWC II claimed their identity as *militants* and as *makers* (of goods, of communities, of movements, of new humans). The method of claiming power was sisterhood. The delegates believed in their own representative power and legitimacy and imagined a "united front" of sisterhood that stretched laterally through Africa and Asia, and that was woven throughout individual countries as well.

The ontological constitution of the Afro-Asian woman as articulated at this conference was a marked theoretical contribution. It nonetheless elided voices and differences that occurred in relation to class and resources. These obfuscations must also be considered with regard to the uneven and formative patterns of violence experienced by Afro-Asian women, and their roles in liberation struggles. The AAWC II named and honored women involved in anti-imperial battle or struggle. These acts—mechanisms to prevent the erasure and affirm the significance of women activists and fighters—were emotive gestures of mourning and of celebration.[12] "Women of all ages in the ranks of the South Vietnamese guerillas . . . ambush the enemy and lay mines and bombs under enemy's installations," the report said, lauding the activities of the rank and file, while memorializing individuals: "We would like to name . . . Le Thi Hong Gam, heroine of the South Vietnam People's Liberation Armed Forces, whose courage and selflessness are a vivid example for the women of the world" (AAWC 1973, 38). The report not only recognized women involved in armed struggle; all entries into the mêlée were validated as reflections of women's politics, and worthy of being honored. In 1972, AAWC II memorialized Palestinian women's "heroic actions of every caliber," emphasizing that "they are using the most various methods in this struggle from armed to political and from economic to social, they conduct manifestations, go on hunger strikes, and engage in all forms of struggle" (AAWC 1973, 41). Over the six days of the conference, the names of heroines, fighters, and militants were folded into the record of the AAWC II to be maintained for perpetuity, covering page after page of the limited historical record: "Palestinian women never to be forgotten in the annals of the Palestinian resistance are: Laila Khaled, Amina Dahbour, Alia Taha, Fatma Barnawi, A'ida Saad, and scores of others" (AAWC 1973, 41). The AAWC II report in 1973 preserved these names for over half a century, so they continue to resonate even though they are written in only two other documents that exist on American soil.

The honoring of militants was an ontological assertion that embodied violence was constantly constituting the Afro-Asian woman as she was written out of and into the archive. "The liberation struggle has forged Afro-Asian women into a great force and has been the first step on the path of their emancipation," the AAWC II wrote in their General Declaration of 1972. And yet, the declaration continued, "our role in the liberation struggle does not and should not end with the winning of independence" (AAWC 1973, 69). Women's role in liberation struggles would continue in two main arenas—first, involving the socioeconomic transformations that nations would need to undergo in the postcolonial era, and second, involving the creation of "genuine equality both in society and in the family" (AAWC 1973, 72–85).

The AAWC II passed two short yet substantive resolutions about women's role in nation building. The first resolution addressed the contributions of Afro-Asian women in economic, social, and cultural development, and the second concerned the status of women in Afro-Asian society and their rights as wives, mothers, and citizens (AAWC 1973, 102–115). The first resolution indicated that conditions of work determine conditions of social life. Correspondingly, the social contours of racism and sexism obstruct women's attempts to access political rights. Rights are not imagined here as entitlements, but rather as a set of interrelated demands unattainable individually (AAWC 1973, 102–108). The AAWC II noted that this was a framework through which all of society—not simply women—could work toward liberation: "The struggle for the social liberation of women is part of the struggle for the rights of all working people who oppose oppression, exploitation, and violence" (AAWC 1973, 107–108). In order for a full-scale new nation to be built, women would have to be centered. Sociality, work, and politics were inextricably linked, and women were necessary for the construction of new political structures that differed from the legacy of colonial rule.

The report enjoined men to see women not as "mothers," but as makers in a complex sense—of women, of men, of nations. This was an essential component of the way in which the AAWC II described motherhood. In sections of their report condemning imperial feminism, the AAWC II stated that: "Imperialist and reactionary forces are trying to keep women apart from social and political life . . . they spread . . . ill-founded allegations about the exclusive role of woman in her <<home>> only as mistress of the house and child bearer" (AAWC 1973, 32). The women of the AAWC II sought to challenge this limited view of women's role. "The healthy and vital elements of women's participation in political and public activities" were not to be overlooked, the report said, but should be subject to negotiation at the national level. Women's solidarity movements were welcomed, but only insofar as each had its own affiliations and "responsibility for the destinies of their countries and peoples." The AAWC recognized that the family was inseparable from the society and country in which it was enmeshed. The freedom and flourishing of family and country were not something attainable through the rights of women alone, however, but required "the liquidation of all forms of discrimination, ethnic prejudices, and tribalism, [the] liquidation of colonialism's consequences regarding women." This "liquidation" was the point of potential transformation; it would release "the creative energy of Afro Asian women and create great possibilities for drawing them into national construction" (AAWC 1973, 108–110). The creative energy of the women of the AAWC II and their sisters would help remake whole societies, freed from the trappings of the past.

The second resolution regarded women as the "producers of intellectual and material goods as well as joint propagators of the human race . . . active and dynamic creator[s]." This resolution described pregnancy and parenting as sites of labor-intensive production, with corollary rights "to family planning and to fully paid maternity leave" (AAWC 1973, 109–110). Marital rights and demands (the rights to divorce, prosecute marital rape, and individual legal personhood) were also folded into this section. The goal was "a revolution within the revolution in terms of post-revolutionary social structure" about women's roles (AAWC 1973, 105). Anti-imperialism was rife with opportunity to design an innovatively socialist, gender-egalitarian, democratic society. Those who dismantled oppressive structures, the logic went, would be the purveyors of justice.

It has been too easy to imagine these women as instruments of decolonizing regimes. They were, instead, actors in their own right, shaping a decolonial democracy. In imagining this class of women from the decolonizing Global South, the problem for historians has not been a lack of archive. In their efforts to organize a democratic conference, the women in these conferences very intentionally created an archive. A brief written text and a few grainy photos remain—but only in a couple of files confiscated by the CIA or tucked into the back of university library bookshelves. This archive has gone unattended because of the political unpalatability of its relationship to socialism or communism. The AAPSO (and its internal cohorts of the AAWC) had an affiliation with the USSR that tainted its legacy. Few approached this archive for decades after the fall of the USSR. But these archives are self-created with historians in mind. It is a way of honoring the political process to attend to the Afro-Asian women who had the opportunity to create this archive of just over a hundred pages, where they defined themselves in rageful hope and sisterhood, and imagined what a decolonial democracy might look like.

Notes

1. The organization was closely watched by the U.S. Central Intelligence Agency for possible communist affiliations. AAPSO conference proceedings were generally redacted from library records and became "missing" from State Department shelves, sometimes just as they arrived there. See, for instance, CIA (1961). State Department records show the conference reports I discuss in this chapter as having been "missing" from the shelves for decades.
2. The conference was truly bicontinental, attended by delegations from Algeria, Arab South, Basutoland (Lesotho), Cambodia,

Ceylon (Sri Lanka), China, Gambia, Guinea, India, Iran, Iraq, Indonesia, Japan, Jordan, Kamerun, Kenya, Korea, Lebanon, Liberia, Libya, Mongolia, Morocco, Nigeria, Palestine, Senegal, South West Africa (Namibia), Sierra Leone, the Soviet Union, Sudan, Tunisia, UAR, Union of South Africa, North Vietnam, Zanzibar, Yemen, and South Rhodesia (Zimbabwe).

3. Prior to the 1960 Preparatory Committee, or the official first AAWC in 1961, a small gathering that included women from Mongolia, India, and Ghana arrived in Colombo and convened briefly in 1958 without the formality of the Afro-Asian People's Solidarity Organization (AAPSO) or a structured committee that organized the research and activities of an ongoing organization. Meetings like this occurred without official record in the moments following the political excitement (and masculine performance) of the Bandung Conference, the April 1955 moment in which Asian-African solidarity affirming an anticolonial democratic future was articulated (Bier 2010, 151).

4. Notably, the word "feminist" was not used once in the conference records or recommendations. One can hypothesize that the use of a rights discourse was favored because self-consciously feminist writing in 1961 did not speak to the experience of women who were not Western, white, liberal, or cisgender. Today there are numerous excellent sources that illuminate racial, classed, geographic, and colonial exclusions from feminism. See Stephen (2009); Anzaldúa (1987); Moraga and Anzaldúa (1981); Lorde (2007).

5. I use the term "Big Man" history to gesture to a particular historical method: the biographical tradition of elevating a single person's actions and written reflections, portraying them as representative of a historical moment, or imagining them as shaping a political era. This person was typically a wealthy man who had the resources—and the foresight—to leave behind a much thicker archive than a slim conference report of under

a hundred pages for a conference with more than a hundred participants. Bahia Karam had the capacity to print a few hundred pamphlets in Cairo; Thomas Jefferson had the capacity to copy every piece of correspondence he wished to preserve for future biographers. See Trouillot (1995); Hartman (2008).

6. The existence of only one copy of the conference report on U.S. soil is likely because of the imagined association of decolonial democracy with terror and communism. I am indebted to the wonderful archivists and research librarians at the Hoover Library, Stanford University, for providing me access to that singular record.

7. The United Arab Republic (UAR) was a state that derived from a union between Egypt and Syria in 1958. Syria seceded in 1961 and thereafter the state had the approximate borders of modern Egypt.

8. The second conference was fruitful in new and inventive ways, taking place in Ulan Bator, Mongolia, in 1972. The third, in Cairo, Egypt, in 1975, prepared the Afro-Asian women's alliances to enter into conversation with those treated in the reports as feminine colonizers and neocolonialists themselves at the 1975 Berlin Conference during the UN Women's Year. Subsequent conferences were in Cairo in 1995 and 1998.

9. Women's conferences, correspondence, and conversation have too often been relegated to the sphere of history alone, but there is productive cause to read this as the writing of theory.

10. This particular rendition of the name of the Mongolian capital, "Ulan-Bator," is taken from the 1972 Conference's spelling. In classical Mongolian, you will find the transliteration Ulagan-bagatur, or in Mongolian Cyrillic, Улаанбаатар.

11. In the process of imagining decolonial democracies and envisioning a world beyond the contemporary state of affairs in the 1960s and 1970s, there was an ongoing usage of many of the terms and practices of colonizers. The "second and third worlds"

were terms used by conference participants as a part of marking out their standpoint, and a way of claiming the particularized power of colonized peoples. This is a tradition that would be echoed by feminist-of-color campaigns and scholars contemporaneously and in the decades to follow.

12. There are echoes of this in the contemporary #SayHerName campaign, which counters both police violence against women and social amnesia that women suffer these forms of institutionalized violence. These resonances are worth exploring in relation to the claim that gender is constituted by and constitutive of a movement for racial justice.

References

Abu-Lughod, Lila. 2013. *Do Muslim Women Need Saving?* Cambridge, MA: Harvard University Press.

Afro-Asian Symposium on Social Development of Women. 1975. *Documents of the Afro-Asian Symposium on Social Development of Women, Alexandria, 8–10 March, 1975.* Cairo: Permanent Secretariat of Afro-Asian Peoples' Solidarity Organisation.

Afro-Asian Women's Conference (AAWC). 1960. *The International Preparatory Committee, Afro-Asian Women's Conference, Cairo, 15–24 September 1960.* Cairo: Dar El-Hana.

———. 1961. *The First Afro-Asian Women's Conference, Cairo, 14–23 January 1961: Reports, Messages, Speeches, Resolutions.* Cairo: Amalgamated Press of Egypt.

———. 1972. *Role and Rights of Women of Africa and Asia in the National Liberation and Development: Preparatory Documents.* Cairo: Permanent Secretariat of Afro-Asian Peoples' Solidarity Organization.

———. 1973. *Documents of the Second Afro-Asian Women's Conference, 13–18 August 1972, Ulan-Bator, Mongolia.* Cairo: Permanent Secretariat of the AAPSO Afro-Asian Publications.

Akyeampong, Emmanuel, and Pashington Obeng. 1995. "Spirituality, Gender, and Power in Asante History." *International Journal of African Historical Studies* 28, no. 3: 481–508.

Anzaldúa, Gloria. 1999 (1987). *Borderlands/La Frontera.* San Francisco: Aunt Lute Books.

Badrī, Balqīs Yūsuf. 2017. *Women's Activism in Africa: Struggles for Rights and Representation.* London: Zed Books.

Bier, Laura. 2010. "Feminism, Solidarity, and Identity in the Age of Bandung: Third World Women in the Egyptian Women's Press." In *Making a World after Empire: The Bandung Moment and Its Political Afterlives,* edited by Christopher J. Lee, 141–172. Athens: Ohio University Press.

Central Intelligence Agency (CIA). 1961. *The All Africa People's Conference in 1961.* https://www.cia.gov/readingroom/docs/CIA -RDP78-00915R001300320009-3.pdf.

Chaudhuri, Nupur, and Margaret Strobel. 1992. *Western Women and Imperialism: Complicity and Resistance.* Bloomington: Indiana University Press.

Fallon, Kathleen M. 2008. *Democracy and the Rise of Women's Movements in Sub-Saharan Africa.* Baltimore: Johns Hopkins University Press.

Finnane, Antonia, and Derek McDougall. 2010. *Bandung 1955: Little Histories.* Victoria: Monash University Press.

Fisk, Robert. 2012. "Syria Is Used to the Slings and Arrows of Friends and Enemies." *The Independent,* February 1, 2012.

Grewal, Inderpal. 2013. "Outsourcing Patriarchy." *International Feminist Journal of Politics* 15, no. 1: 1–19.

Hartman, Saidiya. 2008. "Venus in Two Acts." *Small Axe* 12, no. 2: 1–14.

Hassim, Shireen. 2015. *The ANC Women's League: Sex, Gender and Politics.* Athens: Ohio University Press, 2015.

Kalpakian, Jack. 2004. *Identity, Conflict, and Cooperation in International River Systems.* New York: Ashgate.

Khudori, Darwis. 2007. *Rethinking Solidarity in Global Society: The Challenge of Globalisation for Social and Solidarity Movements 50 Years after Bandung Asian-African Conference 1955*. Selangor, Malaysia: Strategic Information and Research Development Centre.

Lee, Christopher J. 2010. *Making a World after Empire: The Bandung Moment and Its Political Afterlives*. Athens: Ohio University Press.

Leslie, Agnes Ngoma. 2006. *Social Movements and Democracy in Africa: The Impact of Women's Struggle for Equal Rights in Botswana*. New York: Routledge.

Lorde, Audre. 2007. *Sister Outsider: Essays and Speeches*. Berkeley, CA: Crossing Press.

Mahmood, Saba. 2011. *Politics of Piety: The Islamic Revival and the Feminist Subject*. Princeton, NJ: Princeton University Press.

Mohanty, Chandra. 1988. "Under Western Eyes: Feminist Scholarship and Colonial Discourses." *Feminist Review* 30, no. 1: 61–88.

———. 2003. "'Under Western Eyes' Revisited: Feminist Solidarity through Anticapitalist Struggles." *Signs* 28, no. 2: 499–536.

Moraga, Cherríe, and Gloria Anzaldúa. 1981. *This Bridge Called My Back: Writings by Radical Women of Color*. Watertown: Persephone Press.

Najmabadi, Afsaneh. 2005. *Women with Mustaches and Men without Beards: Gender and Sexual Anxieties of Iranian Modernity*. Berkeley: University of California Press.

———. 2006. "Beyond the Americas: Are Gender and Sexuality Useful Categories of Analysis?" *Journal of Women's History* 18, no. 1: 11–21.

———. 2014. *Professing Selves: Transsexuality and Same-Sex Desire in Contemporary Iran*. Durham, NC: Duke University Press.

Roces, Mina, and Louise P. Edwards. 2010. *Women's Movements in Asia: Feminisms and Transnational Activism*. New York: Routledge.

Rupp, Leila J. 1997. *Worlds of Women: The Making of an International Women's Movement*. Princeton, NJ: Princeton University Press.

Steady, Filomina Chioma. 2006. *Women and Collective Action in Africa: Development, Democratization, and Empowerment, with Special Focus on Sierra Leone.* New York: Palgrave Macmillan.

Stephen, Cynthia. 2009. "Dalit Women and Feminism in India." *Countercurrents*, November 16. https://www.countercurrents.org /stephen161109.htm.

Ting, Helen, and Blackburn, Susan. 2013. *Women in Southeast Asian Nationalist Movements: A Biographical Approach.* Singapore: NUS Press.

Tripp, Aili Mari. 2009. *African Women's Movements: Transforming Political Landscapes.* Cambridge: Cambridge University Press.

Trouillot, Michel Rolph. 1995. *Silencing the Past: Power and the Production of History.* Boston: Beacon Press.

Vaz, Kim Marie, and Gary L. Lemons. 2012. *Feminist Solidarity at the Crossroads: Intersectional Women's Studies for Transracial Alliance.* New York: Routledge.

6

"The Kind of World We Wanted to Be In"

"Protocol Feminism" and Participatory Democracy in Intersectional Consciousness-Raising Groups

ILEANA NACHESCU

Consciousness-raising groups were a defining organizing strategy for the women's liberation movement, its "most widespread organizational unit" (Hole and Levine 1971, 26). In these groups, women "pooled" their feelings, "studied" them, generalized based on shared stories, and imagined a world where their pain would no longer exist (Allen 1970). The consciousness-raising group was emblematic and defining for the women's movement to such an extent that any debate underscoring its potential for social change, its ability to rearrange subjects and desires, and its political dimension is by necessity a debate about the scope and results of the women's liberation movement.

Early participants in women's liberation insisted that the practice of sharing personal experiences in groups was inspired by the participatory democratic practices of the civil rights and Black Power movements, as well as the more distant models used by Chinese revolutionaries or Colombian guerrillas (Evans 1979). They were adamant that consciousness-raising was different from therapy, a narrative that has dominated movement historiography for decades. More recently, historians have revealed the entanglements of psychotherapeutic practices with consciousness-raising by documenting the productive nature of psychotherapy for the political practices of postwar social movements, arguing, as historian Ellen Herman (1995) put it, that psychology constructed the feminist. Consciousness-raising was entangled not only with the therapeutic establishment, but with the training groups practiced in postwar American industrial settings as well (Murphy 2012). Murphy adds that consciousness-raising, given the multiple guidelines teaching women how to practice it, was a form of feminist protocol, similar to other practices creatively seized by feminists from the medical establishment, such as the vaginal self-help exam or menstrual extraction. For Murphy, feminist protocols follow a "procedural script that strategically assembles technologies, exchange, epistemology and so on" in order to establish "how to do" something (2012, 25).

In these historical and theoretical debates, the subject of feminism is in most cases white. However, African American feminists both theorized consciousness-raising and adapted therapeutic practices in their organizing. In this chapter, I use the works of forgotten 1970s Black feminists to build on Murphy's discussion of feminist protocols in women's liberation. I argue that while white and African American feminists both used therapeutic practices in their organizing, some of these practices can be understood as pro-tocols (a concept borrowed from medical science), while others are not well served by this conceptualization. More specifically, assertiveness training, enthusiastically borrowed from psychotherapy by white and Black feminists, especially activists associated with the National Alliance of Black Feminists (NABF), fits the description of feminist proto-cols. Yet consciousness-raising, the preferred mode of fem-inist organizing, was polyvalent, had multiple results, and is best understood by referring to its genealogy in the civil rights movement.

The predominantly white historians of a predominantly white movement have attempted to conceptualize Black fem-inisms' place in women's liberation in various ways. Benita Roth (2004) devised the theory of separate roads to feminism, arguing that women of color developed feminist discourses on their own in racial and ethnic organizations, without white feminists' input. However, feminists of color saw themselves as part of the women's liberation movement, as evidenced by their creative use of consciousness-raising and other move-ment practices, such as assertiveness training. My work on the history of the women's liberation movement centers Black feminism. I argue that while assertiveness training represented a form of protocol feminism, intersectional consciousness-raising as practiced by the NABF exceeded the concept of protocol, a distinction that has consequences for our current understanding of feminism. Consciousness-raising's antecedents in the civil rights and Black Power move-ments better explain the political project of 1970s feminism.

Histories of Consciousness-Raising

Early historians of the movement have traced the origins of the practice of consciousness-raising to the participatory democratic groups of the civil rights and Black Power movements. The principle of "let the people decide," the idea that oppressed people should be leaders in the social movements meant to liberate them, and the focus on personal experience as a source of political insight, were as foundational for feminist consciousness-raising groups as they had been for SNCC (Student Non-Violent Coordinating Committee), where early women's liberationists, predominantly white, had learned these principles.

This genealogy burnished the radical credentials of early feminists practicing consciousness-raising and has dominated movement historiography for decades. Yet more recent historians have been open to recognizing the entanglements of the 1960s and 1970s therapeutic discourse and consciousness-raising. Herman (1995) has documented the productive power of psychotherapeutic knowledge for feminism. The late 1960s women's liberation movement was highly critical of the therapeutic establishment, which had touted "adjustment" as a treatment for women experiencing depression. Therapists counseled these women, the vast majority of whom were white and suburban, to "adjust" to the circumstances of their lives rather than try to change them, to appreciate their roles as mothers and wives, and to subsume their individual aspirations to the needs of their families. The postwar therapeutic establishment had defined the norms of feminine psychology as dependent and oriented toward nurturing behavior, and then punished the women who failed to live up to these ideals. Women's liberationists, unsurprisingly, saw therapy as a means to shore up patriarchy. Yet, as Herman argues, psychology also constructed the feminist, in various ways, as in Betty Friedan's use of the language of humanistic psychology and the therapeutic sensibility that seeped into the movement via consciousness-raising and feminist therapy (1995, 290).

Michelle Murphy (2012) further elaborates on the connection between therapeutic knowledge and consciousness-raising by documenting the genealogy of the small group as a social technology borrowed from both the therapeutic establishment and industrial training groups. Her work focuses on the loosely named women's health movement, which sought to establish women's control over their own bodies via feminist protocols such as the self-help exam, the Pap smear, and menstrual extraction. In Murphy's use, protocols—a term borrowed from medical science—are procedural scripts that strategically establish sets of practices with a well-defined purpose. Protocols prescribe "how to compose the technologies, subjects, exchanges, affects, processes, and so on that make up a moment of health care practice" (2012, 25–26). Referencing specifically the feminist self-help practices of the 1970s, Murphy further explains protocols as "the scripting of relations between component entities—the instruments, labor, gestures, identities, emotions, and so on—assembled to compose feminist practices" (2012, 29). These protocols circulated both within the movement and outside of women's liberation; they were adopted by nonprofit organizations, corporations, and state agencies, sometimes for neocolonial projects. These feminist protocols, the self-help exam especially, were supposed to have a consciousness-raising effect. However, Murphy insists that consciousness-raising itself, women's liberation's preferred organizing practice, was a type of feminist protocol, which helped rearrange selves, affects, and political commitments by hailing women as subjects of feminism: "Consciousness-raising . . . set protocols for using language and for interacting, as well as for feeling, aligning, and bonding" (2012, 82).

Both Herman and Murphy assume a subject of feminism that is unraced, hence white. Yet while Herman does not include any discussion of race in her volume, Murphy acknowledges that this unraced subject can consolidate "the unmarked and normalized work of whiteness" (2012, 41). Her narrative occasionally explores activism by feminists of color, most notably the Combahee River Collective and the National Black Women's Health Project, acknowledging that health-related activism occurred in a multiplicity of sites by feminists who "generated myriad expressions of counter-conduct, often oriented around racialized communities, ties, necropolitics, and service provision" (Murphy 2012, 56). What is absent, however, is an analysis of the power relations between U.S.-based feminists of different races. Their projects were "animated out of the uneven racial formations composing Cold War America and hence generated entangled and yet divergent diagnoses of the 1970s" (Murphy 2012, 46). However, the extent to which power differentials between white and Black feminists shaped the women's movement and its history or made possible the marginalization or even erasure of Black feminist analyses remains unmentioned.

Unfortunately, Murphy herself participates in this erasure of Black feminist intellectual work. Her argument asserts the entanglement between consciousness-raising and industrial training groups, an argument very similar to that made by Black feminist Celestine Ware in her 1970 book *Woman Power*. Ware's work, entirely forgotten today, is not referenced in Murphy's account, although it is one of very few book-length texts about women's liberation that were published in the 1970s and authored by African American feminists. Another volume, Toni Cade's *The Black Woman* (1970), has received comparatively more attention from historians.

It is important to correct this oversight because Murphy's project is "to rethink how the history of feminisms in the United States of the 1960s and 1970s, often called 'second wave feminism,' might be written" (2012, 11), and the works of feminists of color, even if marginalized, need to be a part of this rewriting. The kind of erasure that Ware's work has encountered more generally in the historiography of the women's movement should be thought-provoking. On the one hand, Ware, who was a participant in very early radical feminist groups formed in New York in the late 1960s, offers in *Woman Power* a firsthand account of these histories, a narrative that, as Pearson (1999) shows, has been absorbed into metahistories such as Alice Echols's *Daring to Be Bad* (1989). On the other hand, several other arguments that Ware advances in her volume have simply been met with silence. With the exception of Herman and Murphy, feminist historians have not addressed the entanglements of consciousness-raising with industrial training groups and the encounter groups promoted by humanistic psychology.

Similarly, Ware's prediction that by the mid-1970s, college-educated African American women from working-class backgrounds would become interested in the women's movement has received very little attention from historians. But Ware's prediction anticipates the building of national organizations such as the National Black Feminist Organization (NBFO) in 1973 and the NABF in 1976. At the height of the women's liberation movement, in the mid- to late 1970s, Black women throughout the country attended consciousness-raising groups and assertiveness training, took courses on African American women, and became involved in the women's liberation movement in myriad other ways. White feminists, however, were adamant that in a women's movement, gender-driven concerns were paramount, while race remained at best marginal.

Intersectional Consciousness-Raising

For African American women who were interested in the women's liberation movement, the genealogy of consciousness-raising groups harked back to the civil rights and Black Power movements. Frances Beal, member of the Third World Women's Alliance, recalls that activists were using similar terms in the days of the Student Non-Violent Coordinating Committee: "That term was very common. 'You have to get your consciousness raised, brother,' you know, 'sister.' It wasn't just in term of women. That had to do with what it meant to be black and to fight for freedom and be an activist as opposed to accepting racism and being like that. That term of consciousness-raising was not—I don't know if it came out of the black movement, but we sure used it. We sure used it there" (quoted in Springer 2005, 118). Other African American women active in civil rights and Black nationalism gathered in rap groups where they theorized their everyday experience and collectively wrote position papers that synthesized their analysis. Such writings were published in Toni Cade's *The Black Woman* (1970).

In larger organizations for Black women, consciousness-raising was a prerequisite for groups that wanted to become local chapters. The NBFO (1973–1975) required any group wishing to become a chapter to hold at least four consciousness-raising sessions (NBFO 1973). NABF's most famous offshoot, the Combahee River Collective, based its famous Black Feminist Statement on consciousness-raising group experiences.

Yet Black feminists were aware of consciousness-raising's other genealogy, entangled with the therapeutic establishment. In her book *Woman Power* (1970), Ware compared small women's groups to T-groups (industrial training groups) and the encounter groups of the Human Potential Movement. Consciousness-raising, she states, is the "greatly improved descendant of the T-groups that industrial psychologists instituted to effect a working team out of a group of men in competition for a promotion" (1970, 108).

Developed after the war at the National Training Laboratories in Bethel, Maine, T-groups (T for training) were used to train a variety of professions from supermarket executives to stewardesses, professionals, policemen, and clerics. As a means of socializing employees, the T-group was meant to help overcome friction due to personality clashes in order to ensure greater work effectiveness. Training groups were also used in the Peace Corps, where an apparently open-ended process was actually a way to ensure "group conformity to government standards." Ware was critical of such endeavors that in the end pitted participants against each other through endless "evaluations" and used "group processes" in order to induce cooperation and submission. She insisted that, while T-groups purposefully socialized employees, consciousness-raising groups were rather created as a way of gathering information about women's lives in order to formulate the goals of the women's movement (1970, 108).

The process of consciousness-raising, for Ware, similarly evokes the Human Potential Movement, given its attention to minute details from an individual's life. The Human Potential Movement, led by Abraham Maslow, was inspired by his famous hierarchy of needs (ranked from survival needs such as those for food and shelter to higher needs, such as the need for self-actualization) and the insight that modern society repressed individual drives for self-actualization. Personal growth centers such as the Esalen Institute in Big Sur, California, were an important part of the movement, and encounter groups became a mass phenomenon during the 1960s. The encounter was meant to confront the participants' most deeply held beliefs, in the hope that this would foster their emotional growth. Practitioners argued that people needed to discover and confront their deepest feelings, and that the intense experience of a weekend's worth of training could bring about a radical change in one's outlook on life.

During marathon sessions lasting days, in small groups, participants were supposed to express their feelings directly—even feelings of hostility, usually repressed by social norms—and thus discover their authentic personalities, choose communication styles that worked best, and behave in ways that felt the most fulfilling. Nevertheless, these groups were emphatically apolitical, and herein lies the difference from consciousness-raising groups, as seen by Ware, as the latter tried to develop a political outlook based on fragmented and seemingly unrelated experiences and feelings, by building feminist theory (1970, 110).

The National Alliance of Black Feminists and the Practice of Consciousness-Raising

Black feminists who joined the women's movement in the mid-1970s encountered consciousness-raising as a well-established feminist practice. Manuals, instructions, and guidelines circulated in the movement, ranging from books that discussed various stages of consciousness-raising to mimeographed lists of topics. At the second meeting of the Chicago chapter of the NBFO, the precursor of the National Alliance of Black Feminists (NABF), an organization that would last into the early 1980s, Brenda Eichelberger, its president, volunteered to attend meetings at the Chicago Women's Liberation Union, a predominantly white group, in order to learn more about consciousness-raising. The NABF archived and circulated copies of various guidelines for feminist consciousness-raising, and insisted that the process needed to be adapted to include discussions of race.

Eichelberger, who later became executive director of the NABF, submitted a paper titled "Black Feminism" to the Association of Black Psychologists' Seventh Annual Convention (1974). In her paper, Eichelberger carefully differentiates feminist consciousness-raising groups from encounter groups. The two types of groups are comparable in that they involve discussing personal experiences, and that participation in the group can be at times "emotionally heavy." Moreover, both types of groups can help members change their behavior if they wish to do so. Yet the similarities end there; as in the encounter group, the final purpose is adjustment to social conditions, while in consciousness-raising, the direction is "to move away from seeing pain as a personal problem to perceiving the social issue" (Eichelberger 1974, 16).

Eichelberger makes a further distinction between individualized therapy and consciousness-raising. Women in therapy, she argues, are assumed to be sick by their (usually male) therapists and encouraged to repress their feelings and develop a "non-threatening personality." In contrast, feminists, and Black feminists especially, attempt to change social conditions. Eichelberger quotes extensively from Black feminists such as Angela Davis and offers detailed guidelines for intersectional consciousness-raising, including lists of topics that would address the issue of race, thus overcoming the blind spot of the guidelines circulating in the women's liberation movement, and even attempting to bring in African American men, who would attend their own groups (Nachescu 2017). In a similar vein, Eichelberger invites Black male psychologists to participate in a consciousness-raising exercise of their own:

> Do I dismiss as unimportant the concerns of my female clients, especially in those areas which are peculiar to women, such as: menstruation, rape, pregnancy, abortion, childbirth, miscarriage, menopause? Do I expect my female clients to adjust to "woman's role"? If so, what does woman's role mean to me? Do I feel compelled to flirt

with all my female clients, even though I may not feel a
physical attraction? Do I tend to perceive the problems of
my male clients as being more "mature," more important
than my female clients? Do I take a paternalistic posture
in my therapy sessions? (Eichelberger 1974, 18)

These pointed, specific questions are meant to raise the consciousness of Black male therapists in regard to their own
assumptions about gender roles. In her conclusion, Eichelberger recommends that the handful of Black women psychologists present at the conference study feminist psychology
and pay particular attention to the issues of rape and health
care, which few psychologists were addressing in their interactions with African American women clients.

Eichelberger's paper exemplifies the entanglements between feminist consciousness-raising and therapy outlined in
Murphy's reading of women's liberation. Eichelberger is
careful to delineate the feminist practice of consciousness-
raising from encounter groups, while recognizing their com-
monalities. Yet she goes one step further, challenging the
relatively new but predominantly male Black therapeutic
establishment to analyze its assumptions about gender by
engaging in consciousness-raising. Her paper shows that
the entanglements of consciousness-raising with therapeutic knowledge went both ways, as feminists saw the therapeutic influence on consciousness-raising, yet challenged,
through that same medium, gendered power relations within
the very sites where therapeutic knowledge was being produced and circulated.

While most NABF Black feminists were located in Chicago and neighboring cities such as Gary, Indiana, others
participated in this dialogue from farther locations. In Cleveland, Ohio, NABF member LaVerna Caldwell started a
Black women's consciousness-raising group in 1976, which

continued until 1979. Based on her experience leading small groups, Caldwell collaborated with other Chicago-based members in a project that aimed to formalize guidelines for intersectional consciousness-raising (NABF 1979c). Another NABF affiliate group, in the New York Tri-City area of Albany, Schenectady, and Troy, whose purpose was "to study literature by and about Black women and give each other support," met regularly in 1979 at the house of Elizabeth Campbell, another NABF member involved in developing consciousness-raising guidelines for Black women (NABF 1979d). The fact that Elizabeth Campbell, from upstate New York, LaVerna Caldwell, from Cleveland, Ohio, and many other NABF members from Chicago were engaged in developing consciousness-raising guidelines for Black women attests to Black feminists' interest in theorizing the process of consciousness-raising intersectionally, and the collective and cross-regional aspects of this process.

An undated document from the NABF archive includes an elaborate list of questions encouraging Black women to explore their self-perception from the point of view of both race and gender. Many questions had to do with beauty standards, body image, and awareness of racial difference, such as, "Do I now or have I ever used bleaching creams?" and "Do I ever compare my style of dress to that of other Black women, to that of white women?" and "Did my siblings or playmates ever mistreat me because my complexion or hair was different from theirs?" (NABF n.d., Consciousness-Raising Topics). These introspective exercises allowed participants to discuss their socialization experiences in terms of both gender and race. If white women's consciousness-raising groups uncovered the workings of patriarchy in women's daily lives, African American women's groups discussed the impact of racism and sexism on their deepest sense of self.

In addition to race and gender, discussions of class were intrinsic to the consciousness-raising sessions unfolding at the NABF. In 1975, reporter Carol Kleinman from the *Chicago Tribune* attended a meeting of the Chicago Black feminists and wrote an article about the experiences of Black women in consciousness-raising: "Black women follow the same guidelines as white women in consciousness-raising sessions—but a lot of the subject matter and concerns are different." Based on interviews with Eichelberger and other members, she lists some of the "very special, painful problems" that Black women faced, including discrimination in employment, health care, credit, and housing; lack of adequate health care and day care for Black women; negative stereotyping and colorism in the Black community, as well as the popularity of soul food, the myth of Black matriarchy, and relationships between Black men and white women (Kleinman 1975). The personal revelations of intersectional consciousness-raising helped Black women build a community and a collective understanding of their lives.

While consciousness-raising groups were the sites of personal and in-depth self-analyses, of individual stories, their purpose was to imagine a world that would transgress sexism and racism and to erase their traces on the participant's individual psyche. Like other Black organizations of their time, the NABF not only studied Black women's experiences as expressed in personal narratives, but also studied books by Black women, from sociological treatises to fiction. Race was intimately embedded in their discussion of gender, as history both distant (slavery) and very recent (lynching) shaped their experiences as women. Race and gender were also linked to class, and the discovery that Black women earned the least compared with other racial/gender groups (Porter 2013).

For Black women, participating in consciousness-raising was transformative. Poet C. A. Lofton recalls, "I was talking to my baby brother and . . . he said, are you aware of how much your ideas about feminism and consciousness raising permeate what you do? And I was, it's so second nature to me. Now. I mean, it's like, it's like, it was always a part of me, but it wasn't always a part of me. I actually grew up into this" (Lofton 2016). Lofton occupied leadership positions in the NABF and continued her work as labor organizer after the organization ended in 1983. While her personal philosophy and understanding of social justice seem like a given, she developed them through consciousness-raising.

Consciousness-Raising and African American Men

NABF, like other organizations created by women of color, saw African American men as comrades in struggle, and constantly attempted to reach out to them. The NABF invited African American men to certain meetings, tried to organize consciousness-raising groups for them, and encouraged them to support their female partners. Occasionally, in an attempt to continue their consciousness-raising efforts beyond the small groups of members, NABF organized community forums on "Authentic Black Male/Female Relationships" (NABF 1976). The forum organized in the fall of 1976 was attended by a group of prominent African American men—organizers, politicians, business owners, intellectuals—and in its aftermath the participants decided to establish a committee for Authentic Black Male/Female Relationships, including LaVerne Bennett and Pamela Miller of the NABF and Edwin C. Washington of Operation PUSH/Black Men Pushing. This committee was also in charge of developing consciousness-raising guidelines for Black men (NBFO Chicago Chapter 1975). The guidelines they developed included discussion topics on masculinity, demanding from men the same degree of emotional openness that women had. As Black feminists envisioned it, consciousness-raising would lead men to reflect on the experiences, institutions, and practices that had shaped their own understanding of masculinity. Questions invited men to reflect on their own "experiences of becoming a man," and their relationships with women, inviting them to question their own investment in patriarchal notions of male superiority. Some guidelines had practical dimensions, encouraging men to change not only their mindsets but also their lives by becoming more involved in childcare, for instance. While encouraging men to apply the lessons learned in in consciousness-raising, the guidelines invited them to decide individually on how to proceed.

Consciousness-Raising and Protocol Feminism Compared

Intersectional consciousness-raising as used by the NABF exceeds the idea of "protocol feminism" as outlined by Murphy—a "procedural script that strategically assembles technologies, exchange, epistemology and so on" in order to establish "how to do" something (2012, 25). Consciousness-raising, in Murphy's reading, was a protocol that helped feminists to assemble the evidence of women's experience, "revealing the workings of a patriarchy beneath" (2012, 84). Although Murphy states that for most white groups, this evidence was supposed to uncover a certain commonality of experience, she allows for the possibility that the evidence of experience could also reveal "the production of difference and contradictions," as in the works of the Combahee River Collective. Yet consciousness-raising, as used by the NABF, not only created evidence of Black women's experiences but worked to erase internalized racism and sexism in a collective way.

Understanding consciousness-raising as protocol presupposes that at least some of its results, not to mention the stages and the assemblage of actors, could be known in advance or had to be followed strictly in order to be successful. The feminist self-help exam and menstrual extraction, two of the protocols that Murphy analyzes, had well-defined steps, assembled specific objects and actors, and followed rules that had to be obeyed exactly in order for the protocol to achieve its desired results.

The same was not true regarding consciousness-raising. While some manuals, most notably Pamela Allen's *Free Space*, discussed stages in consciousness-raising—opening up, sharing, analyzing, and abstracting—and even prescribed a timeline marking these stages, most consciousness-raising guidelines simply provided lists of topics to be discussed in the group. The process could be highly unstructured. Black feminists understood consciousness-raising as a mechanism to build a narrative of their own experience, understand the works of white patriarchy, grasp the commonality of their oppression, generate writings, build friendship and community among group members, educate women and men, create theory that would lead to political activism, or inspire activism itself. Consciousness-raising dramatically exceeded any purpose that feminist protocols might have had. Yet other practices of women's liberation, such as assertiveness training, come closer to exemplifying this concept.

Assertiveness Training: "Can You Say No without Feeling Guilty?"

By the mid-1970s, the women's liberation movement embraced a new practice, assertiveness training, borrowed from psychology and popularized by countless books and articles. "Dedicated to teaching women to express themselves better and more often, especially in the face of opposition," assertiveness training was intended for women who had already participated in consciousness-raising groups and were now ready to continue their personal transformation. Built on reinforcing the "tactful skills" women already had and aiming to provide them with the "problem-solving skills" men had been trained to use, assertiveness training envisioned a different kind of social change: to "enable women, finally, to be equal partners with men" (Cummings 1974, 27).

Assertiveness training was an example of psychological knowledge seized by feminists in the service of the women's movement. With its roots in behavioral techniques, assertiveness training had become very popular by the mid-1970s, when a series of bestsellers with titles such as *Your Perfect Right* (Alberti and Emmons 1974); *When I Say No, I Feel Guilty* (Smith 1975); and *Don't Say Yes When You Want to Say No* (Fensterheim and Baer 1978) were published in quick succession. Even *Time* magazine featured an article on AT, as it was abbreviated at the time, thus popularizing the practice ("Assignment: Assertion" 1975). In small groups led by one or two facilitators, participants usually determined a set of individual rights and then role-played various situations in which they stood up for them (Hardaway and LaPointe 1974). Although many practitioners and members of the general public enthusiastically embraced assertiveness training, some cautioned that a too narrow focus on individual rights could promote antisocial behavior, and that practicing one's newly acquired assertiveness skills might disrupt participants' lives (Zerbe Enns 1992).

Feminist psychologists especially saw AT's potential to foster women's "growth," as Patricia Jacubowski-Spector (1973) put it in a much-quoted article. Major women's organizations supported the publication of assertiveness training manuals, such as Elan Cummings's *Woman, Assert Yourself*, published in 1974 with the support of the Seattle King County chapter of NOW. Other manuals followed suit, such as *Assertive Training for Women* (Osborne and Harris 1975), *The Assertive Woman* (Phelps and Austin 1975), reprinted three times within less than a year of its publication, and *The New Assertive Woman* (Bloom, Coburn, and Perlman 1975). Perhaps to prove that assertiveness training could address not only gender-related power disparities but also those related to race, Donald Cheek published *Assertive Black . . . Puzzled White* in 1976. Cheek, a Black male psychologist, concluded that African Americans were constantly being perceived as being too assertive in their interactions with white people, and that Black clients needed to assess carefully the situations they were in and calibrate their assertiveness based on the power differentials between themselves and their white interlocutors.

Always up to date on the latest trends in psychology, NABF first offered assertiveness training to its members in June 1976, with Marge Witty from the Chicago Counseling and Psychotherapy Center (an offshoot of the Counseling and Psychotherapy Research Center founded by Carl Rogers in 1945 at the University of Chicago). These seminars became a source of much-needed revenue for NABF, who delivered them initially through the Alternative School. The Alternative School run by the NABF opened its doors in 1978 and, for a small course fee, offered an anti-racist, anti-sexist education to those who sought it. The school's initial offering included classes on Black women's history, feminism, Black women's sexuality (open only to women), and assertiveness training. The latter two proved to be the most popular courses. NABF offered assertiveness training courses on-site at various Chicago institutions, such as Credit Women International (NABF 1979a) and the Argonne National Laboratories in Argonne, Illinois, through the Federal Women's Program of the U.S. Department of Energy (NABF 1979b). "We seek to unshackle ourselves from our 'place' as Black women to become individuals free to live to the fullest of our potential," states the Philosophy of NABF section of the Alternative School Program. For NABF, assertiveness training promoted a new, liberated Black woman, who could be empowered to create social change in her personal life and in society at large. Whether through consciousness-raising or assertiveness training, in programs designed for Black women's education and advancement, the expectation was always that personal liberation would serve a collective political purpose.

Like other feminist psychologists, NABF leaders hoped to harness the behavioral knowledge that was at the root of assertiveness training in order to create both new selves and political change for Black women. NABF trainers popularized the knowledge dispensed in the self-help assertiveness training manuals designed for white women or, more rarely, Black men. Black female students might or might not have recognized themselves in, for example, the "Characterological Lifechart of People We All Know." This handout describes Doris Doormat, a paragon of passive behavior, who allows others to make decisions for her and puts herself down; Agatha Aggressive, who often overreacts and attacks others; Iris Indirect, who wins by manipulating others; and, finally, the much more likable April Assertive, whose point of view is "I'm OK and you're OK," who chooses for herself, receives respect from others, "acts directly," and "wins honestly." (NABF n.d., "Characterological Lifechart"). Of course, Doris, Agatha, Iris, and April are unraced, hence white, although their behaviors, described didactically, could perhaps be recognizable in cross-racial contexts. It is possible that skills taught in assertiveness training could, in fact, help Black women improve their lives. "Can you . . . say no without feeling guilty?" asks the NABF Alternative School Program on the page advertising assertiveness training courses (NABF n.d., Alternative School Program). As practitioners argued, the ability to deny a request represented an assertive skill: "The assertive woman can say no to requests when she is already busy, and she can give herself time to decide when she will do" (Phelps and Austin 1975, 92). As Springer agrees, assertiveness could in fact address Black women's needs, given their long history of unsung labor for their communities and society at large (2005, 104).

A closer look at the materials used in NABF's assertiveness classes shows that they might have allowed students to discuss their experiences not only in gendered, but also in racialized terms. The assertiveness training seminars always started with a discussion of assertiveness and women's particular needs, or "areas of concern," an exploration of participants' assertiveness problems, followed by "role playing alternative responses to difficult situations in small groups" (NABF 1976). The assertiveness inventory, completed at the beginning of each class, asked participants to analyze interactions in a variety of contexts, as consumers, patients, students, family members, and members of the community, and develop an assertive (as opposed to a passive or aggressive) response. A professional (unraced) woman responding to a male collaborator's comments on her looks; a customer standing her ground in front of a rude salesperson; a returning female student demanding feedback from a professor who ignores her work—these situations, for which assertiveness training attempted to develop polite yet firm responses, could be recognized as instances of microaggressions by participants. After all, Black women had had the historical experience of being viewed as sexually available, discriminated against as customers because of their race (not just their gender), and considered less intellectually gifted than their peers. Other handouts, such as the Survival Ladder handout borrowed from *Assertive Black . . . Puzzled White*, an assertiveness training manual that discussed race, listed various social situations in terms of the control African Americans had over the circumstances and the level of assertiveness in which they could safely engage (Cheek 1985, 77). While the assertiveness training class was less focused on personal narrative than consciousness-raising groups had been, such a course could still provide a forum where raced and gendered experiences could be discussed.

If assertiveness training was designed to help white women overcome their supposed lack of assertiveness in front of white men, especially in professional situations, NABF believed that Black women could benefit from learning "alternative ways of negotiating stereotypes in the dominant culture" (Springer 2005, 104). While NABF's seminars were successful and represented a way for the organization to generate much-needed revenue, it is nevertheless easy to imagine the limitations of this method. NABF followed Jacubowski-Spector's (1973) definition of assertiveness as a way of defending one's rights: "Assertion is the kind of behavior in which a person stands up for her legitimate rights in such a way that the rights of others are not violated. Assertive behavior is an honest, direct, and appropriate expression of one's beliefs and needs, in a way that communicates respect—though not deference or submission—toward the other person" (NABF 1976). This type of interaction presupposes a certain level of shared concern for each other's rights and, up to a point, an egalitarian relationship. It is not necessarily true that African American women's superiors, coworkers, or even community and family members were eager to uphold Black women's rights. Cheek states that white society perceives assertiveness differently when it is exercised by African Americans: "There are ready-made words for assertive blacks—impudent, impolite, arrogant, hostile, aggressive, and abrasive" (1976, 91). Even if fluent in the communicative codes of dominant society, African Americans could still be perceived as aggressive when trying to stand up for their legitimate rights in a racist society. NABF suggests that assertiveness training could teach Black women to respond to microaggressions ("Can you respond with humor to someone's putdown of you?"), yet the onus of developing these humorous responses that could hopefully deflect unequal power relations falls on Black women after all.

But while assertiveness training was useful, albeit in a limited way, for African American women, could it perhaps help Black and white women work together? Could assertiveness training become a way to explore new racial relations among women in the aftermath of both the civil rights and women's liberation movement? Eichelberger was adept at using consciousness-raising to discuss gender and race relations in mixed groups of men and women, and thus had quite a lot of experience organizing and moderating conversations about gender and race. Sometimes she used this experience in her assertiveness training seminars, especially when she taught them to both Black and white women. What kind of conversations about race occurred between Black and white women in the 1970s in workplaces that invited Eichelberger to teach assertiveness training to their employees? Twenty-four completed handouts (seven by white women, seventeen by African Americans women) are stored in the archives, and they offer a glimpse into conversations that unfolded at the time (NABF n.d., "Assertion Session Evaluation").

The undated, untitled handout asks participants to define assertiveness in general, from a gender perspective, and from a racial perspective. It is not clear whether the handout was given at the beginning of a class, in the middle of a discussion, or as an evaluation form, although the responses show that most participants had similar understandings of assertiveness, which means that perhaps the handout was completed toward the end of the class. We know the race of each participant because writers were asked to identify themselves as B or W in the upper right corner. It appears that all participants were women.

Perhaps unsurprisingly, most writers understand assertiveness, defined generally, in similar ways: expressing one's views, standing up to a group of people, not feeling guilty, saying no, or, more specifically, asking people not to smoke in one's car. From a gendered perspective, some respondents, both Black and white, define assertiveness as asking their husbands to take on more housework or participate in childcare. Others mention initiating sex play, buying a drink for a male colleague, and refusing to make coffee or assume traditional female roles at work. Some feel that being assertive in gender terms would mean the ability to act in ways that are considered "feminine" without being judged for this behavior. One Black woman sees being assertive from a gender perspective as being paid to stay at home with her children.

From a racial perspective, Black and white women's understandings of assertiveness diverge rather sharply. African American women define it in a variety of ways. Some explain it as expressing individual tastes and not being judged for them ("being able to have so called white lifestyles, not being put down by Black peers"), while others equate it with the ability to avoid stereotypes ("responding as oneself and not playing the racial role of compliance or non-compliance because of race but rather as an individual. Ex. Being able to say, 'I'm not a fan of Jesse Jackson'"). Several responders see assertiveness as the ability to stand up for one's rights in a racist society ("insisting on my right to be waited on next in line when overlooked by clerk who asks the person behind you what you want"; "responding to a white woman I don't know addressing me by my first name"). Others define assertiveness as being competitive in a white world ("choosing a white sorority while being in residence in an all-white dorm," "showing whites I am as competent and knowledgeable as they are"), or as being comfortable with their white friends ("inviting your white friends to your black neighborhood"). One respondent saw assertiveness as rethinking old assumptions about race and class ("Not assuming the white person is the doctor and the black person is the janitor when I don't know which is which"). Others had a hopeful definition of assertiveness as "making a difference in the world we live [in] so that race relations are improved," or as "being able to express my love for all people, be they purple . . . starving in India or living next door to me and making people feel comfortable with this expression" (NABF n.d., "Assertion Session Evaluation"). Assertiveness training, beyond simply creating more assertive subjectivities for African American women, allowed them to discuss microaggressions, imagine their own definition of self, and create an alternative vision of a world of improved race relations.

The responses submitted by white women, while fewer, show a rather different understanding of race. Perhaps Eichelberger imagined that white women would define assertiveness in racial terms as asserting an anti-racist worldview, or as a commitment to fighting white privilege. The answers she received show that white women did not understand racism as something that affected them personally, and their definition of assertiveness in terms of race range from liberal benevolence to directly asserting racial privilege. One white woman defines assertiveness from a racial point of view as not engaging in tokenism, while another one defines it as establishing "bonds of communication" and a good, easy rapport with African Americans. Another white woman understands assertiveness from a racial point of view as "having black friends and being able to view the race condition in a humorous/loving way. Learning from them how they feel about their condition." This liberal woman expects to learn from African Americans how they feel about "their condition" instead of trying to educate herself. Finally, some white women understood assertiveness training from the point of view of race as upholding white privilege by telling Black women, "I believe you are not open or frank" or, even worse, as "offering a watermelon to a black" (NABF n.d., "Assertion Session Evaluation"). While fewer white women than Black women attended the assertiveness training session, their responses show that some define assertiveness as willingness to learn from a different perspective—albeit expecting people of color to teach them. For other white women, assertiveness means claiming equality with men while upholding white privilege.

When African American women attended assertiveness training with their white counterparts, they could learn that some white women were willing to actually fight against racial oppression (avoiding tokenism), while others were willing to learn about race, provided a person of color was willing to teach them "their perspective." Yet they might have also learned that assertiveness training empowered white women not only to stand up to their husbands and male bosses, but also to uphold white privilege.

Conclusion: Reconsidering Protocol Feminism

Assertiveness training is a perfect example of what Murphy called protocol feminism. It set up steps, skills, and affects, and modes of interaction in order to create a new subjectivity, the liberated Black woman, free to fulfill her human potential. In contrast, consciousness-raising, at least in the version experienced by African American women, focused less on protocols, and instead allowed for a multiplicity of results, ranging from building community to activism, from personal liberation from sexist and racist expectations to educating Black women about their history, and from testifying about Black women's experiences to encouraging them to pursue their dreams. Entangled with psychotherapy, Black feminist consciousness-raising intervened in the very location where therapeutic knowledge was produced, exchanged, and validated: professional conferences of the Association of Black Psychologists.

Assertiveness training likewise assembled feelings, actors, modes of interaction, and so on, but its prescriptive dimension was clear. Women had to learn how to "act assertively," and several assertiveness inventories or scales were developed by practitioners. In contrast, there were no definite criteria by which to judge the success of consciousness-raising, because feminists themselves could not agree on what the final purpose of consciousness-raising was, or perhaps because it could have multiple outcomes for women. The women's movement had borrowed the focus on the small group, the narration of feeling, and the value placed on personal experience from the therapeutic establishment. While this genealogy helps historicize the movement, it leaves unanswered the question of why consciousness-raising was profoundly memorable for women's liberationists and defining for the movement, while other practices, such as assertiveness training, the self-help exam, and menstrual extraction, are remembered as peripheral practices.

This genealogy of the entanglements of consciousness-raising with therapy provides an explanation for consciousness-raising's immediate and lasting popularity with suburban women. They were familiar with the therapeutic setting; when educated white feminists argued that consciousness-raising was similar to and yet different from therapy, they rightfully presumed that they shared cultural knowledge with their audience. The therapeutic genealogy of consciousness-raising can also explain why the practice was less successful with working-class women, regardless of race.

Yet 1970s activists recalled consciousness-raising's other genealogy, going back to the civil rights movement, where the vision of participatory democracy animated the practice of anti-racist organizers. In her biography of Ella Baker, Barbara Ransby elaborates on the ethos of participatory democracy: "Her philosophy was not simply to 'let the people decide' as the popular SNCC and SDS slogan suggested. Rather, it was to let the disenfranchised vote, let the silenced be heard, let the oppressed be empowered, and let the marginalized move to the center." In SNCC, Ransby continues, "Black leadership had to be emphasized and poor people's voices amplified because in absolutely every other facet of social life the opposite pressures and privileges were in force" (Ransby 2003, 368–369).

To the extent that this vision of participatory democracy animated the consciousness-raising groups of the women's movement, it subsumed the protocols of the therapeutic establishment and the small groups as a technology of democracy to a wider project of social change. Protocols could circulate between social movements, corporations, and state agencies that might have had contrary political goals. But the extent to which feminist consciousness-raising groups were animated by a vision of participatory democracy, even if in temporary, fleeting ways, shows the specificity of a movement. Feminist consciousness-raising allowed educated white women, more rarely women of color, and occasionally sexual minorities to move to the center of a social movement that was their own, create their own narratives, and act on the political insights they had collectively gained. SNCC's consciousness-raising groups based on race could reassemble as political groups for women, morph into intersectional groups for women as well as men, and incorporate discussions of class and sexuality. Consciousness-raising, and through it the women's movement, had the potential to be led by those multiply oppressed—a participatory democratic goal. All the protocols governing the building of politics out of feelings, the creation of a narrative from the perspective of those silenced, were subsumed to this vision of the world Black feminists, and perhaps feminists of other races, wanted to build and inhabit.

Acknowledgments

I would like to thank the panelists and attendees of the conference Feeling Democracy: A Conference on Feelings and Emotions (April 2020), organized by the Institute for Research on Women at Rutgers University, for their comments and suggestions, and to the Rutgers University Research Council for a grant that allowed me to travel to Chicago for archival research. I am incredibly grateful to the former NABF members who have granted me interviews and shared their memories with me: C. A. Lofton, Gayle Porter, and most importantly Brenda Eichelberger, former executive director of the NABF (1939–2017). I am also very much indebted to Arlene Stein and Sarah Tobias, the volume's editors, for their detailed editing suggestions.

References

Alberti, Robert, and Michael Emmons. 1974. *Your Perfect Right.*
New York: Impact.

Allen, Pamela. 1970. *Free Space: A Perspective on the Small Group
in Women's Liberation.* New York: Times Change Press.

"Assignment: Assertion." 1975. *Time* 105, no. 21: 65.

Bloom, Lynn Z., Karen Coburn, and Joan Perlman. 1975. *The New
Assertive Woman.* New York: Dell Publishing.

Cade, Toni, ed. 1970. *The Black Woman: An Anthology.* New York:
Mentor.

Cheek, Donald. 1976. *Assertive Black . . . Puzzled White: A Black
Perspective on Assertive Behavior.* San Luis Obispo: Impact.

Cummings, Elan. 1974. *Woman, Assert Yourself: An Instructive
Handbook about Assertiveness Training for Women.* New York:
Harper and Row.

Echols, Alice. 1989. *Daring to Be Bad: Radical Feminism in America,
1967–1975.* Minneapolis: University of Minnesota Press.

Eichelberger, Brenda. 1974. "Black Feminism: A New Directive:
Consciousness-Raising Guidelines for Black Women and
Men." Paper presented at the Association of Black Psychologists'
Seventh Annual Convention, August 26–28.

Evans, Sara. 1979. *Personal Politics: The Roots of Women's Liberation
in the Civil Rights Movement & the New Left.* New York:
Vintage.

Fensterheim, Herbert, and Jean Baer. 1978. *Don't Say Yes When You
Want to Say No: THE Assertiveness Training Book!* New York:
Dell Publishing.

Hardaway, Yvonne, and Karen LaPointe. 1974. *Facilitating Assertive
Training Groups: A Manual.* Carbondale: Southern Illinois
University at Carbondale Counseling Center.

Herman, Ellen. 1995. *The Romance of American Psychology: Political
Culture in the Age of Experts.* Berkeley: University of California
Press.

Hole, Judith, and Ellen Levine, eds. 1971. *Rebirth of Feminism*. New York: Quadrangle Books.

Jacubowski-Spector, Patricia. 1973. "Facilitating the Growth of Women through Assertiveness Training." *Counseling Psychologist* 4, no 1: 75–86.

Kleinman, Carol. 1975. "When Black Women Rap, the Talk Sure Is Different." *Chicago Tribune*, June 1, 13.

Lofton, C. A. 2016. Oral history interview by author, Chicago, IL, January 14, 2016.

Murphy, Michelle. 2012. *Seizing the Means of Reproduction: Entanglements of Feminism, Health, and Technoscience*. Durham, NC: Duke University Press.

National Alliance of Black Feminists (NABF). 1975. Letter to "Dear Brother." Brenda Eichelberger Papers, Research Center, Chicago History Museum, Chicago, Illinois. Box 17, Folder 7, March 24, 1975.

———. 1976. Calendar of Events. Brenda Eichelberger Papers, Research Center, Chicago History Museum, Chicago, Illinois, Box 4, folder Calendars of Events, May 1976.

———. 1979a. Calendar of Events. Brenda Eichelberger Papers, Research Center, Chicago History Museum, Chicago, Illinois, Box 4, folder Calendars of Events, February 1979.

———. 1979b. Calendar of Events. Brenda Eichelberger Papers, Research Center, Chicago History Museum, Chicago, Illinois, Box 4, folder Calendars of Events, June 1979.

———. 1979c. Membership Letter. Brenda Eichelberger/National Alliance of Black Feminists Papers, 1974–1997, Chicago History Museum Research Center, Chicago, Illinois, Box 4, folder Membership Letters, June 1979.

———. 1979d. Membership Letter. Brenda Eichelberger/National Alliance of Black Feminists Papers, 1974–1997, Chicago History Museum Research Center, Chicago, Illinois, Box 4, folder Membership Letters, July/August 1979.

———. n.d. Alternative School Program, National Black Feminist Organization Collection, Special Collections, University of Illinois at Chicago Library Chicago, Illinois, Box 1, Folder 1.

———. n.d. "Assertion Session Evaluation." Brenda Eichelberger Papers, Research Center, Chicago History Museum, Chicago, Illinois, Box 24 [Mailing Lists, Correspondence, Membership Forms, Women's Affiliates], untitled folder.

———. n.d. "Characterological Lifechart of People We All Know." Brenda Eichelberger Papers, Research Center, Chicago History Museum, Chicago, Illinois, Box 4, Folder "Assertion Training Handouts."

———. n.d. Consciousness-Raising Topics. Brenda Eichelberger/ National Alliance of Black Feminists Papers, Vivian G. Harsh Research Collection of Afro-American History and Literature, Chicago Public Library, Box 9, Folder 22.

Nachescu, Ileana Voichita. 2017. "Pro Black Women, Yet Anti No One: Intersectional Consciousness-Raising, Black Women Intellectuals, and the National Alliance of Black Feminists." In *Bury My Heart in a Free Land: Black Women Intellectuals in Modern US History*, edited by Hettie V. Williams, 205–228. New York: Praeger.

National Black Feminist Organization (NBFO). 1973. "Statement of Purpose." National Black Feminist Organization Collection, Special Collections and University Archives, University of Illinois at Chicago, Chicago, Illinois, Box 1, File 12.

NBFO Chicago Chapter. 1975. *Newsletter* 2, no. 4: 3. Brenda Eichelberger Papers, Research Center, Chicago History Museum, Chicago, Illinois. Box 17, Folder 6, April.

Nelson, Janie. 1981. "Attitude Behavior Consistency among Black Feminist and Traditional Black Women." PhD dissertation, Kent State University.

Osborne, Susan M., and Gloria G. Harris. 1975. *Assertive Training for Women*. Springfield, IL: Charles C. Thomas.

Pearson, Kyra. 1999. "Mapping Rhetorical Interventions in 'National' Feminist Histories: Second Wave Feminism and Ain't I a Woman." *Communication Studies* 50, no 2: 158–173.

Phelps, Stanlee, and Nancy Austin. 1975. *The Assertive Woman*. San Luis Obispo: Impact.

Porter, Gayle. 2013. Phone interview by author, September 5, 2013.

Ransby, Barbara. 2003. *Ella Baker and the Black Freedom Movement: A Radical Democratic Vision*. Chapel Hill: University of North Carolina Press.

Roth, Benita. 2004. *Separate Roads to Feminism: Black, Chicana, and White Feminist Movements in America's Second Wave*. New York: Cambridge University Press.

Smith, Manuel J. 1975. *When I Say No, I Feel Guilty*. New York: Dial Press.

Springer, Kimberly. 2005. *Living for the Revolution: Black Feminist Organizations, 1968–1980*. Durham, NC: Duke University Press.

Ware, Cellestine. 1970. *Woman Power: The Movement for Women's Liberation*. New York: Tower Publications.

Zerbe Enns, Carolyn. 1992. "Self-Esteem Groups: A Synthesis of Consciousness-Raising and Assertiveness Training." *Journal of Counseling and Development* 71, no. 1: 7–13.

Acknowledgments

Feeling Democracy: Emotional Politics in the New Millennium is the second volume of the Institute for Research on Women's *Feminist Bookshelf* series, which collects innovative feminist research presented at Rutgers University. We thank Rutgers University Press's editorial director Kimberly Guinta for initiating the series and shepherding this volume through its various stages of production. This book originated from IRW's programming in the 2019–2020 academic year, when our annual theme was "This Is What Democracy Looks Like: Feminist Re-Imaginings," and we held a spring conference on democracy and emotion. Originally scheduled as an in-person conference, the event, like much of our lives, moved online with the advent of COVID-19. We thank all the speakers at that conference: Kathryn Abrams, Nermin Allam, Nancy Chi Cantalupo, Belinda Davis, Deborah Gould, Kirin Gupta, Barbara Koziak, Noëlle McAfee, Ileana Nachescu, Holloway Sparks, and Ciara Torres-Spelliscy. We are particularly grateful to those participants who allowed us to publish their work in this volume.

We thank the Rutgers School of Arts and Sciences, especially dean of humanities Rebecca Walkowitz and former dean Michelle Stephens, for supporting IRW's programming. We thank current IRW director and former IRW executive committee member Chie Ikeya. We also thank current and recent IRW executive committee members: Tyler Carson, Asenath Dande, Kayo Denda, Anette Freytag, Chie Ikeya, Suzanne Kim, Suzy Kim, Sara Perryman, Nancy Rao, Kyla Schuller, Ethel Brooks, and Cat Fitzpatrick. We greatly appreciate the skills and kindness of our former administrative assistant Andrea Zerpa, who helped with the logistics of our 2019–2020 programming and pivoted effortlessly to Zoom when lockdown occurred. We also thank Moazima Ahmad, who worked tirelessly in the IRW physical and virtual offices throughout the academic year.

Arlene thanks Sarah for her dedicated leadership and hard work in guiding IRW, organizing the "Feeling Democracy" conference at Rutgers, and assembling this volume.

Sarah thanks Arlene for her generous (and generative) leadership and for six years of extraordinary collegiality that have made IRW a great place to work. She also thanks Beth, Talila, and everyone who has sustained her in ways large and small during the process of editing this volume.

Notes on Contributors

KATHRYN ABRAMS is Herma Hill Kay Distinguished Professor of Law at the University of California, Berkeley. Her interest in emotion arose from two decades of work in feminist theory, in particular on storytelling, and on challenges to the dichotomy between reason and emotion. Since 2011, she has focused on the role of emotion in social movements, most recently in the movement of undocumented immigrants. She is the author of *Open Hand, Closed Fist: Practices of Undocumented Organizing in a Hostile State.*

NERMIN ALLAM is associate professor of politics at Rutgers University–Newark. Allam's work has appeared in *Social Research: An International Quarterly, Middle East Law and Governance, Politics and Gender,* and *Sociology of Islam.* Her book *Women and the Egyptian Revolution: Engagement and Activism during the 2011 Arab Uprisings* offers an oral history of women's engagement in Egypt's modern contentious politics.

KIRIN GUPTA is pursuing a JD/PhD (history and gender/ sexuality studies) at Harvard University. She studies women terrorists in the former British Empire, working transnationally across fields of rebellion/security studies, gender studies, and African studies, in the interest of de-imperializing frameworks. Her legal scholarship focuses on reproductive justice. Her dissertation is concerned with reframing categories of gender, insurgency, and military history.

NOËLLE MCAFEE is professor and chair of philosophy at Emory University, where she also holds a secondary appointment as professor of psychiatry and behavioral sciences and is on the faculty of the Emory University Psychoanalytic Institute. In addition, she is affiliate faculty in the women's, gender, and sexuality studies program. Her monograph, *Democracy and the Political Unconscious*, explores the potential of deliberative dialogue and public testimonies to address traumas that keep political communities from developing democratic spaces and practices. Her book *Fear of Breakdown: Politics and Psychoanalysis*, using psychoanalytic theory to explore the growth of nationalism and populism, won the Courage to Dream Book Prize by the American Psychoanalytic Association for the book that best promotes the integration of the academic and clinical worlds of psychoanalysis.

ILEANA NACHESCU, originally from Romania, is assistant teaching professor and associate undergraduate director in the women's, gender, and sexuality studies department at Rutgers–New Brunswick. Her monograph titled *The National Alliance of Black Feminists (1974–1983): A History* is under contract with the University of Illinois Press. She is at work on a book-length project, *Memoirs of a Socialist Childhood*, which explores the articulations of gender, class, and race in a society of equals. Her essay "Ukraine: Beyond the Postsoviet," published in the *Boston Review*, has been translated into Spanish, Russian, Mandarin, and Romanian.

ARLENE STEIN is distinguished professor of sociology at Rutgers University. She was the director of the Institute for Research on Women between 2016 and 2022. Her research focuses on the intersection of gender, sexuality, culture, and politics. She recently published "Gender, Authoritarian Populisms, and the Attack on Democracy" in *Sociological Forum*. She is also the author of *Unbound: Transgender Men and the Transformation of Identity* and *The Stranger Next Door: The Story of a Small Community's Battle Over Sex, Faith, and Civil Rights (or How the Right Divides Us)*, which was recently reissued with a new preface.

SARAH TOBIAS is executive director of the Institute for Research on Women at Rutgers University, where she also serves as affiliate faculty in the women's, gender, and sexuality studies department. She recently published "Donald Trump, The Resistance, and The Queering of Democracy" in *Signs: Journal of Women in Culture and Society*. She is co-author of *Policy Issues Affecting Lesbian, Gay, Bisexual, and Transgender Families* and co-editor of *Trans Studies: The Challenge to Hetero/Homo Normativities*, which won the Sylvia Rivera Award for the Best Book in Transgender Studies from the City University of New York Center for Lesbian and Gay Studies, and *The Perils of Populism*.

CIARA TORRES-SPELLISCY is professor of law at Stetson University College of Law, where she teaches courses in election law, corporate governance, business entities, and constitutional law. Prior to joining Stetson's faculty, Professor Torres-Spelliscy was counsel in the Democracy Program of the Brennan Center for Justice at NYU School of Law. She was an associate at Arnold & Porter LLP and a staffer for Senator Richard Durbin. Professor Torres-Spelliscy is the author of the books *Corporate Citizen? An Argument for the Separation of Corporation and State*, *Political Brands*, and *The Democracy Litmus Test*.

Index

AAPSO. *See* Afro-Asian People's Solidarity Organization

AAWC. *See* Afro-Asian women's conferences and decolonial democracy

Abbas, Ferhat, 172

Abdellah, Sheikh Khaled, 69

Abouelnaga, Shereen, 69

Abrego, Leisy, 33

Abu-Lughod, Lila, 181

abuse, 12–13

acceptance, as emotional rhetoric, 116, 142–144

ACT-UP organization, 29

advertisers/ advertising, 117–118. *See also* branding

affect vs. emotions, 3–5, 7, 44–45

Afro-Asian People's Solidarity Organization (AAPSO), 168, 177, 185, 185n1

Afro-Asian Women's Conference. *See* Afro-Asian women's conferences and decolonial democracy

Afro-Asian women's conferences and decolonial democracy: absence of word "feminist," 186n4; attendees, 179–180; collective self, 177–178; conditions of social life, 182, 183; conference reports, 172, 185n1; democratic nation construction, 179; family planning rights, 184; gender and political-economic belonging, 175–177, 182, 183; identity as "militants" and "makers," 181; imperial feminisms, 180–185; institutional support, 172; marital rights, 184; memorializing women in anti-imperial struggles, 181–182, 188n12; motherhood described, 183; national liberation as path to gender liberation, 172–175, 178–180, 183; ontology of Afro-Asian womanhood, 179, 180–182; paid maternity leave rights, 184; second world, 180, 187n11; soldiering, 179; third world, 180, 187n11; transnational solidarity, 167–172, 177–178, 182

Åhäll, Linda, 9

Ahdath Maglis al-Wuzara' sit-in, 67

Ahler, Douglas, 123

Ahmed, Sara, 4, 9, 10, 63

Alberti, Robert, 209

Algeria, women patriots, 173

All African People's Conference, 168

Allen, Pamela, 208

Alternative School, 210–211

Amara, Adel, 68, 73
Andiola, Erika, 48–49
anger: defined, 61–63; as emotional
    rhetoric, 116, 134–140; "garden-
    variety," 59–60, 62, 75; in
    philosophy and politics, 61–65,
    68–72; rage, 59, 77n2; retribution
    and, 62–63, 75; revenge vs.
    recognition, 75; secure recogni-
    tion of revenge, 59–61, 73, 75, 76;
    state violence and women's
    political participation, 62, 65–67;
    as tool to expose oppressive
    structures, 64, 77; transition,
    59–60, 62, 72–76; in undocu-
    mented immigrants' movement,
    45–50, 54n21; women as angry
    "killjoys," 63; women's collective
    action and, 58–61, 64, 69, 72–76, 77
anti-AIDS movement, 29, 46
Antifa, 94
anxiety, persecutory, 86–87, 93–94,
    110n2
aphorisms, 42–43, 47, 59
Argonne National Laboratories, 211
Aristotle, 8, 61
Arizona: "attrition through
    enforcement" program, 31–33,
    53n3; Maricopa County, 32; SB
    1070, 32–33, 46, 53n4, 54n21. See
    also undocumented immigrants'
    movement
Arpaio, Joe, 32, 45
Assertive Black . . . Puzzled White
    (Cheek), 210, 213
assertiveness training, 194, 208–217
Assertive Training for Women
    (Osborne and Harris), 210
Assertive Woman, The (Phelps and
    Austin), 210
atrocity fantasies. See fantasies,
    atrocity
Austin, Nancy, 210

authoritarianism, 7, 9, 60–61, 62–63
Azar, Alex, 131

Baer, Jean, 209
Baker, Charlie, 145
Baker, Ella, 219
Bandaranaike, Sirimavo, 175
Bandung (Indonesia) Conference, 168
bargaining, as emotional rhetoric,
    116, 130–134
Barnawi, Fatma, 182
Barr, William, 90, 94
Barrett, Amy Coney, 114
Baum, Matthew, 121, 122–123
Beal, Frances, 199
Belgium, interference in the
    Congo, 173
Benjamin, Elliot, 119
Bennett, LaVerne, 206
Berinsky, Adam, 121, 122–123
Berlant, Lauren, 2
Biden, Joseph, 85, 136, 137, 138–139,
    140, 143, 144
Big Lie. See Trump, Donald J.:
    election loss
"Big Man" history, 172, 186n5
Birx, Deborah, 146
"Black Feminism" (Eichelberger),
    201–202
Black Power movement, 193,
    194–195, 199
Black Woman, The (Cade), 197, 199
Black women: assertiveness
    training, 208–217; consciousness-
    raising and African American
    men, 206–207; right to vote, 6.
    See also Afro-Asian women's
    conferences and decolonial
    democracy; consciousness-raising
    groups and Black feminists;
    people of color as other
Blank, Grant, 120
Blanuša, Nebojša, 107–108

Bloom, Lynn Z., 210

branding: commercial, 116–118, 120; emotional rhetoric, 124–144; information silos, 120–123, 127; political, 118–120 (*see also* COVID-19, political branding of); techniques, 116–120, 125; use of repetition, 119, 127–129

breakdown, fear of, 97, 110n2

Burma, 29–30, 175

cabal and conspiracy theories, 85, 89, 101

Cade, Toni, 197, 199

Caldwell, LaVerna, 203–204

Cameroon. *See* Kamerun

Campbell, Elizabeth, 204

Caputo, Michael, 89–90, 94

Catholics, 14

Central Africa, 174

Ceylon, 175

Cheek, Donald, 210, 214

Chicago Women's Liberation Union, 201

China, 124, 134, 144, 173–174, 175

Chua, Lynette, 27, 29–30, 31

Cinelli, Matteo, 123

civil rights movement, 3, 19, 45, 194–195, 199, 219

Clinton, Hillary, 68, 105

Clinton Foundation, 88

Coburn, Karen, 210

"cognitive liberation," 27, 52n1

colonialism, 95–96, 108–109. *See also* Afro-Asian women's conferences and decolonial democracy

color symbolism, 70–71

Combahee River Collective, 197, 199, 207

communism, 165, 170–171, 185, 185n1, 187n6. *See also* Afro-Asian women's conferences and decolonial democracy

Congo, the, 173

consciousness-raising groups and Black feminists: African American men and, 202–203, 206–207; assertiveness training, 194, 208–217, 219; described, 192–193; discussions of class, gender, race, 201–206, 214–216, 220; encounter groups vs., 202–203; genealogy of, 194, 199, 219; histories of, 193–198; industrial training groups and, 197, 198, 199–200; intersectional consciousness-raising, 198–201, 204; menstrual extraction, 193, 196, 208, 219; microaggressions, 214–216; National Alliance of Black Feminists, 201–206; personal growth centers, 200; practice of, 201–206; "protocol feminism" compared to, 207–208, 218–220; psychotherapeutic practices, 193, 195–196, 203, 219; self-help practices, 196, 205, 208, 219; theory vs., 193

conspiracy theories: aftereffects of, 108–110; anxiety substitute, 87, 93–94, 96, 99, 102–103, 109–110, 111n4; archaic defenses, 91–96; cabal and, 85, 89, 101; chosen trauma, 93; collective insecurities, 87–88, 91–99; conformity and, 97–98; cultural unconscious, 94–95; denial, 86, 93; described, 85–87; desire for ultimate truth, 97–98, 107–108; displacement, 99, 106–108, 110n2; in Egyptian society, 68–69, 78n5; elements of, 87–91; jealousy, 98–99; large-group identity, 91–93, 95, 96, 99, 108–109, 110; mechanisms, 86–88, 99–108; misinformation, 86; misrecognition, 99, 100–101;

conspiracy theories (cont.)
  motivation for, 96–99; paranoia,
  106, 111n3; phobic objects, 99,
  102–103, 104, 107; projection, 86,
  99, 106, 107, 110n2; QAnon,
  88–91; social phenomenon, 97;
  splitting, 86, 96, 99, 103–106, 109;
  use of stereotypes, 94, 102–103
COVID-19, political branding of:
  absentee voting during, 101;
  acceptance as emotional rhetoric,
  116, 142–144; anger as emotional
  rhetoric, 116, 134–140; bargaining
  as emotional rhetoric, 116, 130–134;
  chloroquine myth, 132; cures,
  131–133; deaths from, 139–140, 146;
  as Democratic hoax, 127–129, 144,
  146, 147n1; Democratic reaction to,
  134, 135, 136–137, 139–140, 143,
  144–146; denial as emotional
  rhetoric, 116, 124–130; depression
  as emotional rhetoric, 116, 140–141;
  described, 114–120; impact on
  economy, 130, 135, 147n2; impact
  on hospitality/recreation industry,
  130–131, 145, 147n2; information
  silos, 120–123, 127; mask wearing
  measures, 108, 114–115, 128, 131,
  135–139, 140–141, 145, 147, 147n3;
  misinformation, 86, 89, 115–116,
  124–126, 129, 131–133, 134, 141, 143;
  Republican reaction to, 129,
  132–135, 137, 139, 140, 143, 144–146;
  restriction measures, 131, 135, 139,
  145; shutdown measures, 130, 135,
  139; social distancing measures,
  114–115, 131, 135, 139, 140, 141, 145,
  147n4; stay-at-home orders,
  130–131, 135, 139; super-spreader
  event, 146; Trump's emotional
  rhetoric, 123, 124–144; vaccination,
  140, 142–144; White House daily
  briefings, 130–132

Credit Women International,
  211
critical race theorists/feminists, 11
Cummings, Elan, 210
Cvetkovich, Ann, 5

DACA. See Deferred Action for
  Childhood Arrivals
Dahbour, Amina, 182
Daring to Be Bad (Echols), 198
Davis, Angela, 202–203
de Benedictis-Kessner, Justin, 121,
  122–123
decolonialization. See Afro-Asian
  women's conferences and
  decolonial democracy
Deferred Action for Childhood
  Arrivals (DACA), 48
democracy: authoritarian "backsliding," 9; emotions and, 8–11;
  emotion used to undermine, 2, 9,
  19–20; entwined with self-
  absolving, neoliberal
  neocolonialism, 170; feeling, 8,
  15–19; male dominant norms, 10
  (see also patriarchy); multiple
  meanings, 5–8; normative, 6–7;
  participatory practices, 193, 219; as
  regime type, 9; as type of
  government, 5–6; women
  excluded from, 6, 9. See also
  Afro-Asian women's conferences
  and decolonial democracy
"democracy grief," 7
demonization of others, 109–110,
  111n4
"demosprudence," 11
denial, as emotional rhetoric, 86, 93,
  116, 124–130
depression, as emotional rhetoric,
  116, 140–141
DeWine, Michael, 145
Dickinson, Greg, 125–126

displacement and conspiracy theories, 99, 106–108, 110n2

Don't Say Yes When You Want to Say No (Fensterheim and Baer), 209

DREAM Act, 33–37, 46, 48, 53n6

DREAMers, 33–37, 46

Dubois, Elizabeth, 120

Echols, Alice, 198

Egypt and women's collective action: Ahdath Maglis al-Wuzara' sit-in, 67; al-Nour Party, 66; anger in philosophy and politics, 59, 61–65, 68–72, 74, 76; blue bra symbolism, 59, 67, 68–72; collective activism, 58–61, 66–67, 72–76, 77; conspiracy theories, 68–69, 78n5; cultural gendered roles, 63; Freedom and Justice Party, 66; gender inequalities, 62–63, 65–66, 69–70; inheritance laws, 63; male participation in anti-harassment groups, 74; marginalization of women's voices, 63–64, 66–67; patriarchal authoritarianism, 60–61, 62–63; Salafi group, 66; Sitt el-Banāt march, 58–59, 68–72; state violence and women's political participation, 58–59, 65–67, 69; Supreme Council of the Armed Forces (SCAF), 58–59, 64, 65, 67, 69–72, 73, 74, 76; Transition-Anger and anti-sexual violence campaigns, 59–60, 72–76; victims' use of online platforms, 75–76; virginity tests, 67; women as red line, 58–61, 70

Eichelberger, Brenda, 201–203, 205, 214, 216

El-Said, Karima, 169, 173, 177

Emmons, Michael, 209

emotion: affect vs., 3–5; cultural patterns, 4; democracy and, 8–11, 20; feminine traits, 9; importance of language in communicating, 42–43; management by undocumented immigrant activists, 41; manipulation of (*see* COVID-19, political branding of); relationship between politics and social movements, 3, 10, 11–15, 29–30; reshaping authoritative meaning of democracy, 19; social norms, 4; storytelling and, 11 (*see also* storytelling); as strategy to exclude women from politics, 9; undesirable in political life, 8; use of term, 20n2

emotion culture: built to facilitate activism, 29; described, 27; shift in, 46; storytelling in building, 34; undocumented immigrants' movement, 26–28, 40–45

emotional politics: affect vs. emotions, 3–5; democracy and emotions, 8–11; described, 1–2; emotional movements, 11–15; feeling democracy, 15–19. *See also* Afro-Asian women's conferences and decolonial democracy; consciousness-raising groups; conspiracy theories; COVID-19, political branding of; Egypt and women's collective action; undocumented immigrants' movement

emotives, 54n17. *See also* aphorisms

Esalen Institute, 200

Facebook and misinformation, 125

Fanon, Frantz, 102

fantasies, atrocity, 104–105

Fauci, Anthony, 138

fear, 44, 102

Fear of Breakdown (McAfee), 86

feelings. *See* emotions

feminism: "angry feminist," 63, 77; anticolonial rebellion (*see* Afro-Asian women's conferences and decolonial democracy); Black feminists (*see* consciousness-raising groups and Black feminists); critical race feminists, 11; focus on white women, 193, 196–197; fourth wave, 74; imperial, 180–185; "protocol feminism," 207–208, 218–220; psychotherapeutic knowledge, 195; relationship between emotions, politics, social movements, 3; second wave, 12, 197; self-help practices, 196, 205, 208, 219; separate roads theory, 194; as tool, 3. *See also* women

Fensterheim, Herbert, 209

"fetish," 102–103, 110

Filter Bubble, The (Pariser), 122

Floyd, George, 94

fourth-wave feminism. *See* feminism: fourth wave

Fox News, 128, 132

France, action against Guinea, Kamerun, Mauritania, 174

franchise rights, 6, 19, 175

Free Space (Allen), 208

Freud, Sigmund, 74, 100, 102–103, 109

Friedan, Betty, 195

frustration, met with cognitive and affective strategies, 44–45, 46–47

Gaetz, Matt, 128

Ganz, Marshall, 53n11

Ganzouri, Kamal al, 67

Garrett, Laurie, 115

gaslighting, 126, 136

Gay, Volney, 88, 104–105

gender: consciousness-raising activities, 202–203, 206–207, 214–216; emotions, 2, 9; gendered being, 181; inequalities, 62–63, 69, 77, 182, 183; male participation in anti-harassment groups, 74; national liberation as path to gender liberation, 170, 172–175, 178–180; norms, 2, 10, 63, 74, 77; ontology of Afro-Asian womanhood, 179, 180–182; overturning ideology, 14; political-economic belonging, 175–177, 179; power relations and therapeutic knowledge, 203

Ghana, 174, 175

Ginsberg, Ruth Bader, 114

globalization, 91

Goa, 174

Google, search engine algorithms, 122

Gould, Deborah, 4, 11, 29, 46

Great Britain, 173, 174

Greece, normative democracy, 6–7

Grewal, Inderpal, 181

grief, stages of, 116. *See also* COVID-19, political branding of: Trump's emotional rhetoric

Guinea, 174, 176–177

Guinier, Lani, 11

Hafez, Sherine, 68, 70

Hagman, George, 119, 120, 126

Hamblin, James, 125, 133

Harris, Gloria G., 210

Hasan, Manal Abul, 78n5

Hatch Act, 133

Hemmings, Clare, 19

Herman, Ellen, 193, 195, 196, 198

hoax, use of term, 127–129

Hobbes, Thomas, 8

Hochschild, Arlie, 4, 29

Hofstadter, Richard, 86

Hogan, Larry, 145
Holocaust, 13
Homolar, Alexandra, 126, 134
Hooker, Juliet, 7
Hristov, Todor, 107–108
Human Potential Movement,
    199, 200

Ilouz, Eva, 4
immigrants. *See* undocumented
    immigrants' movement
imperial feminism. *See* feminism:
    imperial
imperialism, eradication of, 173. *See
    also* Afro-Asian women's
    conferences and decolonial
    democracy
India, 170, 174, 175
Indonesia, 174, 175
infodemic, 124–125, 129, 132. *See also*
    COVID-19, political branding of:
    misinformation
information silos, 120–123, 127
insecurity and conspiracy thinking,
    96–99
Iraqi, 105, 175
İskenderun, 174

Jacubowski-Spector, Patricia,
    209–210, 213
Jaggar, Alison, 10
Japan, nuclearization of, 174
Jasper, James, 71, 72
joy, fostered in countering painful
    emotions, 45

Kamal, Hala, 74
Kamerun, 174
Kant, Immanuel, 8, 9
Karam, Bahia, 167–168, 169, 172,
    173, 179
Kenya, 174
Khaled, Laila, 182

Khodary, Yasmin, 66
Khrushchev, Nikita, 172, 174
Klein, Melanie, 103
Kleinman, Carol, 205
Kobach, Kris, 53n3
Korea, 174, 175
Koziak, Barbara, 8
Kübler-Ross, Elizabeth, 116
Kuwaitis and conspiracy theories, 105

Lacan, Jacques, 100–101, 104
Langohr, Vickie, 74
language, importance for communi-
    cating emotion, 42–43
Laos, 174
Laplanche, Jean, 106, 107
Lasswell, Harold, 106–107
Latuff, Carlos, 76
Lebanon, 175
Le Thi Hong Gam, 181
LGBT movement, 29–30, 46
liberalism, 14–15
Liberia, 175
Lindemann, Hilde, 11
Locke, John, 8
Lofton, C. A., 206
Lorde, Audre, 64

madness, 100–101, 104. *See also*
    misrecognition
Mahmood, Saba, 181
"Make America Great Again"
    slogan, 88
Malaya, 174, 175
Managed Heart, The (Hochschild), 29
Marriott, David, 94, 96, 102, 103
"Masked Avenger" (Latuff), 76
Maslow, Abraham, 200
Massumi, Brian, 3–4
Mauritania, 174
McAdam, Doug, 26–27, 52n1
McAfee, Noëlle, 86
Meadows, Mark, 140

media and information silos, 123, 132–133

melancholia, 74, 75, 77

MENA. *See* Middle East and North Africa

Menjivar, Cecilia, 33

menstrual extraction, 193, 196, 208, 219

MeToo movement, 64

Middle East and North Africa (MENA), 60–61

Miller, Pamela, 206

mind, concept of, 20n2

misogyny, 1–2, 7

misrecognition and conspiracy theories, 99, 100–101

Mohamed (Prophet of Islam), 62

Mohanty, Chandra, 181

Mongolia, 175

Morsi, Mohamed, 65

Moten, Fred, 7–8

motherhood, described, 183

Motyl, Alexander, 1–2

Moving Politics (Gould), 46

Mubarak, Hosni, 65

Mueller, Robert, 128

Murphy, Michelle, 193, 196, 198, 203, 207, 218

Muslim Brotherhood, 65, 66

NABF. *See* National Alliance of Black Feminists

Najmabadi, Afsaneh, 181

Nasridinova, Yadgar, 175

Nasser, Abdel, 172

National Alliance of Black Feminists (NABF), 194, 198, 201–206, 210: Authentic Black Male/Female Relationships, 206–207

National Black Feminist Organization (NBFO), 198, 199

National Black Women's Health Project, 197

nationalism, 173. *See also* Afro-Asian women's conferences and decolonial democracy

National Training Laboratories, 200

NBFO. *See* National Black Feminist Organization

needs, hierarchy of, 200

Netherlands, the, 174

New Assertive Woman, The (Bloom, Coburn, and Perlman), 210

Ngai, Sianne, 4–5

Nigeria, 175

N'krumah, Kwame, 172

Noem, Kristi, 133

normative democracy, 6–7

Not1More Deportation, 48

Nussbaum, Martha, 8, 59–60, 61–62, 75

Nyamache, Tom, 70–71

Nyambura, Ruth, 70–71

Obama, Barack, 41, 46, 48

Obama, Michelle, 139

Operation Anti-Sexual Harassment, 73

Operation PUSH/Black Men Pushing, 206

O'Reilly, Bill, 143

Osborne, Susan M., 210

Ott, Brian, 125–126

Pakistan, 175

Palestine, 173, 182

paranoia, 106, 111n3 *See also* projection and conspiracy theories

paranoid politics, 90. *See also* conspiracy theories

Pariser, Eli, 122

patriarchy, 60–61, 62–63, 108–109, 195, 204

Paul, Harry, 119, 120, 126
Peace Corps, 200
Pearson, Kyra, 198
peer modeling in social movements, 41–42
"the people," as defined in democracy, 6
people of color, as other, 109. *See also* Black women
Perlman, Joan, 210
persecutory anxieties. *See* anxiety, persecutory
Phelps, Stanlee, 210
Phoenix, Arizona, 33
Pizzagate, 88, 99, 105. *See also* conspiracy theories
Plato, 8–9
Plummer, Ken, 13
political branding. *See* COVID-19, political branding of
"Political Ideology Predicts Perceptions of the Threat of COVID-19," 144
politics: paranoid (*see* conspiracy theories); relationship between emotions and social movements, 3, 10; state violence and women's political participation, 65–67; women's anger in, 61–65, 68–72. *See also* emotional politics; gender
Politics of Love, The (Chua), 29
Pontalis, Jean-Bertrand, 106, 107
populism, right-wing, 2, 14, 19
Portugal, control of Goa and African colonies, 174
Prieto, Greg, 38
processes, primary vs. secondary, 100, 109–110
projection and conspiracy theories, 86, 99, 106, 107, 110n2
Protestants, evangelical, 14
Putin, Vladimir, 1–2

QAnon, 85, 88–91, 99, 101, 108. *See also* conspiracy theories

racism: "affective economies of hate," 9–10; in South Africa, 174; Trump as champion of, 1–2; white women's views, 216–217. *See also* Afro-Asian women's conferences and decolonial democracy; consciousness-raising groups; undocumented immigrants' movement; white supremacy
rage, use of term, 59, 77n2
Ransby, Barbara, 219
Recommendations for the Struggle of National Independence and Peace, The, 172–173
red, symbolism in color, 70–71
Reich, Wilhelm, 13
Reston, Maeve, 136
Rhodesia, 174
Robinson, Eugene, 116
Rorty, Amélie, 20n2, 73
Roth, Benita, 194
Roussos, Gina, 118
Russia–Ukraine conflict, talk of feelings about, 1–2
Ruti, Mari, 98

Saad, A'ida, 182
Sahara, atomic tests in, 174
#SayHerName, 188n12
Scholz, Ronny, 126, 134
second-wave feminism. *See* feminism: second wave
sexual violence. *See* violence: sexual
shame, 12–13, 31, 72–73, 76
Shehab, Bahia, 71
Sika, Nadine, 66
Sisi, Abdel Fattah el-, 65, 75
sisterhood, 171–172, 178, 181. *See also* Afro-Asian women's conferences and decolonial democracy

Sitt el-Banāt (The Lady of All
  Ladies), 58–59, 68–72, 73, 76
Smith, Manuel J., 209
SNCC. *See* Student Non-Violent
  Coordinating Committee
socialism, 170–171, 185. *See also*
  Afro-Asian women's conferences
  and decolonial democracy
social movements: blame shifted to
  aggressor, 73; "cognition
  liberation," 26–27; "community
  building" process, 30, 31; cultural
  turn in, 27; defense of those
  shamed, 73; described, 26–28;
  emergence of, 26–28; emotions as
  central component, 11–15, 27, 29,
  30; "grievance transformation"
  process, 30; peer modeling, 41–42;
  relationship between emotions
  and politics, 3; use of storytelling,
  11, 12–15, 34–40; vehicle to effect
  change, 11. *See also specific
  movements*
Sood, Gaurav, 123
South Africa, 174
South Dakota and COVID-19
  rates, 133
South Vietnam People's Liberation
  Armed Forces, 181
Soviet Union, 175
Spero, Robert, 118
splitting and conspiracy theories,
  86, 96, 99, 103–106, 109
Springer, Kimberly, 212
Srinivasan, Amia, 75
"status-focused anger." *See* anger:
  "garden variety"
stereotypes, 94, 102–103, 213
stop the steal conspiracy, 99, 106
storytelling: in building emotion
  culture, 34; as compelling tool,
  10–11, 12, 40; in critical race
  theory, 11; empowerment arising

from, 34–35; interpretation,
  36–37; role of collectivity in
  fostering agency, 35, 36–37, 40,
  53n11; role of listener, 36; role of
  teller, 35–36, 42; sense of identity,
  36–37; in social movements, 11,
  12–15; in undocumented
  immigrants' movement, 34, 45–50;
  valuation of experience, 40
Student Non-Violent Coordinating
  Committee (SNCC), 195, 199, 220
Sturgis (South Dakota) motorcycle
  rally, 146
suffrage movements, 6
Sukarno, 172

Taha, Alia, 182
Tahrir Bodyguard, 73
Taiwan, 174
T-groups, 199–200. *See also*
  consciousness-raising groups:
  industrial training groups and
Thailand, 175
Third World Women's Alliance, 199
Time magazine, 209
tokenism, 217
Tomlinson, Barbara, 63
Torres, Gerald, 11
Transition-Anger. *See* anger:
  transition
transnational solidarity, 167–172,
  177–178. *See also* Afro-Asian
  women's conferences and
  decolonial democracy
Trump, Donald J.: on Biden's mask
  wearing, 137; branding techniques, 118–119, 126–129;
  COVID-19 as Democratic hoax,
  127–129, 144, 146, 147n1;
  COVID-19 hospitalization, 114,
  140; economic shutdown and
  COVID-19, 130–131, 139, 145,
  147n2; election loss, 90–91,

142–143; emotional rhetoric about COVID-19, 123, 124–144, 129; empathy toward COVID-19 victims, 141; failure to address COVID-19, 115–116, 140, 141, 144–146; gaslighting techniques, 126, 136; on governors' COVID-19 messaging, 134–135; loyalists' fundamental identification, 94, 103, 110, 126–127; misogyny, 1–2, 7; paranoia, 106; politicalization of COVID-19, 115, 129, 132–134, 135; populism and (*see* populism, right-wing); QAnon theory on, 85, 89–90, 101, 108; racism, 1–2, 7, 134, 144; Twitter use, 125–126, 135; use of stereotypes, 94–95; use of term "hoax," 127–129, 147n1; use of term "witch hunt," 128; vaccinated against COVID-19, 142–144

Trump, Mary, 140–141
Tunisia, 175
Turkey, 175
Twitter, 125–126, 135

UAR. *See* United Arab Republic
undocumented immigrants' movement: "Adios Arpaio: campaign, 45; anger in, 45–50, 54n21; attrition and enforcement, 31–33, 35, 53n3; changes in self-perception and emotion, 31; collectives and socialization, 27–28, 31, 33–39, 53n11; "coming out" events, 47; cultural traditions, 39; emotion cultures, 26–28, 31, 40–45; family separation, 45–50; fear erased through solidarity, 44; formation of immigrant enforcement policy, 41; frustration met with cognitive and affective strategies, 44–45, 46–47; hostility

toward, 28; isolation and sequestration, 35–36, 38; joy fostered in countering painful emotions, 45; legal status, 51, 54n24; "legal violence," 33; meal sharing, 38–39; organizing skills, 39; outward-facing activism, 27, 40–45; peer modeling, 41–42; political agency showcase, 39, 50, 51; self-assertion, 27, 42; "shells" in self-isolating routines, 38; shift in activists, 46; solidarity and support, 38–39; storytelling and private suffering, 34, 35–36, 45–50; undocumented organizations, 28–31; videos of emotional encounters, 48–50; youth activism, 33–37

United Arab Republic (UAR), 175
United Nations, women and diplomatic posts, 173
United States: action in Vietnam, Laos, Korea, 174; Federal Women's Program, 211; Fifteenth Amendment, 6; January 6, 2021, insurrection, 85–86, 91; Voting Rights Act, 6. *See also* conspiracy theories; undocumented immigrants' movement
Unzueta, Tania, 47
"Uses of Anger, The" (Lorde), 64
Uzbekistan, 175

Vetlesen, Arne Johan, 76
Vietnam, 174, 175
violence: abuse, 12–13; anti-racist movements and, 94–95; intimate, 13; "legal," 33; sexual, 72–76; state and women's political participation, 58–59, 65–67, 188n12
Volkan, Vamik, 91–96, 103
Volpi, Frederic, 71
voting. *See* franchise rights

Ware, Celestine, 197–198, 199
Washington, Edwin C., 206
West Irian of Indonesia, 174
When I Say No, I Feel Guilty (Smith), 209
white privilege, 217
white supremacy, 7, 95–96, 103, 108–109, 110, 174. *See also* racism
Whitmer, Gretchen, 138, 139
Williams, Raymond, 7
Winnicott, D. W., 97
witches, 111n4
witch hunt, use of term, 128
Witty, Marge, 210
Woman, Assert Yourself (Cummings), 210
Woman Power (Ware), 197–198, 199
women: anger in philosophy and politics, 61–65, 68–72; assertiveness training, 208–217; bodily rights, 71, 74, 76; demonization as witches, 111n4; education, 176–177, 211–212; family planning rights, 184; health movement, 196–197; as lacking in intellectual capacity and religious faith, 62; liberation movement and

consciousness-raising groups, 192, 195; marital rights, 184; ontology of Afro-Asian womanhood, 179, 180–182; as other, 109; paid maternity leave rights, 184; participation excluded from democracy, 6, 9; political rights, 175–177; property rights, 176; as red line in Egypt, 58–61, 70; social liberation of, 183; state violence and women's political participation, 65–67; underrepresented in Islamist political parties, 66. *See also* Afro-Asian women's conferences and decolonial democracy; feminism
Woodward, Bob, 128, 142

Yalch, Matthew M., 135
Yemen, removal of British bases in, 173
Your Perfect Right (Alberti and Emmons), 209

Zanzibar, 174
Zelensky, Vlodymir, 1–2
Zuckerman, Ethan, 88–89, 108